W9-AQT-998

ELEMENTARY AND JUNIOR HIGH/MIDDLE SCHOOL SOCIAL STUDIES CURRICULUM, ACTIVITIES, AND MATERIALS, SECOND EDITION

James L. Barth
Purdue University

UNIVERSITY
PRESS OF
AMERICA

Lanham • New York • London

ISBN (Perfect): 0-8191-3197-0

All University Press of America books are produced on acid-free
paper which exceeds the minimum standards set by the National
Historical Publications and Records Commission.

PREFACE

When this book was originally conceived in 1977 and written and published in 1979, the author believed a revision with additions would be needed eventually. The field of social studies is dynamic, and though the reader's experience may not have been dynamic in taking social studies courses, the growing edge of the field itself is changing sufficiently in terms of topics, vocabulary, and even objectives to warrant this revision. For example, the title has changed. The original title was <u>Elementary and Middle School Social Studies Curriculum Program, Activities and Materials</u>, and now, to recognize a change in terminology, the new title is <u>Elementary and Junior High/Middle School Social Studies Curriculum, Activities and Materials</u>. Some states now have programs which designate a specific Junior High/Middle School certification and, therefore, texts need to reflect that change in emphasis.

I wonder if your experience with the social studies curriculum was similar to mine? I cannot, for the life of me, remember a social studies curriculum in school. My first remembrance was of a fifth grade class where students reported on different South American countries. I was assigned to Chile which I described to a room full of invited sixth graders as "a long shoestring." My final remembrance is that of American history in the eleventh grade. The treatment was academic, that is, I remembered with great care presidents, wars, battles, and import taxes, but the course had no relation to real problems and the real world that I knew. Frankly, I find it hard to reflect on my school's social studies curriculum, for if it ever existed, it was well hidden. I did not become aware of a field called social studies until after I graduated from college. It was incredible, for how could I have journeyed through sixteen years of formal education without having heard or seen or sensed that a whole field, which I presumably had taken part in and which was a required curriculum,

i

was missing from my experience?

I hope you will be as intrigued as I was to discover social studies. If you were to examine your experience with your school's social studies curriculum, would you not have approximately the same experience as I did? That is, you would not be able to identify a curriculum that featured the integration of the social studies and humanities for the purpose of instruction in citizenship education. I hope this book will persuade teachers that the social studies they knew years ago is not what social studies educators would wish them to repeat. I want to convince teachers that there is a social studies curriculum that aims at constructing an integrated, developmental series of courses, topics, activities, and materials, all of which are intended to achieve a goal. This book suggests an integrated curriculum for kindergarten through twelfth grade, and presents topics, activities, and materials for kindergarten through eighth grade.

The book is designed for teachers in training, experienced teachers, curriculum supervisors, and social studies consultants who wish to organize a systematic elementary and junior high/middle school social studies program. In particular, this book is volume one of a two-volume set, with the second volume, Secondary Social Studies Curriculum Activities and Materials, written for high school social studies teachers. The author does not intend this book to be a substitute for a methods text, but rather that the activities and materials as found in this book be a companion to the methods text Methods of Instruction in Social Studies Education and to The Nature of the Social Studies or Defining the Social Studies, which are historical and philosophical examinations of the meaning of social studies. Any complete course in social studies methods would include all three books.

This book is organized into nine sections including a prologue called Person to Person, an introductory chapter, and individual chapters for kindergarten/first grade through eighth grade. The reader is urged to read the prologue carefully, for the curriculum suggested is founded on the goal and four objectives for teaching a social studies program. The prologue is followed by the first chapter which describes and illustrates a K-12 curriculum. Each succeeding chapter describes courses taught at that particular grade level and includes illustrative activities and materials through eighth grade.

I would like to acknowledge the hundreds of graduates and undergraduates who have read and critically evaluated the activities and materials, for they are responsible for my belief that the book will help the teacher. Special thanks to the book's editor, Mary Ellen Thrall. In particular, I am indebted to Barbara Bauhof Barth who was the illustrator for this book and who helped to organize the activities and materials in many of the chapters.

Purdue University   J.L.B.
1983

TABLE OF CONTENTS

PERSON TO PERSON

Social studies, as an organized subject field, has traditionally been a requirement of the elementary and junior high/middle school curriculum. Yet many teachers do not know that there is a social studies curriculum, nor are they aware of how the social studies curriculum is to be integrated and taught. In some states elementary social studies is required to be taught no less than one half-hour a day, and in junior high/middle school no less than one period per day. Some states mandate, that is, require, that specific topics and, in some cases, certain content be covered at specified grade levels.

The fact remains, however, that social studies curriculum appears to many teachers as unrelated fragments of history and geography. One's remembrances of social studies are bits and pieces of historical events, an odd pile of geographic trivia, and an assortment of government offices, titles, and person-alities once memorized for a current events test. The odd lot of memories does not call forth a curriculum. No consistent themes, interesting activities, or developmental and integrative materials come forth to remind one that in the end students were being prepared to be fully functioning, responsible citizens in a complex, interdependent, democratic society. Elementary and secondary schools require students to take the social studies curriculum, though, in fact, the separate courses at the secondary level may have been called American history, government, world history, economics, etc., whereas in higher education the curriculum name became social science and the courses are called political science, sociology, psychology, anthropology, and history. The notion of social studies is very confusing to some, for not only is it difficult to remember a social studies curriculum which students undoubtedly followed to graduate from high school, but now in college even the name of the curriculum was changed to social science.

Why Social Studies?

Before there was a social studies field, there was history and geography.
One hundred years ago your great-great-grandparents would have studied history
and geography not social studies. There was no social studies. The field of
social studies was dimly perceived at the end of the 19th Century. Building
on early foundations, social studies was conceived as a curriculum for the
schools in the early 20th Century.[1] Why the change from the traditional subjects of history and geography to a social studies curriculum? That change
occurred because some of the educators at the turn of the century identified
what they thought to be a crisis. America had become by 1900 an industrialized,
interdependent, urban society. That society was in crisis, for the quality of
urban life, including the conditions of the factories, were condemning generations of American citizens to lives that were not consistent with a democratic
heritage. Educators believed that public schools should be places where future
citizens would learn to improve the quality of their lives. The social studies
curriculum in those schools was intended to provide an organized, integrative
education aimed at training decision-makers who could use a democratic foundation to earn their dream of the good life.

In summary, the change from traditional subjects to social studies occurred
because educators believed that education should include practice in democracy,
including decision-making. People could not participate in the control of
their own lives unless they had training in the skills of reasoning, valuing,
and participating. Traditional subject matter of history and geography and
traditional teaching practices could not offer a proper training for modern-day
citizens.

What is Social Studies?

Because social studies was conceived and applied some seventy years ago, it does not follow that all schools or teachers have necessarily adopted the notion of a social studies curriculum. To this day, authorities within the field debate the meaning of social studies, and though there has emerged some agreement, the field is still evolving. The meaning of social studies you should find for yourself in such books as The Nature of the Social Studies or Defining the Social Studies.[2] However, in brief:

> Social Studies is an integration of social science and humanities for the purpose of instruction in citizenship education.[3]

One part of that definition is particularly significant, for the definition tells us that the reason for teaching social studies is instruction in citizenship education.

The Goal of Social Studies

Simply, the goal of teaching social studies is citizenship. If we agree the goal is citizenship, then what must a teacher do to achieve that goal? This is a point on which some social studies educators have agreed.

The Four Objectives for Teaching Social Studies to Achieve the Goal of Citizenship[4]

Social studies educators agree that to achieve the goal of citizenship the teacher should teach social studies to achieve the following four objectives:

1. Gain knowledge about the human condition which includes past, present, and future.

2. Acquire skills necessary to process information.

3. Develop the skills to examine values and beliefs.

4. Encourage the application of knowledge through active participation in society.

For use in this book, the four objectives are shortened to:

---

1. Gaining knowledge (work, roles, services, define, identify)

2. Processing information (interpreting symbols, map skills, fact from fiction)

3. Valuing (evaluate, divergent, clarify, rank)

4. Participating (find and solve, social action, establish rules)

Perhaps it is sufficient to know that the social studies field is young and changing. What I do want teachers to know are the four objectives for teaching social studies. In principle, social studies teachers generally accept the four objectives. Just what does this mean? It means that a teacher will plan to practice all four objectives when teaching social studies, whether in kindergarten or twelfth grade. In short, teachers should help students gain knowledge, process information, develop the skill to examine values, and finally apply knowledge through an active civic participation. The argument is that if students practice the four objectives, then social studies is taught as citizenship education.

Is Knowing the Objectives Important?

Why is it important that teachers know the four objectives before reading this book? Very simply, all activities and materials found in this book are categorized under one of the four objectives. In other words, at each grade level all activities and materials are organized to accomplish the four objectives. At each grade level (first through eighth) there are activities designed to gain knowledge, process information, develop valuing skills, and encourage participation.

One might ask, "Even if activities are identified for each of the four objectives by grade level, why is this different or unique?" This book is one of the first attempts to organize a kindergarten-eighth grade social studies curriculum that says to teachers, "The objectives for which you teach kindergarten are the same as those used in each of the succeeding grades right up through the eighth grade." For the first time teachers know that their teaching is part of a developmental social studies program, that each teacher, though the courses and topics differ, is following the same general objectives. No longer need teachers feel isolated, alone, separated from others who are teaching social studies.

I want to encourage the teaching of social studies that is part of an organized school curriculum. In some states social studies seems to have been included in primary education almost as an afterthought--after reading, language arts, math, etc. Hopefully teachers will be more likely to use social studies content if they know that the lessons taught in their classes are to be followed the next year by lessons that build developmentally upon their lessons. In summary, if teachers know that the social studies curriculum has continuity and is developmental, they might be more inclined to teach the curriculum.

Some Activities and Materials Include All Four Objectives

One could argue that the best type of social studies activities should be organized to provide knowledge, process information, value, and participate. As the activities become more complex in grades four, five, six, and junior high/middle school, distinctions between the four objectives blur. The important points are: that all four objectives should be part of a social studies program; that all four objectives be part of each activity is not important; that activities and materials at least incorporate one of the four objectives is important; that all four objectives be part of a K-12 social studies curriculum is essential.

Social Studies Integrated With Other Fields

Social studies is a distinct subject field, but that does not mean social studies should not be integrated with subject fields which offer opportunities for integration. Many of the activities suggested in this book could be and should be found in methods and activities books in other fields. Some of the social studies materials will look familiar, and I suspect reading through activities at each grade level teachers might say, "I saw that in science methods," or about valuing, "That's talked about in health; I didn't know that's social studies." It is no accident that activities are designed to be integrated with lessons in other fields. Common sense alone tells one that elementary teachers with limited time to teach all subject fields will look for opportunities to integrate some of the fields with the hope of concentrating on those for which they are held accountable.

Social Studies Asks the Important Questions

It is natural to suppose that one's field is the most important. Surely without math, science, reading, and music the world would be different. But for the moment consider the social studies educator's point of view. In other fields questions are asked that have to do with why and how things work. In social studies the really important questions have to do with the quality of life. Social studies questions are: Who am I? Who are you? How are we related? How did we get this way? What was the past? What is the future? Shall we live for the present? Trying to find answers to these questions takes a lifetime. The task of an elementary and junior high/middle school teacher is to help students use social studies to start the search for answers following the process of gaining information, evaluating that information, testing that value, and by making decisions as the basis of participation.

A Final Word on How to Read This Book

Frankly, I do not anticipate that teachers will read straight through
this book. What I think will happen is that teachers will identify their
grade level--primary, intermediate, junior high/middle school--and read only
the pertinent parts. Because I have anticipated how teachers might read this
book, each grade level is designed to be self-contained. The fact that
teachers really ought not to read the book piecemeal probably has little to
do with what they will actually read. Each chapter is purposely written
following the same pattern, so that to know the pattern of one will be to know
the pattern of all chapters. These final thoughts complete our Person to
Person: Use this book as a dictionary, use it as a text, use it to coordinate
a consistent social studies program, because it integrates some of the best
ideas about teaching social studies.

Notes

1 Barth, J. L., & Shermis, S. S. Social studies goals: The historical perspective. In C. Berryman (Ed.), Goals for the social studies: Toward the
twenty-first century. Journal of Research and Development in Education,
1980, 13, 2.

2 Barr, R. D., Barth, J. L., & Shermis, S. S. The nature of the social
studies (Palm Springs, CA: ETC Publications, 1978), and Defining the social
studies, Bulletin 51 (Washington, DC: National Council for the Social
Studies, 1977).

3 Barr, Barth, & Shermis, The nature of the social studies, p. 19.

4 The four objectives were originally identified in Social studies guidelines
(Washington, DC: National Council for the Social Studies, 1971). The four
objectives were also used as the rationale for organizing a social studies
teachers' guide--Indiana Department of Public Instruction, Social studies:
A guide for curriculum development (Indianapolis, IN: Author, 1978), p. B-1.

A SOCIAL STUDIES KINDERGARTEN THROUGH TWELFTH GRADE CURRICULUM

Though the focus is on elementary and junior high/middle school social studies, teachers would agree that conceiving social studies as a subject in kindergarten through eighth grade only would be a narrow perspective. As in any other field, knowing the whole program is undoubtedly necessary so that one can more easily spot one's part in that total program. What is a social studies kindergarten through twelfth grade curriculum supposed to do for a student? One answer is that the curriculum should help students integrate their life experiences including knowledge gained from a study of the social sciences, history, and humanities for the purpose of performing as effective citizens. Fine, teachers say, so what we want is an effective citizen. But just what specifically should an effective citizen be able to do? "I, as a teacher, have to know this; otherwise I cannot very well prepare the student for a task without knowing what knowledge and skills are needed." The reader surely can answer this question, having read the preceding Person to Person. Of course the answer is that the task of preparing effective citizens is best accomplished by preparing the student to practice the four objectives of gaining knowledge, processing information, examining values, and knowing how to participate.

A Systematic Curriculum

Am I saying that at each grade level social studies should be taught so as to emphasize those four objectives? Yes, absolutely. Those four objectives, plus some common activities and materials, offer the best chance for a systematic kindergarten/twelfth grade social studies curriculum. If one agrees that a systematic curriculum should be built primarily upon the teaching of the four objectives at each grade level, then each of the four objectives must be carefully planned at each grade level. Conceive of a funnel as it spirals and broadens upward from the base, then imagine how the four objectives are passed from one grade to another, deepening and broadening the child's ability to understand the world.

Fragmented Bits and Pieces

Now, be honest when asking yourself this question, "What pattern of social studies topics and courses did I follow elementary through high school?" Think about this question for a minute. Odds are that you can't recall the course topics or whether there was a pattern. If your experience was similar to most college students', you remember social studies as history (with emphasis on events and dates) and geography (with emphasis on land forms and exports).

Believe it or not, there was supposed to be all three--courses, topics, and patterns--throughout your scholastic years, and together they were to be called the social studies curriculum. Every school has a social studies curriculum. The fact that you probably don't know this, and also that you don't remember the course, topics, and patterns practiced on you for twelve years, suggests that the school system was not particularly interested in having you know that a prescribed social studies pattern existed. If you are curious at all, you must be wondering why you don't know much about a curriculum that you spent considerable time in school completing.

There are many reasons why you don't know. One reason among many is that teachers--both elementary and secondary--don't know that there might be a state-prescribed social studies curriculum. It is true that most all school systems have a kindergarten through twelfth grade social studies curriculum, a part of which is mandated by the state. That curriculum often is designed by a kindergarten through twelfth grade school system curriculum committee which has produced a study guide that each social studies teacher in the system is supposed to follow. The practice has been for each teacher to ignore the study guide, then proceed to teach whatever course, topic, or pattern fits their individual interests. Of course, the consequences of such liberties have been that little or no continuity exists between courses or topics, and patterns don't emerge, giving the social studies program the appearance of being disjointed, fragmented bits and pieces of government, history, and geography. If math and reading were taught based upon a personal whim of the teacher without planning for continuity, one might guess the consequences. Of course, the same reasoning applies to teaching social studies. Social studies, just as math and reading, requires continuity based upon a developmental system.

Social studies, according to authorities in the field, was never meant to be fragmented bits and pieces. The intent was for a carefully planned curriculum that set forth a pattern of courses and topics. This chapter introduces teachers to the rationale for and the demonstration of a kindergarten through twelfth grade social studies curriculum. Teachers ought to become convinced that social studies should not be taught as disjointed, fragmented bits and pieces, but rather should be taught as part of a total social studies curriculum aimed at the goal of preparing citizens.

Social Studies Curriculum Chart[1]

The following chart is a representation of a curricular pattern that exists throughout the United States. However, this suggested national curricular pattern may not exactly fit any one state pattern.

Instructions:

Examine the suggested national curricular pattern in Column 1, then in Column 2 try your hand at identifying the approved (mandated) pattern in your state, then try to identify your school's approved kindergarten-twelfth grade pattern in Column 3.

Column 1 National K-12 Social Studies Curriculum	Column 2 Fill in your state's approved curriculum	Column 3 Fill in your school system's approved K-12 Social Studies Curriculum
Grade / Basic Theme	Grade / Basic Theme	Grade / Basic Theme
K-2 Individuals and Families	K	K
K & Individuals and Families		
1 Locally and in the USA	1	1
2 Individuals and Families in Selected Parts of the World	2	2
3-4 Communities		
3 The Local Community and Selected Communities in the USA	3	3
4 Selected Communities of the World	4	4
5-6 Countries		
5 The United States Today and Yesterday (Postholing certain periods in our history in the second half of the year)	5	5
6 Selected Countries of the World (to be studied in depth)	6	6
7-8 Basic Problems and Decisions in the USA		
7 Problems and Decisions in the USA Today	7	7
8 Problems and Decisions in the USA Yesterday	8	8
9-10 Cultures		
9 Studies in Depth of the 8 Major Cultural Areas of	9	9
10 the World "Today and Yesterday," Western and Non-Western	10	10
11-12 The United States and the Emerging International Community		
11 United States History	11	11
12 Contemporary Problems in the USA and in Other Parts of the World	12	12

Comment

Some states do not have a suggested kindergarten/twelfth grade social studies curriculum, though there probably are social studies requirements for graduation. The probability is that even if the state does have a mandated curriculum, teachers will not know either their state's or their school system's social studies curriculum. Why is it that school administrators, curriculum directors, social studies teachers, and the students, who obviously are required to pass through a social studies mandated curriculum, do not know what their state's or their school's kindergarten/twelfth grade curriculum is? Teachers prepare materials and teach classes and students graduate, not knowing that they are or ought to be part of a systematic program.

Social Studies Course Content, A Brief Overview

Just what content is included in a total social studies curriculum? The earlier chart lists, under the suggested national curricular pattern, course titles. Though the titles are suggestive, they give only a hint as to content. Remember there is no one prescribed national social studies curricular pattern. Each state establishes its own pattern. There are literally fifty different patterns, but, as suggested in the chart, there are similar state patterns. What follows is only a suggestion of a particular pattern of course offerings and content, but the courses do illustrate what a systematic developmental program might be like if planned according to the four objectives.[2]

KINDERGARTEN

The child and his investigation of himself, his family, home, school, and neighborhood, and the accompanying living and working functions of each in which the child learns to work in groups, to use classroom tools, to share materials, to use simple inquiry skills, and to engage in social participation.

GRADE 1

Individuals, families, schools, and social institutions of the neighborhood; ways of living and working together using available resources at
home, and in other parts of the world (in other environments); yesterday
and today, with extension of, or introduction of, cooperative and problem-
solving skills.

GRADE 2

Local school neighborhoods, neighborhoods in other countries; how local
communities meet common interests and needs of individuals and institutions through human interaction and through services basic to mankind;
the introduction of valuing skills and simple map reading skills; the
development of the value of responsibility.

GRADE 3

Development of the local community, other communities, states and regions
in other parts of the world; ways communities adjust to the environments,
develop and use technology and human and natural resources, and adapt
from other cultures while extending student interests; knowledge of
occupations, values and value systems, map skills, organization, and
inquiry processing skills.

GRADE 4

State (history), region, nation, and world communities influenced by the
past; present use of environment, distribution of human and natural
resources, use of societal controls, ever-present problems, and the influence of geography on development with extension of research skills,
problem-solving and valuing activities.

GRADE 5

The United States, Canada (North American continent), and regions of the
world; the growth and development of nations and regions of the world

with special emphasis on geography, history, physical and cultural environments, and the roles and relationships which develop and exist among
them while comparative study, problem-solving, and awareness of how to
effect change as an individual are emphasized. Note that study of North
America should emphasize historical events between 1400 and the 1850's
including the following topics: discovery, colonization, revolution, and
geographical development of the United States up to the Civil War.

GRADE 6

Western Europe, Latin America (South and Central American Continent), and
other regions of the world, with comparative studies on the growth and
development of nations and regions of the world influenced by geography,
history, physical and cultural environments, and the roles and relationships which develop and exist among them; also stressing pupil-teacher
planning and decision-making.

GRADE 7

Area studies of World Civilization (global studies) including the Middle
East, Asia, and Africa.

GRADE 8

United States history (including instruction in the Constitution of the
United States of America), with special emphasis on 19th Century, pre-
and post-Civil War, industrialization, and internationalism.

GRADES 9, 10, 11, 12

Course offerings of 9-12 are allowable at any level but must provide:
United States History (2 semesters required, with emphasis on the 20th
Century, wars, and social, political, and economic international events;
United States Government (2 semesters required or 1 semester of US govern-
ment or civil government and 1 semester of an acceptable citizenship
course). The classes must deal with the historical, political, civic,

sociological, economic, and philosophical aspects of the Constitution of the United States. In addition to the required courses, each commissioned high school shall include in the curriculum: ancient, medieval, or modern history, and economic or physical geography. Courses approved for the foregoing additional elective offerings and for other electives are: African Studies, Early World Civilizations, Psychology, Sociology, Urban Affairs, Western Civilization, Anthropology, Asian Studies, Economics, Ethnic Studies (US), Latin America, Area Studies, Modern World Civilization, World Civilization, World Geography, Current Problems, Introduction to Social Science, and Values and Issues.

Expanding Horizons

There are several ideas about the organization of social studies courses and basic themes which you should note from the above kindergarten through twelfth grade curriculum. Notice that social studies starts with individuals, families, and school the first years, and ends twelve years later with contemporary problems of the social system with special interest in the emerging international/global world. This approach is called expanding horizons-- starting with oneself and expanding through the school years to an understanding of the social, political, and economic problems of family, neighborhood, community, state, nation, and the world.

Spiral

American history is taught three different times throughout the curriculum at grade levels five, eight, and eleven. Also, content about other cultures, that is global studies, is taught at grade levels two, four, six or seven, ten, and twelve. This repeating of topics at ever greater levels of complexity, kindergarten through twelfth grade, is called a spiral. That is, at specific grade levels certain topics and themes are repeated but at a more complex level each time. Imagine what the funnel of a tornado looks like; the small end of the tornado on the ground is kindergarten, with an increase in the size of the funnel as it reaches for the sky representing the higher grades. In practice, when teaching about Latin American, Asian, or African societies in sixth or seventh grade, teachers would be building on topics and themes developed in grades two and four and preparing students for further study in grades ten and twelve.

Current Events and Comparative Studies

Social studies educators for the past seventy years have strongly recommended that current events and comparative studies be a supplementary part of all social studies instruction. Readiness for current events should originate in first grade and current events is recommended for second grade and each succeeding grade. Each year students should gain additional experience and skill in learning how to inquire into contemporary events and into processing the information about those events. A common thread throughout the entire kindergarten through twelfth grade curriculum is current events along with comparative studies. Teachers are encouraged to recall the notion of expanding horizons and the spiral, both of which help to keep social studies content from being seen as fragmented bits and pieces. Both the spiral which holds the bits and pieces together and expanding horizons provide the depth in subject matter and continuity from one grade level to another.

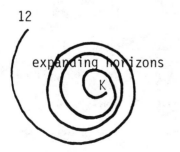

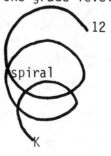

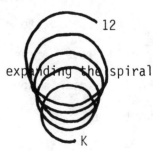

Summary: Expanding the Spiral

Yes, there is a social studies goal, four objectives, themes and concepts, with current events and comparative studies that should be taught in a common kindergarten through twelfth grade social studies curriculum. No matter what grade level, kindergarten or twelfth, at least the following should be basic threads holding all social studies courses together in a common curriculum:

spiraling themes and concepts

expanding personal horizons

comparative studies

current events

Teachers might think that practicing the above "expanding spiral" in a social studies curriculum is nothing less than frightening. One can hear a teacher say, "No way!" Yes, there is a way, a way to make such a complex curriculum work for you. The following chapters on activities and materials at each grade level, in part, offer a real opportunity to help you and all other teachers achieve the goal of preparing effective citizens.

Notes

1 The first column on the National Curriculum Pattern was suggested by Leonard S. Kenworthy, Changing the social studies curriculum: Some guidelines and a proposal. Social Education, (May 1968), p. 485.

2 Indiana Department of Public Instruction. Social studies: A guide for curriculum development. Indianapolis: Author, 1978, p. A-4.

NOTES

CHAPTER KINDERGARTEN/FIRST GRADE

ACTIVITIES AND MATERIALS FOR KINDERGARTEN/FIRST GRADE

CHAPTER KINDERGARTEN/FIRST GRADE

Organization of the Chapter

Each of the succeeding chapters represents a particular grade level, in this case kindergarten and first grade. These two grade levels are combined because in some schools formal social studies does not start until first grade, and therefore what would normally be taught in kindergarten is not begun until first grade. Each chapter consists of three parts: the first part is a brief discussion on topics taught and national trends in teaching kindergarten and first grade throughout the United States; the second part is an illustration of a state kindergarten/first grade program; the third part has activities and materials which conform to topics taught in kindergarten/first grade and are categorized according to the four objectives for teaching social studies-- gaining knowledge, processing, valuing, and participating.

I. Topics Taught and National Trends in Teaching Kindergarten and First Grade

Course, Topics, and Themes Frequently Covered in Kindergarten: "Living Together in a New Environment"

The emphasis in kindergarten is on the child (a study of the self). The study includes how the child identifies his role in the family and the school with special emphasis on living and working with other children. Some teachers prefer to see social studies in kindergarten as a concentration on immediate surroundings. This includes an examination of what the family is, what the relationships between the child, home, and school are, and what functions the members of the home, school, and neighborhood environment perform. The kindergarten social studies program should be integrated with the first grade which, as you will find, emphasizes not only the topics of living and working at home and in the school but also extends to comparisons of living and working in

<u>other parts of the world</u> and to topics such as the various ways families make a living.

Course, Topics, and Themes Frequently Covered in First Grade:
"Self, Home, and School"

<u>Objectives of the Course</u>

Preparing the pupil for school life and community living. Special emphasis is on developing attitudes of self-reliance and cooperation at home and school. The course introduces the concepts of interdependence and variety in human life--in family, school, neighborhood, etc., providing readiness experiences for current events and for skills and concepts related to understanding of space and time relationships (map skills, chronology).

<u>Basic Content of the Course</u>

The Family--its members, the work of various members, rules, recreation; School--the physical plant, "helpers" at school such as the principal, nurse, custodian, patrol persons, bus drivers, and paraprofessionals, and school rules and reasons for them; Safety--in the home, at school, enroute to and from school; Experience with simple maps of the neighborhood and with diagrams of the school and its grounds; Holidays--Thanksgiving, Christmas, birthdays of patriotic heroes.

Just as a reminder, where there is a kindergarten program in social studies, the above content will be treated there and then reinforced in first grade.

In addition to the above, schools include one or perhaps two of the following topics: Pets--emphasis on caring for them; the Farm--attention to farm animals, work of the farmer, seasonal changes in farm work and life, farm products; Transportation--in daily life of the family and neighborhood; and Food for the family--kinds needed for healthy diet with emphasis on the four food groups.

Kindergarten and First Grade Course, Topic, and Themes for Advanced Students: "Home, School, and Neighborhood or Community"

Objective of the Course

Basically the same as for "Home and School" but with an additional dimension: neighborhood.

Basic Content of the Course

In addition to the topics Family, School, Safety, Maps, National Holidays, Transportation, and Health Studies, the course includes selected neighborhood or community helpers and the services they provide: policeman, fireman, postman, milkman, newsboy, doctor, nurse, librarian, bus driver, garbage collector, and repairmen of various types. This is content that was formerly reserved for second grade and still is in most schools.

Trends in Teaching Kindergarten/First Grade Social Studies

1. More emphasis on current events readiness. Calling attention to media, newspapers, radio, TV, popular news magazines (Time, Life, and Newsweek) that carry current events.

2. More emphasis on geographic concepts, including more intensive readiness experiences for map-reading and map-making; also discussion on "the quality of life" with emphasis on managing one's environment at home and school.

3. Systematic development of economic concepts, in connection with study of the family. Division of labor, specialization in production, role of the consumer, budgeting limited resources to meet family needs, making choices among the many ways the family can use its resources. Example: Our Working World series.

4. Emphasis on variety in family patterns and ways of living. Some guides for the first grade unit on "family living" develop these main topics:

Families differ in size and composition.

The composition of a family may change.

Homes may be different in many ways.

Families are supported in many ways.

These topics are often explored through "current events" experiences.

5.   Perhaps the most important trend is toward the use of comparative studies--comparing the child's own self, home, and school with alternative lifestyles in America and in Asia, Africa, and Europe; in other words, developing readiness for global studies with emphasis on resources, interdependence, and lifestyles.

II.   Illustration of a State Kindergarten/First Grade Program

Keep in mind that there are fifty states and therefore fifty different state departments of public instruction, descriptions of courses, topics, and themes.   There is no one prescribed social studies program throughout the United States.   However, one state's description of its social studies kindergarten/first grade program will illustrate the content which the state expects to be taught.   This illustration identifies a state's suggested social studies curriculum for the first grade.

> Children examine how they learn in different environments, primarily within family, peer, educational, and social institutions.   They also begin to develop their self-concepts, group and social participation skills.   Reading skills are developed while learning about families in various parts of the world.   Students learn how families differ in composition, lifestyle and role expectations.   Studying the multiethnic nature of societies, children learn how in different environments groups of people use resources available to them, earn a living, and discover how basic social structures sustain themselves.[1]

III.   Activities and Materials Categorized by Gaining Knowledge, Processing, Valuing, and Participating

A rather common practice is to skip purposes and specific objectives which precede the activities, but in this case the objectives are extremely important for an objective in the first grade will be found in succeeding grades. The following activities and materials are part of a <u>developmental</u> program organized to build citizenship skills from one grade level to another.

A.   Purpose: to <u>gain knowledge</u> about oneself and one's family

KINDERGARTEN ACTIVITIES AND MATERIALS

Specific Objective: Develop a concept of self

    1.   <u>Up and Down the Ladder</u> (or <u>Stairs</u>) - (identifying self)

        when: recurring

        what: tape outline of ladder on floor
               tape labels on steps of ladder or use school stairs

        how: Introduce the children to the game "Up and Down the Ladder
              (or Stairs)" to knowing oneself. Explain that each child
              will climb as high on the ladder or steps as the child is
              able to recall the specific information. This activity
              should be continued from time to time until the child has
              successfully climbed the ladder or stairs.

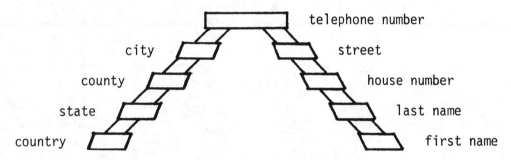

    2.   <u>Here Is My House</u> - (identifying self)

        when: recurring

        what: yarn, construction paper

        how: Construction paper is cut in the general shape of the
              student's house (A-frame, rectangle, square) and is pasted
              on manila paper with room to write name, address, and tele-
              phone number as the child learns them. Houses are placed on
              a construction paper street with paper telephone poles
              attached to houses with yarn to show how houses in the neigh-
              borhood are connected to each other.

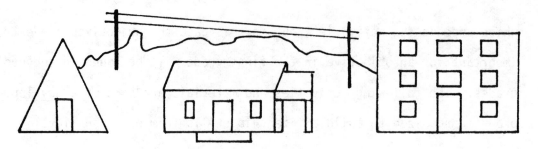

3.   <u>My Birthday</u> - (identifying self)

   when: recurring

   what: calendars (free from businesses)

   how: Help child find birthday and mark it on child's own calendar.
          Also mark it on the room calendar.   Children can look for
          birthdays and holidays.   May wish to start in January to
          illustrate entire year.

4.   <u>Birthday Cake</u> - (identifying self)

   when: recurring

   what: large paper cake and paper candles

   how: Label paper cake with current month.   Children with a birthday
          in that month put their name and date on candle and put on
          cake.   May re-use same cake each month or make a new cake,
          posting previous cakes in another part of the room.   This has
          the advantage of showing the months, the passage of time, and
          the relationship of the child's birthday to the month.

Specific Objective: Develop a concept of one's family relationships.

5.   <u>Who's Who</u> - (identifying family)

   when: two periods

   what: magazines, catalogs (Sears, Penneys, Wards)

   how: Each child finds pictures of figures that represent own family
          members, cuts them out and pastes them on separate sheets of
          paper.   Child or teacher prints label on sheets.   Fasten
          sheets into booklet for each child.

6. Who's Home - (identifying family)

    when: two periods

    what: paper cut into window shapes by teacher

    how: Child draws a house on paper. Child takes from teacher a
           paper window for each person in house, draws face of that
           person on window, and pastes it on house. Names are written
           under windows. This activity is particularly appropriate for
           children who have people living in their home who are not
           necessarily relations.

7. Relationship Clothesline - (identify close family and other relation-
                                ships)

    when: two periods

    what: clothesline, clothespins (or string and paperclips), paper

    how: Children draw pictures of family members and cut them out.
           Hang them on lines marked: brothers, aunts, fathers, grand-
           mothers, and others who may be living in the home but are not
           necessarily related.

8. Routing My Roots - (identifying family)

    when: one period

    what: dittos of geneology root form

    how: Have each child route own family roots with names and pictures.

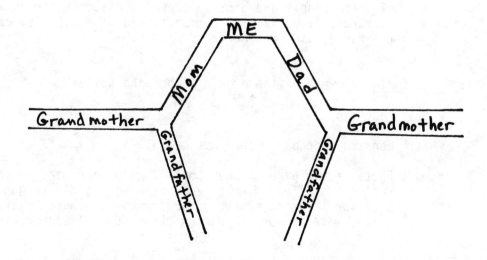

Specific Objective: Identifying one's immediate world and how it changes.

9. <u>Our Class Roots</u> - (identifying school classmates)

   when: one period

   what: tree branch (or small tree), paper leaves

   how: Child prints name on leaf and fastens on photo. Leaves are
          taped to tree branch.

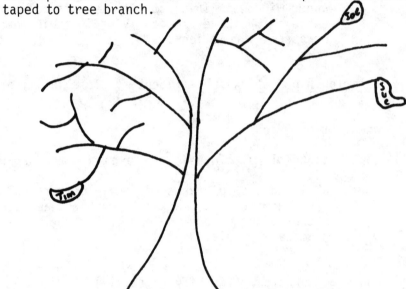

10. <u>Our Book</u>^{2} - (identifying school people)

   when: recurring

   what: paper

   how: Make booklet of children's experiences of going to school for
          the first time. After visiting with different school per-
          sonnel (nurse, principal, etc.), have children draw pictures
          of these people and dictate experience stories to go with the
          pictures, i.e., "I will not be afraid to visit Mrs. Jones,
          the nurse, if I get hurt."

11. <u>Flourishing Flowers</u> - (the growing, changing self)

   when: recurring

   what: construction paper and tape measure

   how: Fasten a big paper flower to wall with tape measure for stem.
          Fasten small leaf with child's name at child's height (may be
          necessary to make another stem if several leaves overlap).
          Leaves move up during year as child grows (measure every few
          months). May make new flower for each month.

12. <u>Seasons</u> - (changing weather or seasons)

   when: recurring

   what: material scraps and construction paper

   how: Label four separate sections of the room for each season.
          Use tree branch for little tree. Have children color leaves
          appropriately for each season and fasten to tree. Dress
          large girl and boy paper dolls in the clothes appropriate for
          the current season. Move tree and change dolls' clothes as
          seasons change. Seasonal stories can be placed near section.

FIRST GRADE ACTIVITIES AND MATERIALS

Specific Objective: Identify family relationships.

13. <u>Me and Mine</u>[3] - (identifying self and family)

   when: one period

   what: large manila paper

   how: Students make booklet pages by folding paper in half. On
          first page they put title "Me and Mine" and one sentence on
          each page which they illustrate, i.e., "This is my house."
          "This is my animal." "This is my mother."

Specific Objective: Identify family members' roles and compare with other
                     cultures.

14. <u>Family Helpers</u>[4] - (identify work roles of the family)

   when: two periods

   what: chart or questionnaire

   how: Children fill out family members including self on chart,
          what they do at home, and how it helps the family.

Family member	What member does	How it helps
grandmother	washes dishes	dishes ready for next time
older brother	mows grass	keeps lawn neat
father	paints house	makes home look nice

If children cannot fill out chart, they may take it home. Compare
and contrast jobs, i.e., Are certain jobs done by the same people
in each family? Do all older brothers cut grass?

Specific Objective: Identify how weather and surroundings affect (change) what we eat and wear and where we live.

15. Weather Person - (identifying change)

> when: recurring
>
> what: large cardboard doll, cloth or paper clothes (teacher cuts out doll and various pieces of clothing, i.e., boots, shirt, skirt, raincoat, mittens)
>
> how: Each day a different child dresses the doll according to the weather. Stick clothes to doll with rolled masking tape.

16. Weather Chart - (identifying change)

> when: recurring
>
> what: large weather chart, cards printed with days of week and weather symbols
>
> how: Each day a different child fills out the chart according to the weather.

17. Playhouse - (identifying different environments)

> when: recurring
>
> what: large packing carton
>
> how: Make a playhouse out of carton and have children decorate it using a certain theme: holidays, different cultures, life-styles.

18. Houses Around the World - (identifying different environments)

    when: two weeks

    what: resource materials, art supplies, boxes

    how: Discuss houses in own community and other climates and cul-
          tures, how they are made, and how they help people.
          Make: shoe box houses
                 cardboard carton apartment buildings
                 clay igloos and pueblos
                 "thatch" huts
                 cloth tent
          Make paper dolls to go with houses.

Specific Objective: Identify national holidays.

19. Holidays - (identifying one's culture)

    when: recurring

    what: resources, art supplies

    how: Use holidays to identify with history.
          Thanksgiving - Make Pilgrim and Indian costumes using con-
                         struction paper to make paper headbands and
                         feathers, collars and hats, cardboard shoe
                         buckles covered with aluminum foil.
          Sculpture Indian and Pilgrim faces on bottom
             of paper plates, pasting on hair, hats, etc.
          Make log cabins from Lincoln logs or rolled
             brown paper.
          Also consider foods that would be appropriate.

Specific Objective: Define neighborhood/community and examine different
                     communities.

20. A Walking Tour[5] - (identifying neighborhood)

    when: three days

    what: boxes, art supplies

    how: Take a walking tour of community. Have students listen to
          sounds (machines, traffic), look at houses, stores, pools,
          parks, places to worship, streets, trash, etc. Using what
          children learned, make a scale model on table or floor of
          their community.

21. <u>Communities Chart</u> - (identifying neighborhoods and communities)

   when: two periods

   what: chart

   how: Have children help fill out chart with things common to all
          communities (homes, transportation, schools, food, etc.).
          Children can collect illustrations or tell about where they
          have visited. May want to concentrate on a community in
          another part of the world.

22. <u>Early American Community</u> - (identifying historical communities)

   when: two weeks

   what: Lincoln logs, boxes, art supplies

   how: Use the children's understanding of their neighborhood and
          community as compared with historical American community,
          relating the present needs to the past. Have children plan
          and build an early American table top community using Lincoln
          logs, paper scenery, and people. May be play area when
          finished.

B. Purpose: to develop skills necessary to <u>process</u> information

KINDERGARTEN ACTIVITIES AND MATERIALS

Specific Objective: One skill of processing information is learning to
                     locate places such as home, land, and water on a
                     model, map, or globe and compare distances (shorter,
                     longer).

1. <u>Head to Feet</u> - (develop readiness in measurement, a skill in pro-
                     cessing information)

   when: recurring

   what: art supplies

   how: Use distances from one object or area in room to another to
          identify concepts of longer than or shorter than. Pick area
          of room for home (teacher's desk). Lay blue paper for sea
          going to the art supplies, lay brown paper for land to block
          play area. Have two lines of children lay down on paper
          (head of first child against teacher's desk on brown paper
          with toes pointing to blocks, second child's head at feet of
          first child, and so on, same for blue paper). Which line had
          the most children and so was longer? shorter? Teacher should
          make map of layout for children to color. Students can
          measure distances with yarn. Simple teacher-drawn maps for
          similar activities.

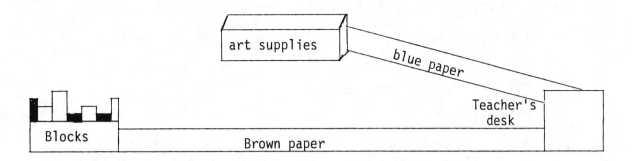

2. <u>Arrows</u> - (developing readiness in measurement, a skill for process-
           ing information)

   when: recurring

   what: colored or masking tape, simple teacher-made floor plan of
          school or kindergarten wing of school, yarn or string

   how: Arrows for walking are taped to floor. Have the children
          walk the arrows, then study arrows drawn on floor plan map.
          Children can measure distances with yarn or string and com-
          pare to see which is longer or shorter.

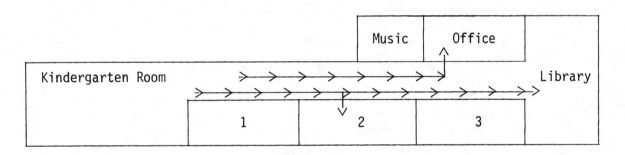

Specific Objective: Learning to group and classify.

3. <u>Let's Line Up</u> - (developing the concept of classifying, a skill in
                processing information)

   when: recurring

   what:

   how: When class must line up to leave room (library, recess), use
          categories. Teacher says, "I'm taking a potato." Each child
          must name another item in the category (vegetable) or go to
          back of line. Different categories are used so each child
          has a chance to succeed in classifying: fruits, colors,
          games, clothes.

Specific Objective: Learn to distinguish fact from fiction.

4. <u>Keep Your Ears Open</u> - (developing readiness skills for classifying information)

    when: three periods

    what: stories

    how: Read fairy or fantasy story to children and then raise specific questions, i.e., Can birds talk? Can people fly by themselves? Can objects do things people can do? Read another story and have children make a sign (clap, raise hand) when events are not based on fact.

5. <u>Strangers</u> - (identifying community safety)

    when: three periods, good at Halloween

    what: stories

    how: Read story of your choice such as "Hansel and Gretel." Discuss story in terms of present day situations: witch was a stranger who allowed children to eat house. Discuss strangers today who might offer candy or toys to children. Have children make up, draw, or tell modern versions of fairy tales. Share stories.

FIRST GRADE ACTIVITIES AND MATERIALS

Specific Objective: Learning to identify student's part of many social systems, i.e., family, neighborhood, class, school, and community.

6. <u>My Part in the School System</u>[6]

    when: two class periods

    what: picture puzzles. Before starting, make sure all puzzle pieces are color-coded or marked in some way so that the puzzles may be easily separated if they become mixed. Place each set of puzzle pieces in a separate bag. Remove and save several puzzle pieces from half of the bags (or mismatch pieces).

    how: Divide the class into groups. Give each group a bag with a complete puzzle and a bag with an incomplete puzzle. Do not tell them one puzzle is incomplete. (Groups of two each are ideal, but group size will depend on the size of your class and the number of puzzles you have.) Encourage students to complete a whole puzzle from each separate bag. After sufficient time, have students identify which bag had a complete puzzle and which did not. Have groups tell why one bag or set of pieces fit together and one did not, reinforcing such words as "parts," "whole," "fit together," and "connected."

Explain to students that each completed puzzle is a "system," using the words stressed above. Make sure they also understand that an incomplete puzzle is <u>not</u> a complete system because it is not whole. Relate this concept of system to student's part in school system, meaning student is part of a family, part of the class, part of the community, and all of these--family, class, school, and community--are systems.

7.   <u>You Depend on Me</u> - (identifying the concept of interdependence)

    when: three periods

    what: butcher paper (enough to make a full-scale cutout of each child)

    how: Make a picture of each child by having the child lie down on the paper and then tracing around his or her outline. Cut out figures and allow children to color in features, clothes, etc. Hold a class discussion:

    Start with how parts of the body help (depend on) each other. For example, <u>hand</u> combs <u>hair</u>, <u>eyes</u> see where <u>feet</u> walk, <u>hand</u> turns pages of book so <u>eyes</u> can see pictures. The concept of interdependence can then be extended to family members depending on each other and then extended to class members depending on each other.

    The teacher may wish to talk about the physically handicapped during this activity. What happens when a body part breaks down or is missing? Usually the other parts of the body have to work harder (a blind person's hearing may become more acute). Extend the idea to the family. When a family member is sick or away, others must work harder to get chores done, etc. Extend the idea to the class members as part of a group.

    As a conclusion the teacher may want to put the children's pictures with hands linked in a circle on the classroom walls, a sign not only of interdependence but of cooperation--an attitude which is emphasized as important for the completion of any group activity.

Specific Objective: Learning to group and classify.

8.   <u>Fish Pond</u> - (developing the processing skill of classifying and categorizing)

    when: recurring

    what: sticks with magnets attached, boxes or buckets

    how: Cut pictures from magazines, attach paper clips, and place in a box called "Fish Pond." Children fish with poles and separate what they catch into correct box or bucket by categories (food, animals, transportation, etc.) May also use things people use or make such as artwork, food, clothes, and have children categorize in buckets as to country or culture.

9.   Toys From Home - (developing the processing skill of classifying and categorizing)

when: one period

what: toys from home

how: Children bring a favorite toy. Children name categories. Categories should be discussed and voted on: games, wheeled toys, dolls, etc.

10.   What We Need - (developing the processing skill of classifying and categorizing)

when: three periods

what: magazines, catalogs (Wards, Penneys, Sears)

how: Divide children into committees. Have each member cut out pictures of things child thinks are necessary in order to live. Committees place like things (i.e., clothing) in construction paper folders. Label one folder "Committee Problems," do not label other folders yet.

       Have a class meeting. Each committee shows folders to entire class. Are there similarities? Put all like pictures together and name group, i.e., food, tools. Committees discuss "problem" pictures and see if they fit a category, need a new category, or if item is not necessary. Teacher should help committees as they work.

11.   Grouping - (developing the processing skill of classifying and categorizing)

when: one period for each activity

what: materials for each activity

how: groups -
       foods--use paper plates to hold cut-out pictures of foods
           grouped by breakfast, lunch, dinner. Group by color,
           by likes and dislikes, by holidays, by hot and cold.
       clothing--plan a fashion show and include categories such
           as work clothes, school clothes, party clothes, play
           clothes, costumes, adult clothes. Invite another class
           or parents for audience.
           Make puppets and dress by categories.
       shelter--
       transportation--

Specific Objective: Interpreting symbols, a skill in processing information.

> NOTE: This is an extremely important skill because children do not necessarily recognize that symbols represent a real object.

12. <u>Symbols</u> - (symbolizing: a processing skill)

    when: two periods

    what: classroom objects

    how: Begin with maps and globes and the colors for land and sea. Take a large piece of paper and place small objects on it (pencil, chalk, paper clips, block, etc.) and let children examine it. Remove objects and ask a child to replace them exactly as teacher had them. Children will argue about placement and end up not being sure. Replace articles and have children draw around each one. Remove articles and have same child replace them. Discuss use of symbols and how paper is a simple map. Trace six rulers and six scissors on a paper. Remove and place legend in corner of paper:

Show as map.

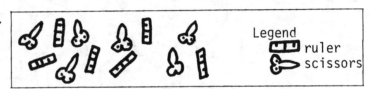

13. <u>Floor Plan</u> - (symbolizing: a processing skill)

    when: two periods

    what: doll house furniture or little boxes to represent furniture

    how: Same activities as "Symbols" above. Make a room plan of furniture and then decide on symbols you will use to represent furniture.

    ☐ BED   ☐ TABLE   ◯ CHAIR   Etc.

Make a new floor plan using only symbols.

Specific Objective: Learn to distinguish fact from fiction.

14. <u>Is It True?</u> - (process of identifying facts)

    when: two periods

    what: copies of commercials heard or seen by children

    how: Discuss how commercials may influence people. Did you beg mother to buy cereal because of prize and then did not want to eat cereal? Are brand name toys better than other toys? Toys brought from home might be compared (would help if parents could recall price of toys).

C.   Purpose: to develop the skill to examine <u>values</u> and beliefs

KINDERGARTEN ACTIVITIES AND MATERIALS

Specific Objective: Valuing the knowing of oneself.

1.   <u>Put Me Together</u> - (valuing the uniqueness of self)

when: three weeks

what: brown (butcher) paper, masking tape

how: Trace around each child naming parts of the body, then have
       child paint or color tracing. Cut portrait outline and then
       cut into separate body parts (one person at a time). Attach
       little rolls of masking tape to the back of each piece. Have
       child stand in front of mirror and reassemble parts, working
       from head to feet. Remove tape and place pieces in envelope
       for further practice away from mirror.

hair

face

ears

neck

arm

wrist

hand

thumb

fingers

trunk

legs

thigh

calf

ankle

foot

shoe

2. <u>Me, Myself, and I</u> - (valuing the uniqueness of self)

    when: two weeks

    what: coat hangers, paper

    how: Make a booklet including sheets for: my name, my picture, my hand, my footprint, my house, my friend, my room, my toys, etc. Make a mobile using a coat hanger.

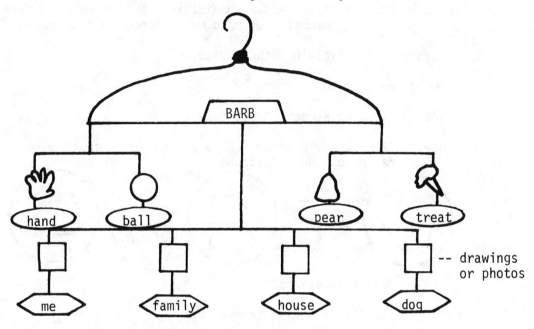

Specific Objective: Identify actions or feelings that are similar or different from storybook characters.

3. <u>Reactions</u> - (valuing feelings)

    when: recurring

    what: stories, films, etc.

    how: Read a story or show film and ask questions, i.e., "What would you have done or felt if 'it' had happened to you?" Have children draw pictures about what they liked best and then let child dictate sentences about drawing, i.e., "I liked the part where . . ." Make papers into a book.

4. <u>Feelings</u> - (valuing feelings)

    when: recurring

    what: stories

    how: Read stories showing emotions (fear, love, etc.). Choose a feeling such as "I felt angry . . ." Have children draw pictures of themselves in a situation that made them angry (friend broke favorite toy, etc.) and then have child dictate story that goes with picture. Vary emotions. Discuss how all people have similar emotions. Discuss mixed emotions, i.e., want to start kindergarten but afraid to go to school.

FIRST GRADE ACTIVITIES AND MATERIALS

Specific Objective: Realize people in different societies may behave differently but have many things in common.

5.   <u>Glad or Sad</u> - (valuing other cultures)

when: one period

what: ditto or stencil questionnaire

how: After studying other cultures, children could do a value rating on the questionnaire.

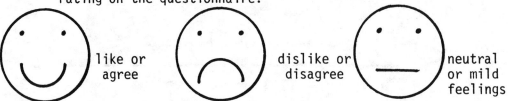

like or agree   dislike or disagree   neutral or mild feelings

Sample questions:

1. I like German sauerkraut _____.

2. I like Chinese fortune cookies _____.

3. I like Dutch cheese _____.

Discuss the fact that though people may disagree on what they like to eat, they all still eat.

6.   <u>What to Choose</u> - (practicing evaluating questions, a readiness activity preparing for the asking of questions)

when: two periods

what: Teacher prepares stencil or ditto of questions that require child to make a choice between several alternatives.

how: Have children fold and cut large manila paper into booklet. Have them cut stencil and paste each evaluation question on a separate page of booklet. Then they can illustrate their answers on those pages.

Use after studying other cultures, times, and weather.

```
The weather I like to dress for is _____

and I wear _____ .
- - - - - - - - - - - - - - - - - - - - - - - - - -
On Halloween I would like to wear a costume from another

country.  I would be _____ .
- - - - - - - - - - - - - - - - - - - - - - - - - -
If I were in a play about the first Thanksgiving, I would

dress as _____ .
```

Specific Objective: Identifying "advantage" and "disadvantage" value judgments.

7.   Our Classroom - (practice valuing on real problems)

   when: one period

   what: chart

   how: Use classroom to identify meaning of advantage and disadvantage. Discuss good and bad things about classroom and then make a chart.

Our Classroom	
Disadvantages	Advantages
1. Plants don't grow well	1. Shady side of building
2. Noisy	2. Close to playground
3. Late lunch schedule	3. Short afternoon
4. Can't chew gum	4. Don't get "stuck-up" with gum

8.   What Can We Do About It? - (practice valuing on real problems)

   when: several periods

   what:

   how: Refer to classroom chart on advantages and disadvantages. Discuss ways disadvantages might be changed where possible. Some things cannot be changed but list suggestions and try. For example, let children chew sugarless gum. If they are responsible for carefully throwing it away, they get to keep the privilege.

9.   <u>Improving the Neighborhood</u> - (practice valuing on real problems)

   when: several periods

   what:

   how: Discuss advantages and disadvantages in neighborhood, such as crossing streets, safety, facilities for play, library. Discuss suggestions for improvement that children might do: pick up litter, get permission to do some planting.

D.   Purpose: Apply knowledge through active <u>participation</u> in society

KINDERGARTEN ACTIVITIES AND MATERIALS

Specific Objective: Participate with others to solve problems and find solutions.

1.   <u>Award</u> - (practicing participation by achieving goals)

   when: recurring

   what: paper tree and ladder, paper awards

   how: Teacher helps child decide on area which needs personal improvement such as putting toys away. On large paper draw a tree with kitten stuck high up in the branches. Draw a ladder reaching up to cat. Put child's name on little paper. Each time child succeeds in task, child's name moves up a rung of the ladder. When child reaches the top, child gets the kitten award. The award is a kitten and a paper blue ribbon which the child gets to wear for the rest of the day and then take home. Repeat with new goals.

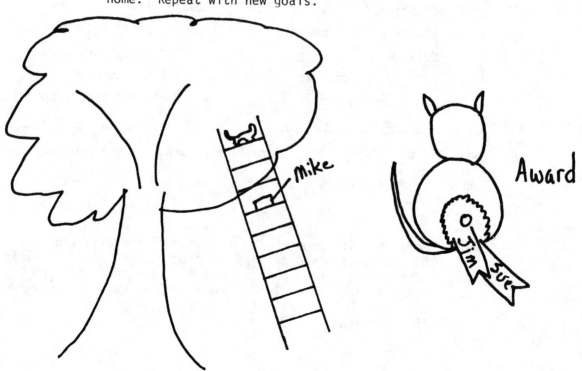

KINDERGARTEN AND FIRST GRADE ACTIVITIES AND MATERIALS

Specific Objective: Preparation in developing rules for classroom behavior.

2. Trusty Tricks - (developing readiness for practicing participation)

when: recurring

what:

how: (a) During first days of school teacher circulates, giving praise where good behavior is observed. "I like how Tim and Mike are sharing the Lincoln logs. I like how Sue and Jane are sharing the doll house." If child is not using good rule (behavior), help to correct it on the spot. "I like to use a clean paint brush when I start to paint. Help me clean the brushes you just used so that they will be ready to use again."
(b) Appoint child of the day to be line leader, announce show and tell, etc. Child will pick theme: "We will all be kittens." Children pretend to be kittens when walking in halls, etc. They evaluate if they were quiet as a cat. Let child use imagination.
(c) Discuss possible problems with total group. Suppose two people want to use all long blocks at the same time. Let them offer solutions. No need to write all rules down because "class members are so considerate and know what to do."

Notes

1 Indiana Department of Public Instruction. 1978 Indiana textbook adoption categories for social studies. Indianapolis: Author, 1978, p. 2.

2 Barth, J. L., & Shermis, S. S. Teaching social studies to gifted and talented students. Indianapolis: Indiana Department of Public Instruction, 1981, p. 18.

3 Ibid., p. 21.

4 Ibid.

5 Ibid.

6 This activity was suggested by Education for a world in change, INTERCOM 84/85 [D. C. King, M. S. Branson, & L. E. Condon (Eds.), Center for Global Perspectives, 1976, p. 34] and was adapted for use in this text.

INTEREST FORM

You have just completed the Chapter Kindergarten/First Grade. In an effort to have you identify activities and materials that seem most promising at this grade level to you, please fill out the following interest form.

Instructions:

Identify two activities from this chapter. Name the activities and breifly describe why these particular activities are of interest to you.

ACTIVITY 1

ACTIVITY 2

CHAPTER SECOND GRADE

ACTIVITIES AND MATERIALS FOR SECOND GRADE

CHAPTER SECOND GRADE

Organization of the Chapter

Each succeeding chapter represents a particular grade level, in this case second grade. Each chapter consists of three parts: the first part is a brief discussion on courses, topics, and national trends in teaching second grade throughout the United States; the second part is an example of a state second grade program; the third part has activities and materials for the second grade categorized by the four objectives for teaching social studies-- gaining knowledge, processing, valuing, and participating.

I. Topics Taught and National Trends in Teaching Second Grade

Course, Topics, and Themes Frequently Covered in Second Grade: "Neighborhood and Community"

Objectives of the Course

Continuing from the first grade, emphasis should be upon a concept of interdependence, the notion that we are not alone, that we depend on many others (food, oil, raw materials from overseas). Highlight the services and activities in the neighborhood community that affect everyday life and processes of living with the purpose of teaching a comparative study of communities other than the child's own. Also continue from the first grade emphasis on fostering the positive attitude of cooperation among people. Encourage current events-mindedness and lay foundations for a systematic geographic study.

Basic Content of the Course

Second graders study community helpers with emphasis on names and places and type of work, i.e., fireman, policeman, postman, milkman, store keeper (grocery, drugstore, bank), librarian, transportation workers, doctors, repair-men of various types (TV, electrician, plumber, gas, telephone), and others who affect daily life. In addition, one or more topics such as transportation within the community, communication within the community, or food types required for good health are usually studied in the second grade. Besides the study of the community, second graders often have units of work on the relationship between types of clothing and seasons of the year, the difference between city life and country life, and special observance of national holidays and the birthdays of national heroes (Washington, Lincoln, Martin Luther King).

NOTE: As you surely have already noted, second grade objectives, topics, courses, and content may seem not to be significantly different from those suggested for first grade. There is a difference. The difference is in the depth of the topic to be studied and in the breadth to which the study should be expanded to cover more people, places, and things than were covered in first grade.

Second Grade Course, Topic, and Themes for Advanced Students:
"The Community"

Objectives of the Course

Essentially the same as for neighborhood community with emphasis on basic needs of people.

Basic Content of the Course

How needs of people in the community for goods, clothing, shelter, protection, transportation, and communication are met. A typical illustration of a curriculum guide that emphasizes community living is the following:

Geographic Overview (relating to the community as a whole, and to basic needs of food, clothing, and shelter)

Our Community (background of geography; homes; types of stores; factories; places of interest)

Food (kinds, balanced diets)

Clothing (traced from raw material to product; wool, cotton, flax, silk, synthetics)

Shelter (how a home is build--not just the shape of the home as in first grade but place emphasis on planners, workers, materials, utilities)

Trends in Teaching Second Grade Social Studies

1.   The chief trend is toward an in-depth study of neighborhood and community. Some programs approach this by moving the "food, shelter, clothing" themes from the third grade into the second and including in them the treatment of "helpers" who have not already been studied in first grade. Comparative studies of food, clothing, and shelter in communities, in other cultures, and/ or in an earlier period of time (as in pioneer days) are often topics at the second grade level.

2.   A popular trend is to study each "helper" and his job more fully, and to include a greater variety of helpers, such as the street cleaner, the shoe repairman, the TV repairman, the bus driver, the filling station attendant, the librarian, and the playground director, as well as the traditional fireman, policeman, etc. Helpers may be studied through such questions as these: What is his job and why is it important to us? What education and training does he have to have? What special skills? What special equipment does he use? Who pays him (leading into some study of local governmtnt)? How are the services this helper gives us provided for in other communities, in other cultures, and in different types of rural, suburban, or city communities, and how were they provided for in past times--as in pioneer days? Is the helper's job really necessary? Could the community, could I, do without the helper's service?

3.   A continuing trend is toward emphasis on basic social science concepts, such as specialization of labor and production, how goods are distributed in our economic system through private business organizations, etc., as the various services and institutions within the community are studied.

4.   Some teacher's guides and textbooks are beginning to suggest units on the study of local government. This is partly an attempt to stimulate a positive and constructive civic attitude, and partly an attempt to show how

the political system delivers neighborhood and community services. It is a
continuing effort to demonstrate that garbage pickup, paving and fixing of
roads, and street lights do not just happen, they are the consequences of
political decisions.

5.   Recall that current events in the first grade was limited to readiness exercises. By second grade current events should be a regular part of the
social studies program. Teachers are being encouraged to continue readiness
experiences for map reading and in other geographic skills such as symbol interpretation.

6.   As in the first grade, a popular trend is toward comparative studies
with emphasis upon global studies. Comparisons are often made between climates
and family roles in other cultures. Again the emphasis is on broadening the
child's outlook. Within recent years this emphasis has increased because
children view TV programs that are filmed in other nations and in consequence
are exposed to other cultures.

II.   Illustration of a State Second Grade Program

There is no one prescribed social studies program throughout the United
States. However, one state's description of its social studies second grade
program will illustrate the content which the state expects to be taught.
This illustration identifies a state's suggested social studies curriculum for
the second grade.

> Students study the role of the individual in the neighborhood com-
> munity in which they live and how needs are met through human inter-
> action and communication. Neighborhood and world interdependence
> are studied while examining how needs are met for transportation,
> for government, and in the market place. Students continue to
> develop self-concept, reading, group and social participation, cur-
> rent events, and comparative study skills.[1]

III. Activities and Materials Categorized by
Gaining Knowledge, Processing, Valuing, and Participating

A common practice is to skip specific objectives which precede the activities, but in this case the objectives are extremely important since an objective in the second grade will be found in succeeding grades. The following
activities and materials are part of a developmental program organized to build
citizenship skills from one grade to another.

SECOND GRADE ACTIVITIES AND MATERIALS

A.   Purpose: to gain knowledge about the human condition which includes past,
     present, and future

   Specific Objective: Learn about roles and services performed by people who
                        live or work in the neighborhood/community.

   1.   Prop Box[2] - (identifying work roles in neighborhood/community)

        when: recurring

        what: sturdy boxes and various items students contribute

        how: A prop box is composed of specialized items combined to foster
                a specific type of play. This combination of ordinary house-
                wares can afford a child hours of enjoyment while providing
                an educational experience. A prop box contains the kinds of
                things which prevent play from becoming stale or from stopping
                altogether. Watch the play. Where is it going? What will
                keep it going?

                What does a mechanic need when he/she wants to repair cars or
                bikes, trains or planes? Tools, parts, wires, flashlight,
                etc. What does an astronaut need when he/she is about to
                visit the moon? Proper clothing, instruments, a space panel,
                food containers, camera, etc. What might a nurse require in
                order to tend an emergency case? Bandages, medicine bottles,
                hot water bottle, uniform, etc.

                Boxes of props may be started as children need materials to
                extend their play (electrical switches, wires, and pliers for
                the electrician; plastic flowers and vases for the florist).
                The props are real and that is their appeal. Or they are
                made to order by the players over at the art center or the
                carpentry table. And so they are meaningful because they are
                made the way a child thinks they should be made. As an open-
                ended material, prop boxes can be developed for children to
                use at home or at school. At home they may be joint creations
                of parent and child, or created as a gift for a young child.

At school they are developed by children and staff together. They constantly grow. They fill up and probably start to spill over as everyone finds things or makes things to add. Since these are really separate boxes for various kinds of role-playing, they can be made easily identifiable to children by appropriate pictures cut from magazines or drawn by children and/or adults and pasted on boxes.

Specific Objective: Identify family member roles and compare with other cultures.

2.   What Is It and Who Uses It? - (identifying work roles in other cultures)

when: three periods

what: articles from other cultures, perhaps brought from home by children. Other cultures means foreign lands (such as Canada, Mexico, Europe), but it also means other cultures within the United States (such as ethnic groups, American Indians, New England, Appalachia, the South, etc.). Remember that grand-parents and older relatives may very well represent a different age of cultural development in the United States and therefore qualify as having articles from "other cultures."

how: Separate class into groups and divide the articles between the groups. Move articles from group to group so that each group can see all articles. Questions to ask: What is it? What does it do? What is it made of and how (by hand)? Does it have a name? Who uses it? Do we have anything like it? Can you tell anything about people who use it? Is it useful?

Have class separate articles into various displays as to who in the family they think uses them. Study information about articles used by people in other cultures and then see if articles had to be moved from one display to another. Have children explain moves.

3.   Picturing Cultural Difference - (identifying work roles in other cultures)

when: one week

what: painting supplies

how: After studying roles of people in other cultures, have each child pick a person in another culture to paint, showing role that person plays. May also paint whole family engaged in activity typical to their culture.

Have children write stories to go with paintings.

Specific Objective: Define neighborhood/community and examine different
                    communities.

4. Ants and Bees[3] - (identifying another community)

    when: two or three weeks

    what: ant colony and/or bee hive or audiovisual aids

    how: Study an ant or bee community either by bringing them into
           the classroom or by using pictures and films. Questions
           could include: Is there a group? Do they all do the same
           work? Do they share anything? Do they have similar problems?
           Do they do any activities together? Is there a sign of indi-
           vidual initiative? How do you feel about the ants and bees
           community? Suppose you could join such a community, would
           you?

5. Community Criteria - (identifying community)

    when: two periods

    what: four or five pictures--one of city, one of plains, one of a
           farm, one of a small town

    how: Post the pictures, then have children identify which are
           communities and which are not. The important part of the
           exercise is listing under each picture why it is or is not a
           community. Out of the reasons will come the criteria for
           identifying what is or is not a community. The final step in
           this exercise is to apply the criteria to communities near
           the school. One additional exercise might be for the children
           to collect pictures from magazines showing different types of
           communities throughout the world. Be sure they apply the
           criteria they have learned above to their magazine "scrapbook"
           communities.

Specific Objective: Learn about services performed by community members.

6. Who Will We Be? - (identifying different kinds of work)

    when: three periods

    what: large paper, art supplies

    how: Make a display of workers in the community. Separate children
           into two groups. Groups must select a worker they want to
           depict. Have group of children trace one other group member
           on paper. Figure of child on paper is then colored or painted
           in the clothing or uniform of their chosen worker.

           Variation: Make puppets instead of using figures of children.

7. <u>What Would Happen?</u> - (identifying different kinds of work)

    when: one period

    what: paper

    how: Choose a worker in community and ask, "If all workers were bakers . . . ." Children must finish sentence and tell what would happen if there were no variety of workers in the community. Children could also draw pictures to illustrate their description. To illustrate a community with only bakers and no other services, draw people without cars, shoes, clothes, houses, etc.

8. <u>Play Time</u> - (identifying different kinds of work)

    when: recurring

    what: materials needed for each activity listed

    how: Pantomime: One child or a group of children pantomime work done by a specific worker. Class tries to guess the worker. Discuss what training this worker needs and whether worker is needed in neighborhood community.

    Envelope: Place picture of worker cut from magazine or drawn by children in envelope (one worker to one envelope). Have child pick envelope. Class must try to guess worker by asking questions that can only be answered by yes or no. One who guesses worker gets to draw next envelope.

Specific Objective: Learn to distinguish between urban, suburban, and rural communities.

9. <u>From City to Farm</u> - (identifying contrast between communities)

    when: four or five periods

    what: resource materials, pictures

    how: Give children plenty of time to examine resource materials and pictures, then make a chart on the differences between rural, suburban, urban. Discuss similarities and differences and list items that are interdependent. Pick one topic such as bread and describe how each community might be involved in making or using it. Have children categorize pictures of communities into urban, rural, suburban.

COMMUNITIES

	Urban	Suburban	Rural
Buildings			
Transportation	taxi, bus, truck	cars, school bus, commuter train	car, truck, horse
Homes			
Pollution			
Etc.			

10. Clean Clothes for Everyone - (identifying community service showing interdependence)

when: five or six periods

what: field trip

how: Visit a service-type industry such as bakery, food processing or canning plant, small factory, dry cleaning plant. Almost all neighborhoods have a dry cleaner. Have children prepare questions to ask on trip such as: Where do workers live who work at dry cleaning plant? How far do they commute? Who are cleaner's customers (individuals, restaurants, businesses, etc.)? Where does cleaner get supplies (chemicals) to clean clothes? After field trip, discuss answers and plot answers on a map showing interdependence of urban, suburban, and rural people, products, etc.

Specific Objective: Learn to distinguish between characteristics of different climates and how one lives in each.

11. Let's Visit - (identifying climates)

when: three or four periods

what: shopping bags or suitcases made from cartons

how: Children plan make-believe trips to places having different climates. Children can cut out or draw pictures of items (clothing, etc.) they will need in new climate and "pack" them in suitcases. They will be staying a long time in new climate, so they should include shelter, tools, etc. Children can show suitcases to class, explaining relationship between clothing, shelter, tools, and climate.

12. <u>This Climate Calls For . . .</u> - (identifying climates)

   when: two or three periods

   what: magazines, several tree branches or paper-made trees

   how: Spread trees around room, labeling each tree with a different
          climate. Children cut out pictures that show ways of life
          for different climates and hang on appropriate tree.

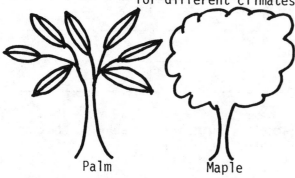

Palm   Maple   Pine   Cactus

B.   Purpose: Develop skills necessary to <u>process</u> information

Specific Objective: Learning to group and classify.

1. <u>Recall and Categorize</u> - (developing the concept of classifying, a
                              skill in processing information)

   when: three or four periods

   what: collection of small objects, tray

   how: Teacher arranges small objects such as pencils, paper clips.
          thumb tacks, plant on a tray. Children view the tray for one
          minute. Remove tray and have children draw or write down all
          the items they can remember. Discuss how categorizing things
          (food, writing materials) helps you remember. Winners are
          those children who remember the most items.

Specific Objective: Interpreting symbols, a skill in processing information.

   NOTE: This is an extremely important skill because children
   do not necessarily recognize that symbols represent a real object.

2. <u>Our Own Symbols</u> - (symbolizing, a processing skill)

   when: three periods

   what: paper, crayons

   how: Discuss symbols that could be used in landscape pictures:
          hills, mountains, roads, bridges, trees. Children decide
          what symbols should be and draw them on a chart. Label

symbols. Each child draws a landscape picture and then he/she makes a map of picture using only symbols.

 mountains   tree    road

Specific Objective: Learning to locate areas on community map.

3. <u>Mapping Our School and Neighborhood</u> - (developing map skills)

   when: four or five periods

   what: large paper, little blocks or pieces of cardboard or colored paper

   how: Take a walk around school and neighboring area, having children take notes or make sketches of what they see. Separate class into groups and give each group a large piece of paper to be used as map. Children place school (using blocks or cardboard) on map, and then draw in or use colored paper for grounds of school, surrounding streets, buildings, area (pool, woods, etc.). If children cannot remember or disagree, repeat the walk. Continue until map is complete. Same activity could be done for neighborhood shopping area.

4. <u>Tracing Our Community</u> - (developing map skills)

   when: three or four periods

   what: Prepare transparency that shows the streets, buildings, and major land forms around the school and immediate neighborhood and/or community.

   how: Project transparency from projector onto a large piece of butcher paper. Have children trace in streets, land forms, buildings, etc. Then each child should locate his own home and label it. Have children locate and label stores, schools, etc.

5. <u>Planning New Community</u> - (developing map skills)

   when: two or three periods

   what: art supplies, boxes

   how: Cover large table with paper. Children decide what community needs and use milk cartons, boxes, etc. to lay out what they believe to be a good community. Then each child makes a map of the new community that includes a legend which symbolizes land forms, buildings, parks, shopping centers, etc.

Specific Objective: Learning our nation is composed of states and locating states and their capitals.

6. <u>Same States Game</u> - (map skills)

    when: two or three periods

    what: large map of US

    how: Using children's initials, match them to first letter of state and/or state capital names. For example:

    Ivy, Irene - Iowa, Indianapolis
    Matt, Mike - Massachusetts, Montana
    Tim, Tom - Texas, Trenton

    Have students write their names on states that have the same first letter. After students have written names on map, discuss those states that have no student names on them. Identify for those states without students' names people that the students might know by name such as national figures and community and school people.

7. <u>Multiethnic Map</u> - (map skills)

    when: one period

    what: large US map, magazines

    how: Have children cut out pictures of <u>people</u> (all kinds of people) from magazines and cover the map with the pictures (collage). Teacher places state outlines over collage with magic marker. Display the collage and title it, "Each of the 50 States and Its People Are Part of the US." The pictures of people probably represent the multiethnic character of the country. This exercise reinforces the notion that this is a pluralistic nation.

8. <u>State Songs</u> - (location and direction skills)

    when: recurring

    what: records, song books

    how: Add music to your program by listening to or singing songs that mention states or particular parts of the country.

    "Rocky Mountain High"   "My Old Kentucky Home"
    "Deep in the Heart of Texas"   "This Land is Your Land"
    "Sidewalks of New York"
    "Fifty Nifty States" - (the best one for learning all the
      states. It begins, "Fifty nifty United States from thirteen
      original colonies . . .")

Specific Objective: Learn to distinguish fact from fiction.

9.   Addled Ads - (process of identifying facts)

   when: three or four periods

   what: paper

   how: Have children draw an advertisement, then tell or write about
           it. Make up a funny commercial such as "Dirty Dishes are
           Delicious." Can use TV set (below) to show commercial.
           Place emphasis upon importance of identifying commercials,
           noting that commercials are not necessarily interested in
           offering facts but rather in stimulating interest. The funny
           commercials the children make up should point up the differ-
           ence between stimulating interest and the giving of accurate
           information.

           TV Sets: Make TV by cutting part of side out of carton and
           covering the hole with cellophane. Make holes in top and
           bottom in back of cellophane screen big enough for two sticks
           to pass through. Draw pictures, in order, on long paper and
           roll from one stick to another to give the effect of a moving
           picture.

           Variation: Make TV set the same as above but use puppets
           attached to popsicle sticks stuck through holes in top.

           TV sets can be used for showing commercials, current events,
           summarizing field trips, and other experiences.

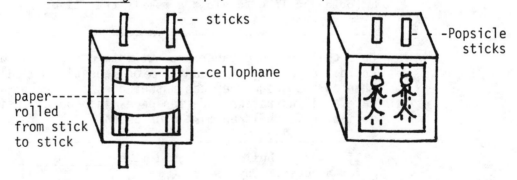

10.   How Do They Do It? - (process of identifying facts)

   when: one or two periods

   what: visits from people who create special effects

   how: To explain how some of the "super heroes" such as Superman do
           things they do, invite someone who works with or understands
           special effects to demonstrate how things are made to look
           real on TV and in movies. The best place to find people who
           create special effects is in the theater where the set design-
           ers are required to simulate the real. The point being that,

in part, the world of TV, movies, theater (entertainment) is created fiction and that it is important to learn to distinguish between the real and the unreal, between fact and fiction, for in the end we are talking about belief and disbelief. The very essence of processing information is at times identifying those things which are true and should be believed.

C. Purpose: Acquiring the skill to examine <u>values</u> and beliefs

Specific Objective: To encourage an attitude that people around the world are both alike and different.

1. <u>Would You Like . . . ?</u> - (practicing evaluative questions, a readiness exercise building skills on asking questions)

   when: two periods

   what: paper, ditto made by teacher that questions what other cultures (of those studied) children would like to visit:

   > Would you like to visit a family that lives in a high rise or on a farm?
   >
   > Would you like to visit a family that lives in an igloo?
   >
   > Would you like to visit a family that lives in a pueblo, kibbutz?

   how: Have children fold paper and cut into pages. Children should cut ditto so that they can paste one question on each page, then on that page they can answer question, tell why, and make an illustration. Fasten pages into book. Using same format, have children make book on roles:

   > If I were a builder, I would make _____ for a house. Why?
   >
   > If I were a man or woman, I would like to work in a _____. Why?

Specific Objective: Practicing value judgments by identifying "advantages" and "disadvantages."

2. <u>Questions, Questions, Questions</u> - (practicing valuing on real problems)

   when: four or five periods

what: valuing questionnaires prepared by teacher

how: Prepare questions for children to answer individually concern-
        ing what they think are good and bad things about their com-
        munity. Example:

> In my neighborhood I like _____ best.
> In my neighborhood I would like to see
>   _____ changed.
> If I were a worker in my community I would
>   _____.
> The job I would like least in my community
>   is _____.

Prepare similar questionnaire for children to take home for
parents to answer. Prepare survey sheet for community members
and have children interview people. Survey should have people
rank what they think the community's three greatest advantages
and three greatest disadvantages are. Compare children's,
parents', and community members' answers. Do they agree or
disagree? Why?

3. What Can We Do? - (social action, practicing valuing on real problems)

when: two or three weeks

what: data from questionnaires in previous activity

how: Using answers from questionnaires, have class choose a social
        problem that they identify as a real problem to them. Discuss
        the different responses the class might make to the problem.
        If the children perceive the social/community problem as real
        to them, they might wish to not only study but also act upon
        the problem. The teacher's role is to help students identify
        and if possible to act through some form of participation.
        What is important for the children at the second grade level
        is to know that they are capable of identifying and partici-
        pating.

        An illustration of a real problem for second graders might be
        something like this: Suppose stray dogs were manacing the
        children while they were walking to and from school, barking,
        chasing, and generally frightening children off the sidewalk
        into the street. Having identified this as a real problem to
        some members of the class, the class could consider what would
        be appropriate action to deal with the problem. The children
        might well identify such problems as: How did the dogs get
        there? What happens to dogs when they are not cared for?, What
        might happen if the dogs were captured and sent to the Animal
        Shelter? What officials in the community are responsible for
        dealing with this problem? The class might decide to ask the
        appropriate official to visit the class and discuss the prob-
        lem. The children may discover that what seems like an easy
        solution to their problem may represent a fatal solution for
        the dogs. What decision will the class make?

D.   Purpose: The application of knowledge through active <u>participation</u> in
                society

     Specific Objective: Participate with others to solve and find solutions.

     1.   <u>Nonverbal Communication</u>[4] - (participating in observation experience
                                           to note nonverbal behavior)

          when: two class periods

          what: materials for note taking

          how: Explain the meaning of nonverbal communication to children.
                 For example, a person makes a "face" when tasting something
                 unpleasant, a mother slaps a child's hand away from something
                 that should not be touched.

                 Plan a short walk through school and on playground to observe
                 nonverbal communication. Establish some ground rules for
                 conduct on this walk. As far as possible let students set the
                 rules.

                 Take the walk and have students write down brief notes or
                 draw pictures that illustrate the behavior (nonverbal) they
                 observe along the way. Hold class discussion on what students
                 observed, letting students both describe and demonstrate the
                 behavior if they wish. List behavior on the board. Can the
                 behavior be classified in any way?

                                      teacher behavior?
                                      student behavior?
                                      one-to-one behavior?
                                      group behavior?
                                      negative behavior?
                                      positive behavior?

     2.   <u>We've Got Problems</u> - (practicing social action through participation)

          when: recurring

          what: puppets

          how: Two or three children plan and present a puppet show on a
                 problem situation or conflict (may wish to use TV set made and
                 used in an earlier activity). The children can stop the show
                 before the problem is resolved. Class discusses possible
                 solutions. Children presenting puppet show pick solution
                 they will use to complete show.

Specific Objective: Preparation in developing rules for classroom behavior.

3. Looking Over the Rules - (participating in establishing rules)

   when: one period

   what: copies of school rules and class regulations

   how: After identifying and discussing the rules of school with the
          class, use the following strategy:
          (1) Discuss by reviewing and evaluating the rules:
              (a) Are there any complaints about the rules?
              (b) Did we follow the rules?
              (c) Are there times when you feel we shouldn't follow the
                  rules?
              (d) Did following/not following the rules help/hurt us in
                  any way (accomplish more, being held after school,
                  length of recess, etc.)?
              (e) Would you change any rule?
              (f) Add rules?
              (g) Do you follow rules without being told?
              (h) Do you need to be responsible to follow rules others
                  make?
              (i) Are you responsible to follow rules you help to make?
          (2) Evaluate pupil progress during report period conference.
          (3) Role-play fairy stories or true stories where people fail
              to follow rules.

          Emphasize with the children participation in evaluation and
          the practice of real rule-making. The point should be made
          (repeatedly) that along with participation goes responsibility.

4. Why Rules, Can They Be Changed? - (participating in establishing
                                        rules)

   when: two or three periods

   what: newspaper and magazine pictures

   how: (1) Have children tell, write, or draw: If I could change
              the school, I would _____. Discuss with class.

          (2) Have children act out illustrations of people following
              or breaking rules.

          (3) Compare and contrast pictures of people at home, school,
              in community who are following rules.

          (4) Take a field trip to find examples of rules for all
              people, i.e., traffic light, no parking sign, no
              smoking sign.

Notes

[1] Indiana Department of Public Instruction. 1978 Indiana textbook adoption categories for social studies. Indianapolis: Author, 1978, p. 2.

[2] Barth, J. L., & Shermis, S. S. Teaching social studies to gifted and talented students. Indianapolis: Indiana Department of Public Instruction, p. 19.

[3] Ibid., p. 22.

[4] This activity was suggested by Education for a World in Change, INTERCOM 84/85 [D. C. King, M. S. Branson, & L. E. Condon (Eds.), Center for Global Perspectives, 1976, p. 37] and adapted for use in this text.

INTEREST FORM

You have just completed the Chapter Second Grade. In an effort to have you identify activities and materials that seem most promising at this grade level to you, please fill out the following interest form.

Instructions:

Identify two activities from this chapter. Name the activities and briefly describe why these particular activities are of interest to you.

ACTIVITY 1

ACTIVITY 2

NOTES

CHAPTER THIRD GRADE

ACTIVITIES AND MATERIALS FOR THIRD GRADE

CHAPTER THIRD GRADE

Organization of the Chapter

Each succeeding chapter represents a particular grade level, in this case third grade. Each chapter consists of three parts: the first part is a brief discussion on courses, topics, and national trends in teaching third grade throughout the United States; the second part is an example of a state third grade program; the third part has activities and materials for the third grade categorized by the four objectives for teaching social studies--gaining knowledge, processing, valuing, and participating.

I. Topics Taught and National Trends in Teaching Third Grade

Course, Topics, and Themes Frequently Covered in Third Grade: "Living in the Community"

Objectives of the Course

The continued development of the concept of interdependence with emphasis on an in-depth examination of the community. That in-depth treatment includes local history of the community and government with special emphasis upon how the community delivers services such as water, power, and waste disposal. Along with this in-depth study is the continued emphasis upon current events, the development of geographic skills and concepts, and the stressing of a constructive civic attitude through responsible decision-making.

Basic Content of the Course

Food, clothing, shelter, communication, transportation, government in the community; how education is provided in the community; and how the community grew (local history). A typical third grade teaching guide might include the following units:

Man's Dwellings (influence of geography, customs; materials, tools, and workers involved; buildings of early settlers and Indians; how children can take care of the home and help at home)

Where We Get Our Foods (from plants and animals; from different geographic areas; workers who produce, transport, and process food; food-getting today and long ago)

Clothing Materials (materials from plants and animals, and from man-made fibers; different geographic areas that produce different raw materials for clothing; the many people who work to provide clothing-- the workers and their interdependence; producing clothing long ago and today)

Responsible Civic Citizenship (emphasis is upon decision-making with reminders that responsibility is an obligation that goes with making decisions. Participation in decision-making is intended to encourage the attitude of cooperation and constructive civic-mindedness)

Our City, Past and Present (local history which examines why the community was created, why the community has persisted, were there native Americans living on the community site first, how has the community changed through the years, what do you suppose the future of the community to be)

Ways of Travel (transportation used within the community and to take goods and people out of the community; transportation workers; travel today compared with pioneer days)

Keeping in Touch With You (CB radio, postal service, telephone, radio, movies, television, newspapers, books, magazines).

Third Grade Course, Topic, and Themes for Advanced Students: "Comparative Study of Communities"

Objectives of the Course

Similar to those cited for "Living in Our Community" but with emphasis on comparative study of how people meet basic life needs. This course develops a global studies view by comparing communities in other cultures as well as in other regions of the United States with the child's community. The primary objective is to broaden the child's concept of community in a world of many different communities.

Basic Content of the Course

The comparative study of communities course usually has a beginning unit on a community familiar to the child, followed by community studies in different regions of the United States. Additional units emphasize communities around the world. These units of study usually center on geographic factors, technology, cultural traditions, and in recent years upon the interdependence on earth of all peoples and communities.

Trends in Teaching Third Grade Social Studies

1.   The strong trend is toward comparative studies. However, what is new in recent years is the increasing attention to basic social science concepts as these concepts are applied to the study of community life. For example, a portion of the elementary social studies texts are organizing their comparative content on such basic social science concepts as interdependence, scarcity, environmental adjustment, and social control, among others. This is an important trend to note because it illustrates a recent tendency to move topics from higher grades to lower grade levels. Content and concepts are becoming more pronounced in kindergarten through third grade with the advent of the new elementary social studies texts that emphasize "basic social science concepts."

2.   There is little question that third grade materials are aimed not only at comparative studies but at higher levels of thinking such as analysis, synthesis, and evaluation with the goal of preparing students for decision-making.

3.   Some of the more recent curriculum materials for third grade include units such as: Primitives of Africa, Peoples of the Hot Dry Lands, The Boat People of Hong Kong, The People of Switzerland. What is particularly noteworthy about these units are the questions that students are expected to answer about each of the comparative communities: How do these people provide their basic needs? What rules govern the family? How do the people educate their children? What traditions do they pass on to their children? What evidence of

change is there? The study of foreign cultures is no longer the traditional study of land forms and exports, the emphasis is on people and lifestyles.

4.   As in first and second grade, the trend is toward systematic instruction in geographic concepts and emphasis upon current events as a regular part of any social studies instruction, because current events are a reflection of the past but when put into contemporary times they make the past and present relevant.

II.   Illustration of a State Third Grade Program

There is no one prescribed social studies program throughout the United States. However one state's description of its third grade program will illustrate the content which the state expects to be taught. This illustration identifies a state's suggested social studies curriculum for the third grade.

> Children examine how different communities around the world develop
> based on environmental, cultural, and technological factors. They
> study similarities and differences in cultures and how contact be-
> tween cultures often brings about changes in social institutions.
> The present condition of people is an outgrowth of the way human and
> natural resources are developed. All skill development is continued.
> Students read about people who specialize and contribute to society
> in a unique way by developing their own potential to the fullest.[1]

III.   Activities and Materials Categorized by Gaining Knowledge, Processing, Valuing, and Participating

A common practice is to skip objectives which precede the activities, but in this case the objectives are extremely important for an objective in the third grade will be found in succeeding grades. The following activities and materials are part of a developmental program organized to build citizenry skills from one grade level to another.

THIRD GRADE ACTIVITIES AND MATERIALS

A.   Purpose: To gain knowledge about the human condition which includes past, present, and future

Specific Objective: Identify how weather and surroundings affect (change) what we eat and wear and how we live.

1. Keeping the Weather - (gathering and gaining knowledge about the environment)

    when: recurring

    what: outdoor thermometer, weather chart for graphing

    how: Keep a temperature chart for each month. Have children check temperature each day at a set time (when school starts or after lunch) and record it on a chart. Once a week have two or three children illustrate what clothes we should wear and what activities are going on (boots, shovel snow). Attach illustrations to chart.

           Alternative: Give each child a big calendar to record temperature, special activities, seasons, special events.

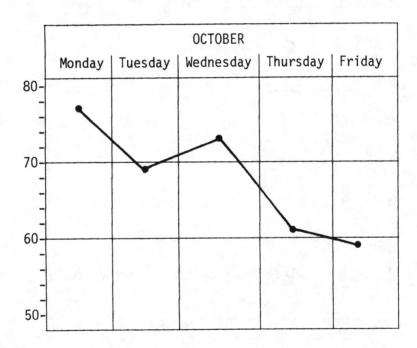

Specific Objective: Identify different types of climate and ways of living in those climates.

2. Climate Center Activities - (gathering and gaining knowledge about the environment)

    when: two or three weeks

    what: art supplies, scraps, resource materials, clay

    how: The activities listed are designed to encourage children to think about the relationship between climate and different

ways of living. One's environment has a direct personal
effect upon the child's daily life.
(1) Teacher prepares cards giving climate conditions. Child
    picks card and makes picture or diorama using whatever
    materials are available.
(2) Children make collage of something "wrong" with climate
    (snowsuits in summer, swim suits in snow).
(3) Children study pictures and see what can be observed about
    climate by looking at landscape, people, in pictures.
(4) Papier mache (newspapers soaked in paste of equal parts
    flour and water) sculpture of landscape scene can be
    molded, allowed to dry, and painted. Clay landscape
    scene.
(5) Paper dolls dressed for climates around the world.

Specific Objective: Identify causes of pollution (air, water, noise, etc.)
                     in children's community and what is being done about it.

3. <u>Gathering Your Own Trash</u> - (gathering and gaining knowledge about
                                  the environment)

    when: two or three periods

    what: art supplies, gallon containers (ice cream store might supply
           these free)

    how: Clean and dry containers. Have each child decorate a container
           to take home to use as wastebasket. Spray completed container
           with commercial fixative to protect decoration.

4. <u>Learning to Conserve Your Environment</u> - (gathering and gaining knowl-
                                              edge about the environment)

    when: one period

    what: two shallow boxes or flats obtained (usually free) from a
           nursery

    how: Line boxes or flats with aluminum foil so water cannot leak
           through holes. Fill with soil; using finger or pencil make
           furrows in dirt in one flat crosswise, in other flat length-
           wise. Cut one end of each flat in a V shape. Tip flats on a
           slant and water slowly with sprinkling can. Which flat lets
           the most water run off quickest? Discuss how contouring is
           important to farmers in conserving rainwater for their crops.
           The point of this activity is that by learning to work with
           our environment we can conserve it, but first we must learn
           how nature works.

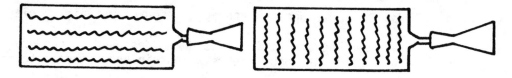

5. Action to Take - (gathering and gaining knowledge about the environ-
                        ment)

    when: two or three weeks

    what: pictures, tape recorder, camera

    how: Identify problems by taking a walk around neighborhood and
           school, watching work at home, taping noises in school and
           out, inviting older person to discuss pollution, visit sewage
           treatment plant, etc.
           Action: Children make personal decisions, i.e., I will clean
             my table after lunch; I will use only returnable bottles.
             Take picture of pollution conditions in community, and talk
             to officials who are responsible for this and discuss
             solutions.
           Other activities to examine the effect of man on the environ-
           ment:
           Noise: Using tape of noises made earlier, have one group of
             children read under normal conditions and have other group
             read while tape of noises is being played. Which group was
             able to read the best?
           Auto Exhaust: Must be done with teacher. Put a few earth-
             worms and beetles in a plastic bag and hold it over the
             exhaust pipe of a car while the motor is running. When bag
             is full, tie it closed. Watch effect of exhaust on bugs.
             What did you think would happen? What actually did happen?
             Try first with leaded gas and then with unleaded gas; was
             there any difference?

Specific Objective: Learning about work performed by community members.

6. Interviewing - (identifying different types of work)

    when: two or three periods

    what: tape recorder, cassettes

    how: Interview different workers. This may be done by inviting
           people to the classroom (principal, nurse) or by making an
           appointment to interview them in their office (maybe after
           school). Help children prepare questions to use in interview
           such as:

           What kind of work do you do?   If you had a chance, would
                                               you choose this type of
           Did you need special training?   work again?

           How does your work help community?

           When you were little, did you plan to be what you are today?

           How did you get this job?

7. Workers and Jobs - (identifying different types of work)

    when: two or three periods

    what: chart for workers and jobs

    how: Chart workers and their jobs using people children know or
          people they have interviewed or people they make up. Do
          certain jobs seem to be for only men or women? Does it have
          to be that way? Why or why not?

Worker	Job	What is made	What is done for someone
Dr. Smith	doctor		keeps people healthy
Mr. Olsen	baker	breads, cakes	provides food
Mr. Phillips	President of power company	electric power	power to run labor-saving devices
Mrs. Jones	bus driver		helps children get to school and home
Miss Jacks	bank president	loans	a place to keep money and to borrow money

8. Workers and Job Fair - (identifying different types of work)

    when: two periods to plan, one day for "fair"

    what: booths

    how: Hold a "Workers and Job Fair." Invite parents and community
          members to come to school and man a booth to tell about their
          job, including training they need, products or services they
          provide. Children should visit as many booths as time allows
          using a "job interview card."

          After fair is over children can draw pictures or tell about
          work they would like to do when older. This is a good activity
          for several classes to do together.

Job Interview Card

Occupation _____

Training _____

Will the job be available in the future when I grow up? _____

_____

Specific Objective: Learning to identify criteria for good work habits.

9. How Do We Do? - (identifying good work in school, gaining knowledge
         about oneself)

   when: recurring

   what: bulletin board, children self-portraits

   how: Place bulletin board on section of wall accessible to chil-
         dren. Put the title at top, "How Do We Do?". Post five self-
         portraits of children and underneath each portrait put
         writing paper. During the week any class member can write
         any positive statement about the work done by one of the five
         children under that child's portrait: "Barbara colors good
         pictures." "Jim read well today." Each week teacher posts
         new portraits.

         Start with five children who are easy to compliment, then as
         children understand procedure, mix less successful students
         in among other more popular ones. At times it is difficult
         to identify those things that we do from day to day that tend
         to make us successful at a task. Sometimes we just don't
         stop to think about those things that work for us. Sometimes
         we see only the negative. Occasionally we may need others to
         point out what went right. This may help us to identify and
         repeat good work habits.

10. Letters - (identifying good work in school, gaining knowledge about
         oneself)

   when: recurring

   what: stationery, envelopes, box containing children's names (each
          name printed on a separate card)

   how: Child reaches into box and pulls out a child's name, uses
         stationery to write a note complimenting that child on some
         job or thing he has done well. Do not replace name in box
         until all cards have been used.

         This type of activity tends to strengthen our concept of self
         by pointing out those things which went right. "Letters" may
         help us to identify and repeat good work habits. In a sense
         we gain knowledge about oneself.

B.   Purpose: Identify skills necessary to <u>process</u> information

   Specific Objective: Using map key to interpret and read maps.

   1.   <u>Salt Maps</u> - (developing map skills)

        when: two or three periods

        what: salt mixture (1 cup flour, 1 cut salt, ½ cup water)

        how: Discuss topography in class using whatever resource materials
               are available. Have groups or each child individually make a
               salt map. Discuss how others can read map and have children
               make a key for map.

   2.   <u>Mapping Our Classroom</u> - (developing map skills)

        when: one period

        what: construction paper, paste

        how: Give each child a 9" x 12" piece of construction paper on
               which to map the classroom. Children decide on symbols, cut
               them out of scrap paper, and paste onto map; include key. Be
               sure children try all items (symbols) before they paste to
               make sure they fit.

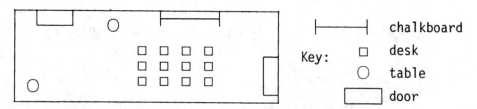

   Specific Objective: Locating areas and places on maps and globes.

   3.   <u>Working With Maps</u> - (developing map skills)

        when: two or three weeks

        what: Post world map so that it is accessible to children.

        how: (1) Each child makes a flag with his/her name on it and pins
                   it to location shere he/she was born. Children place
                   markers on places they have lived or visited and make
                   paper planes to place on oceans they have crossed. Place
                   gold stars on capitals of countries. Locate item on
                   globe that you have labeled on map.
               (2) Outline continents in yarn using a different color for
                   each continent. Make a key for this. Have children pick
                   continent for imaginary trip. Have them tell or write
                   about what cities they would visit and what countries
                   and oceans they would travel over to get there.

(3) Divide children into groups. Each group lines up flat on floor so that the line of their bodies forms a continent. Class guesses what continent it is.

4. Using a Key - (developing map skills)

when: one period

what: ditto of an imaginary place prepared by teacher including key which includes countries, oceans, capitals, continents.

how: Have children locate areas marked by key on map and name them. Children can make up imaginary place maps of their own using their own key or that of teacher.

5. Name Game - (developing map skills)

when: one period per game

what: maps or globes as aids

how: (1) First child says place name such as "Indiana." Second child must say a place that begins with the last letter "a" of the name said before, i.e., "Arkansas." Third child then finds place that begins with "s", i.e., "Syracuse." If child cannot find name, he/she is out. Last person out is winner. Could also be played with teams.
(2) Have one child leave room. Class picks country, city, etc. Child returns and tries to guess place by asking twenty questions that can only be answered by yes or no. Is it small? Is it water? If not successful in guessing, then another child becomes it.

Specific Objective: Learning to use cardinal (north, south, east, west) and intermediate (northeast, northwest, southeast, southwest) directions.

6. Directions - (developing map skills)

when: four or five periods

what: sunny day

how: Pick a sunny day and take children outside early and line them up facing north. The sun should be on their right (east). Repeat at noon (sun overhead) and as late as possible in afternoon (sun on left - west). After each trip, return to classroom and label direction on correct wall.

Pick a starting point in room and give child oral directions: thirteen steps north, four east. Where did child end up (art center, etc.)? Prepare cards that give child starting point

and directions. Did child end up on correct spot? May begin
to use intermediate directions (five steps southwest).

Set up small community map and have children follow directions
(using "Hot Wheel" or "Matchbox" cars brought from home) to
drive to location.

7. Treasure Hunt - (developing map skills)

when: one or two periods

what: cards written by teacher with instructions using cardinal and
intermediate directions, possible treat

how: Divide children into groups and give each group a card. Have
them follow treasure hunt directions on cards. Children could
plan own treasure hunts using directions.

```
┌─────────────────────┐
│  Treasure Hunt      │
│                     │
│  10 steps S         │
│   4 steps E         │
│   2 steps NW        │
│   5 steps N         │
│   7 steps W         │
└─────────────────────┘
```

8. Footprints Up the Wall - (developing map skills)

when: two periods

what: construction paper

how: Have children trace around feet on construction paper and cut
out footprints. Have children print directions on each footprint and place in a traveling pattern around room, even on
walls.

Have teacher make up cards that give directions which children
then follow, laying out a new printed cutout footprint every
two feet. As a reinforcement, have each child walk his/her
footprints giving directions as he/she goes.

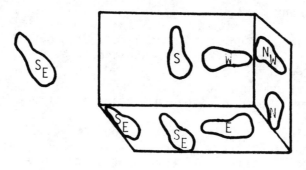

9. Graphing - (developing graphing skills)

when: one or two periods

what: ditto a graph (one inch squares)

how: Give each child a ditto and have him/her plan a city including
      things specified by teacher (hospital, lake, airport, hills).
      Children place items on graph as they wish along with symbols.
      Include symbols in map key on bottom of graph. After children
      learn to graph, they plan a city on a grid. Have them make
      key and tell area where things are located.

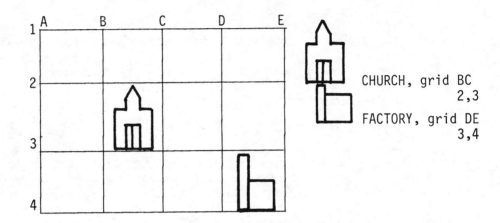

C. Purpose: Develop the skill to examine values and beliefs. Many judgments
              call for values and beliefs first. For example: (1) ranking,
              and (2) identifying advantages and disadvantages, and (3)
              examining similarities and differences imply a set of values.

Specific Objective: Learning to rank based upon a set of criteria.

1. Ranking Jobs - (the skill of ranking)

when: two periods

what: ditto made by teacher listing ten jobs in ten boxes

how: Discuss with class a criteria for establishing the desira-
      bility of a job, i.e., what must a job provide me with? Such
      criteria might be: working hours, money, job satisfaction,
      location of job, working conditions, others. Give each child
      a ditto and have them cut out boxes. Have each child indi-
      vidually arrange boxes in row from most desirable job on left
      to least desirable job on right, in order of preference.
      Tally class results. Discuss results with class. If group
      disagrees on two lowest or two highest ranks, ask children
      for reasons.

Specific Objective: Identifying "advantages" and "disadvantages."

2. <u>Keeping a Record</u> - (advantages and disadvantages)

    when: two or three weeks

    what: resource materials

    how: Have each child pick a community to study. Child keeps a diary as he/she does research on the community recording:

    Things I like in this community.
    Thinks I do not like in this community.

Specific Objective: Identifying similarities and differences in all communities.

3. <u>Finding New Friends</u> - (identifying foreign communities)

    when: recurring

    what: letters, art work

    how: Teacher can write to a minister of education in a foreign country to secure name and address of school with which the children can exchange letters. Have children exchange letters and art work that shows what each community is like. Look for similarities and differences.

    Invite foreign exchange students enrolled in local high schools to visit the class to talk about their countries. The foreign student can be helpful by identifying schools to write. Also, American exchange students who have returned are an important source.

Specific Objective: Identify how values affect solution to personal social problems.

4. <u>Watches</u> - (developing the skill to identify values)

    when: one period

    what: story told by teacher, for example: Cindy and Jack are brother and sister. Cindy is in the fourth grade, and Jack is in second grade. For Christmas their grandparents gave them each a watch. The grandparents wanted to be fair so the watches were identical. Cindy put her watch on after she opened the gift. Jack, who hadn't learned to tell time, put his back in the box but left the box on the floor. While cleaning up the Christmas wrappings, Cindy accidentally picked up Jack's watch box, thinking it was her empty one, and threw it out in the trash. Who should get the watch that is left? Cindy threw Jack's watch away, but Jack left his watch on the floor.

how: Teacher now stimulates discussion that leads to moral develop-
        ment. Encourage disagreement in children's choices. If most
        feel Cindy should keep her watch, teacher could ask, "Couldn't
        Cindy have been more careful about what she threw away? Cindy
        should have looked in watch box to make sure it was empty,
        shouldn't she?" If most think Jack should get the watch,
        teacher could ask, "Shouldn't Jack have put the watch somewhere
        safe like on a table? Shouldn't he have checked what his
        sister was throwing out?"

        Teacher should make children stick to problem and not choose
        easy solutions like getting another new watch. Have children
        role-play by pretending they are either Cindy or Jack and
        giving reasons why they should have the watch, then reverse
        roles. Look for compromises. Valid compromises (sharing
        watch) should be treated as moral choices. When class reaches
        agreement on what should be done, have them pick best reasons
        to support their view.

        Once children have expressed their preference for a solution,
        the teacher's responsibility is to encourage valuing by ask-
        ing, "What are your beliefs (values) that are the basis of
        your solution?" In other words, the teacher will want the
        children to identify (go beyond their reasoning) what they
        value. In this case their values may be rooted in concepts of
        honesty or fairness or perhaps the Golden Rule ("Do unto
        others . . ."). The point is that we have opinions and
        reasons that are usually rooted in values. A step in the
        process of moral development is that we identify and evaluate
        our values, for our judgments are based on our values.

5. Valuing the Feelings of Others - (developing the skill to identify
                                                values)

    when: one period

    what: the situation: Often children are in conflict with each
           other in class. Sometimes the conflicts become so marked
           that a child or children are isolated by their peers. The
           usual reaction is that the teacher intervenes by attempting
           to modify the situation and this may mean modifying both the
           isolates and the dominant group. The following technique is
           one promising way to intervene.

    how: Establish a Socratic small group; purpose: to bring students
           and instructor together to discuss a problem posed by the
           teacher for which an answer can best be determined through
           the open and honest exchange of informed opinion.
           Guidelines: Begin in Stage 1 with teacher encouraging free
             and uninhibited discussion of the problems children identify
             and their feelings about those problems. For example, the
             teacher asks, "How do you act that encourages people to
             respect you?" "Are there things that classmates do that
             you don't like?" "Have you ever been in conflict with a
             classmate?"

In Stage 2 the teacher does a lot of good, hard listening, then becomes a leader and participant by probing, stimulating, challenging, synthesizing. For example, the teacher might ask these questions in the second stage: "Can you think of reasons why you behave in a way that puts you in conflict with others?" "How does it feel to be in conflict?" "Suppose you wish to act differently, could you?" "What would be some of the different ways you could act?" "Are there people who could help you?"

This activity, "Valuing the Feelings of Others," should help the children to examine their behavior, increasing some children's ability to control themselves and help others identify the problems and feelings of others.

D. Purpose: Apply knowledge through active _participation_ in society

Specific Objective: Identify problems of communities and cities.

1. _Plan a City_ - (participate in the process of decision-making)

    when: two or three weeks

    what: large board, carton, boxes, art materials, film strip

    how: Show film strip showing a city. Discuss what makes a city, establishing categories such as homes, stores, schools, services, parks, industry. Assign groups to make things for each category. Prepare board by pinning on pieces of torn construction paper. The torn paper represents trees and the whole board represents unsettled territory. Class must now settle area using categories decided upon previously. Children must think seriously about what type of community they are building (fishing, seaport, lumber, industry, farm community). They must realize that removed trees are gone forever. Children should see some need for organization as groups compete to place their categories. They may need to elect a mayor or planning commission to approve roads, buildings, etc. Discuss how community grew. Did it remain small or become a city with suburbs? Do some communities remain small? Why?

    After children work for a short time, teacher should start to hurry them by saying, "We need a hospital, a baby is about to be born." "We need a bakery, . . . shoe store, . . . etc." The idea is to rush children so they don't have time to plan where things go and the city grows haphazardly (the way most cities grow). Have children examine city and list good and bad features. Suggest ways to improve city.

    Plan a new city without hurrying. Use blocks for buildings so that children can experiment by moving them around. When good working model has been established, make map by tracing around blocks and drawing in streets and landscape. Color it using an agreed upon color code. Attach key to map and display it.

2. Problems Right Here[2] - (participating in the process of decision-
                                                making)

    when: three or four periods

    what: newspaper articles on community problems

    how: After using strategy Plan a City (previous activity), try to
           discover and offer solutions to local problems. For example:
           (1) How would you redesign your own community?
           (2) Visit local library--look up any plans for community
               changes.
           (3) Our community needs a superhighway, or a sewage treatment
               plant, or a new hospital--where would we locate it? Why
               or why not?
           (4) Check newspapers--bring in articles about problems in the
               community.
           (5) At home, have children take snapshots of smog, etc. or
               draw illustrations. Share with the total class. Compare
               these problems to other communities. Are they similar,
               different?
           (6) Invite speakers such as civic association president, chair-
               man of retail association, highway department leaders,
               etc. to give opposing views to problems in local commu-
               nity.

    Specific Objective: Participate with others in deciding on directions to be
                         taken in improving community and then taking action
                         to do so.

3. Social Action on Real Problems - (participating in acting on problem)

    when: three weeks at least

    what: materials as needed below

    how: Have class identify a real community problem. A real problem
           means that the children actually recognize it as a problem to
           them. Remember that because the teacher announces something
           as a problem does not necessarily mean that the children
           accept this as a problem. For example, many elementary
           teachers identify ecological problems (i.e., smog, noise,
           waste disposal including litter) as community problems. How-
           ever, it seems that studying a social problem does not neces-
           sarily enhance the children's personal awareness of that
           problem in their own lives. Problems which children might
           identify as real: being bullied by older students after
           school; no place to play after school; no bike lanes on the
           streets; a lot of trash and litter along the sides of streets
           and in vacant lots.

           Suppose the children decide to participate in resolving the
           problem of rubbish on school property and in the surrounding
           neighborhood. The class might elect to participate in a
           trash pick-up by taking one period to walk about the school

and school grounds collecting and properly disposing of trash. Even though the class trash pick-up temporarily helps, the point needs to be made that other activities need to follow that help in maintaining a cleaner environment which apparently the students value. Possible actions:
(1) Make posters to display in halls such as "Help Snoopy Beat the Trash Problem" with a picture of Snoopy trying to put trash in containers. Suggest trash containers be painted in bright colors.
(2) Set up trash contests--award for class that collects most trash.
(3) Award to cleanest classroom of the week; cleanest desk of the week.
(4) Invite school custodian to class to talk about rubbish and give him recognition for his work in keeping school neat.
(5) Invite someone from city sanitation department to speak to the class about problem and what they can do to help.

Specific Objective: Participating with teacher in changing classroom procedures.

4. Contracts - (creative participation)

when: recurring

what: dittos of contracts

how: Teacher has conference with each child individually. They discuss what the child would be interested in trying. They can fill out a contract card. Often children express desires to try different ideas, new things, but those occasions may not happen if the teacher or parent does not allow for new interests. This is one way to stop the daily routines and provide time for reflection. The contract is a means of stimulating the child to try different ideas. Of course, the contract could also be used to increase the children's attention to those areas in which they need to improve.

Suggestions for contract: to attend a play, to try a hand at carving, to take some time for special reading, to leave home a little earlier in morning, to take an interesting trip. Both teacher and student should have a copy of contract.

Contract date _____

I agree to _____

_____

_____
student's name

_____
teacher's signature

Making Things

The formula for making salt maps was offered in Activity 1 under Process-

ing. Several additional recipes on creating "inexpensive" playdough are:

Salt Clay

> 1 cup salt
> ½ cup cornstarch
> 3/4 cup water
> food coloring if desired

1. Put the salt and cornstarch in top of double boiler and place
    over boiling water.

2. Add water slowly, stirring constantly.

3. When the mixture has thickened (i.e., is difficult to stir),
    spoon onto a cookie sheet to cool.

4. When completely cool, knead to remove lumps and air bubbles.

Store in an air-tight container, as air will harden the mixture.

Craft Clay

> 1 cup cornstarch
> 2 cups baking soda
> 1½ cups water
> food coloring if desired

1. Combine all ingredients in a pan or pot.

2. Cook over medium heat, stirring constantly.

3. Turn out on a pastry board and knead slightly.

4. Cover with a damp cloth until cool to keep it from hardening.

Notes

[1] Indiana Department of Public Instruction. 1978 Indiana textbook adoption
categories for social studies. Indianapolis: Author, 1978, p. 2.

[2] Barth, J. L., & Shermis, S. S. Teaching social studies to gifted and
talented students. Indianapolis: Indiana Department of Public Instruction,
p. 23.

INTEREST FORM

You have just completed the Chapter Third Grade. In an effort to have you identify activities and materials that seem most promising at this grade level to you, please fill out the following interest form.

Instructions:

Identify two activities from this chapter. Name the activities and briefly describe why these particular activities are of interest to you.

ACTIVITY 1

ACTIVITY 2

NOTES

CLARIFICATION AND SUMMARY OF SOCIAL STUDIES
CURRICULUM DEVELOPMENT
KINDERGARTEN THROUGH THIRD GRADE

This is the appropriate time to take a break between grade levels for the purpose of clarifying and summarizing the major ideas discussed over the last three chapters. The suggestion was made in Chapter "A Social Studies K-12 Curriculum" that elementary teachers, and for that matter those who are specially hired to teach the social studies program in junior high/middle school, tend not to know that they are part of an integrated developmental curriculum. It is no small wonder that elementary teachers are reluctant to teach a social studies curriculum which in many cases is not clearly identified as an essential part of the school's program. To put matters simply, elementary teachers are not particularly held responsible for the content of their social studies program.

Hopefully, having read through the course, trends, activities, and materials in the last three chapters, teachers will have identified why it is important that there be a primary social studies program. Imagine the severe limitations that a fourth grade teacher would face if the students had no background in current events, comparative studies, or geographic skills. Suppose further the students lacked any acquaintance with a concept such as interdependence or had never been exposed to themes such as identifying the self and the relationships between home, school, neighborhood, and community. A good many primary teachers might react to some of the activities and materials by saying, "Yes, I recognize some of those activities and, in fact, use a few of them already, it's just that I never thought of them as being social studies. I never really thought of the study of self or of the school as being part of a social studies program. I never really thought of social studies as an integration of the social experiences of the children. I always thought social studies had to do with historical events and geography." Well, now you know that social studies is an integration of life experiences with the goal of citizenship education and, further, you know that the goal is achieved through the purposes of gaining knowledge, processing information, valuing, and participating. Surely those objectives need to be taught systematically kindergarten through twelfth grade, for the expectation is that as citizens in a democracy students will learn to be effective decision-makers.

The notion of a "spiraling expanding horizon" through the first three grades can readily be imagined by the teacher for it is a persistent form of organization that has lasted for over eighty years. Some educational authorities argue that children's environments do not expand in neat concentric circles, and, in fact, the contemporary child, with travel, TV, and increased exposure to a number of alternative lifestyles, is able at an earlier age to be more national and global minded. Therefore, topics which were traditionally taught in upper elementary are now appearing more frequently in the earlier grades. Without question the social studies texts written for the first three grades have increasingly emphasized the integration of basic social science concepts and comparative studies. This trend will probably carry into the twenty-first century because it is rooted in the notion of global interdependence, a concept which names a basic concern for present and future citizens.

Consensus K-3

Even though there may not be complete agreement, there is at least a consensus about what social studies content ought to be taught in the primary grades. In a sense, it is relatively easy to imagine the spiraling expanding horizon, but that consensus does not continue to hold after the third grade. In the fourth, fifth, and sixth grades, one finds a wide variety of different courses. Through the first three grades students are being prepared to "spiral off" in a number of directions. Having completed an in-depth study of one's own family, school, neighborhood, and community with comparative studies of families, schools, neighborhoods and communities, both foreign and domestic, the curriculum could logically spiral to a regional study of cultures throughout the world or alternatively could stay closer to home by emphasizing state and regional studies. In other words, the neat, clean progression of expanding horizons of the first three grades no longer dictates topics and themes after the third grade. The social studies curriculum beyond the third grade resembles a branch with many leaves. Keep in mind that many states do prescribe the curriculum beyond the third grade, and in that case the leaves are arranged by the hands of the state legislature, but, where the law has not laid its hands upon the curriculum, school systems and teachers fill the void with their own notion of citizenship.

In summary, many states follow the social studies K-3 curriculum as described above in the first three years of elementary school, but after the third grade the curriculum diverges from school to school and from state to state.

CHAPTER FOURTH GRADE

ACTIVITIES AND MATERIALS FOR FOURTH GRADE

CHAPTER FOURTH GRADE

Organization of the Chapter

Each succeeding chapter represents a particular grade level, in this case fourth grade. Each chapter consists of three parts: the first part is a brief discussion on courses, topics, and national trends in teaching fourth grade throughout the United States; the second part is an example of a state fourth grade program; the third part has activities and materials for the fourth grade categorized by the four objectives for teaching social studies-- gaining knowledge, processing, valuing, and participating.

I. Topics Taught and National Trends in Teaching Fourth Grade

Fourth grade social studies usually follows one of these three alternative courses: state and United States history, state and communities around the world, or communities around the world. If you recall, in the third grade children studied their own community in depth and compared that community with other communities including pioneer communities, other communities in the United States, and some selected communities around the world. The children supposedly enter the fourth grade with geographic skills including graphing, mapping, and map interpretation; have studied the interrelationship between climate, homes, neighborhood, and communities; and finally they are to have a basic mastery of the four objectives having completed activities based on gaining knowledge, processing information, valuing, and participating.

With the above foundation, a social studies curriculum could logically "spiral" in a number of directions. The student is ready to spiral and expand from community/region to a study of the state and from the state to the nation. Or the student could proceed to study the state as a region, and then compare it to other selected regions around the world (people of the state of Indiana and the Midwest region in contrast with the peoples of Nova Scotia and the people of Mysore State, India). Or students could just as well be launched into a study of the interdependence of people and places throughout the world with emphasis upon Africa, the Middle East, Southeast Asia, and Asia. No one pattern of courses seems to absolutely dominate the teaching of fourth grade social studies in the United States. It is not unusual for one state to mandate the teaching of its state history at the seventh grade level while preferring to teach global studies in the fourth grade. In another state the reverse may be true. Of importance at this moment is not the dwelling upon disagreement over what ought to be taught but rather noting the alternative curriculums and, in consequence, being prepared with activities and materials which will help teachers to be flexible enough to teach any one of the alternatives.

Course, Topics, and Themes Frequently Covered in Fourth Grade:
"State and United States History"

Objectives of the Course

Introducing the child to his home state with special emphasis upon geography, history, and government and stressing the events, places, and people important in the establishment of the state. Usually state history is taught in this course as it directly relates to the development of the United States as a country so that state and national history will tend to flow together to tell the story of how the country has grown and changed. A state objective might sound something like this: Examine the state's physical geography and relative geographic position, where the people live and why, how people lived in the past and present as part of the regional and national community. Fourth grade state and regional history is often followed by fifth grade American history.

Basic Content of the Course

Authors of state history materials at the fourth grade level will often stress that "history content is to be enjoyed," that the study of heritage will help students to develop a better <u>understanding</u> and <u>appreciation</u> of who they are as the new generation of citizens of the state. To develop that understanding and appreciation, the following are illustrations of typical topics: Our State, a Place on the Map; How the Ancient Indians Lived on Our Land; The White Man Comes to America; Our State and the American Revolution; Indian Wars and Early Settlements; Trails and Rivers, Roads and Canals; Our State in the Civil War; People in Government; Our State's Environment. Also, many state history books attempt to show how the state was affected by national issues with such topics as The French and British Fight for the New World, The Black Man Comes to America, The Fight to Be Equal. In other words, American history is not taught as a separate course but only as it relates to specific important events in the state's history. American history when taught as part of the state history is usually intended to prepare students for the formal study of American history in fifth grade.

Course, Topics, and Themes Frequently Covered in Fourth Grade:
"State and Regions Around the World"

Objectives of the Course

The course is intended to provide sytematic instruction in geographic concepts and skills with emphasis on the influence of geographic and cultural factors on the ways people meet needs: work, shelter, food, clothing, transportation. Though the course focuses on state and other regions around the world, it is intended to provide an overview of world geography.

Basic Content of the Course

Keep in mind when thinking about this course that the emphasis is upon certain basic life processes. The regions are studied to show how these basic life processes are viewed from different cultures. The effort is made not to isolate and study each region separately but rather to show how each region deals with work, food, transportation, etc. Typical units on the combined state-world regions approach are: An Interdependent World; A World of Different Regions (essentially a map skills study); People at Work; World of Buyers and Sellers; Transportation; Cities and Their People; Cities Around the World. Though the unit headings suggest the broad outlines of a region study, to identify the essence of regional studies it would be useful to look at what would be covered in one of the units. For example, the Unit Cities Around the World might well include Chicago, Illinois, USA; Rotterdam, The Netherlands, Europe; Osaka, Japan, Asia; and Nairobi, Kenya, Africa; with emphasis on such topics as transportation, manufacturing, trade, shipping, how port cities grow and change, and how the cities were made.

Course, Topics, and Themes Frequently Covered in Fourth Grade:
"Regions Around the World"

Objectives of the Course

As in the case of the preceding course, "States and Regions Around the World," the intent is to provide systematic instruction in geographic concepts and skills with emphasis on the influence of geographic and cultural factors on the ways people meet basic needs: work, food, clothing, shelter, recreation, transportation. This course, though it focuses in depth upon a few regions around the world, is expected to give an overview of world geography. As distinct from the other two courses, "State/National History" and "State/Regional World History," the objective of this course is to focus exclusively on cultures outside the United States and in some cases exclusively on world cultures other than Western cultures.

Basic Content of the Course

The content of this course is usually designed to show sharp contrasts

between the students' lifestyle and those of other cultures, but "the aspira-
tions of all people have much in common." Very often contrasting cultures are
chosen to demonstrate the influence of environment, custom, and traditions in
under-developed countries and the effect technology can have on the lives of
people. For example, typical units might sound like this: The World and Maps;
By a Fjord in Norway; On a Desert in Saudi Arabia; In the Mountains in Ecuador;
or, The People of Mysore State; The People of Osaka Prefecture; The People of
Serbia; The People of Nova Scotia.

Trends in Teaching Fourth Grade Social Studies

1.   Of the three approaches, "State and United States History," "State-
World Regions," and "Regions Around the World," the course "State-World Regions"
is becoming the most popular. This trend will undoubtedly continue. Teachers
view this approach as a compromise between the other two; that is, being able
to link some of the fourth grade content directly to third grade community/
city studies, and yet provide preparation for American history in the fifth
grade by emphasizing state and regional history.

2.   Continued emphasis upon current events with special attention to
world, state, and local affairs with emphasis on following contemporary events
in the regions being studied.

3.   Increased attention to key social science concepts. In the first
three grades students learned such concepts as interdependence, differences,
and cultural change. In fourth grade such concepts as causality, tradition,
social control, and institutions are being emphasized in some social studies
texts. Though both teachers and students are experiencing some problems with
identifying these social science concepts, there remains a strong trend toward
using these concepts when studying a culture. The argument in favor of using
these concepts is that they lend substance (hard content) to the course.

4. The more traditional world culture materials tended to stress regions within western civilization: Norway, Holland, Greece, perhaps a Latin American country. The most recent trend is away from the traditional western civilization world history approach to reflect a more modern world affairs approach which focuses on developing nations: SubSahara Africa, Middle East, Asia.

II. Illustrations of a State Fourth Grade Program

There is no <u>one</u> prescribed social studies program throughout the United States. However, one state's description of its fourth grade program will illustrate the content which the state expects to be taught. This illustration identifies a state's suggested social studies curriculum for the fourth grade.

> The world as the home of humans provides opportunities to compare and contrast how we live in our state, or within a region of our state, and how people of other cultures and regions live and how we are alike and different. Students examine how different cultures and ethnic groups within our state influence the ways in which similar geographic and environmental conditions are utilized. Students note the ways in which human and natural resource distribution affects peoples' lifestyles, and how peaceful interaction among humans is related to social control amidst changing requirements and problems. Reading for context clues, map and globe skills, and social skills is emphasized.[1]

III. Activities and Materials Categorized by Gaining Knowledge, Processing, Valuing, and Participating

A common practice is to skip objectives which precede the activities, but in this case the objectives are extremely important for an objective in the fourth grade will be found in succeeding grades. The following activities and materials are part of a developmental curriculum organized to build citizenship skills from one grade level to another.

FOURTH GRADE ACTIVITIES AND MATERIALS

A.   Purpose: To gain knowledge about the human condition which includes past, present, and future

Specific Objective: Gaining knowledge about the roles people play in society.

1.   What's My Role - (identifying roles and practicing graphic and interview skills)

when: three weeks

what: materials as needed for activity

how: (1) Divide students into groups. Have them discuss and list activities, jobs (roles) they undertake in a typical day. Have groups classify activities under categories such as home roles, school roles, recreation, living, "just messing around."

Home roles:	School roles:
babysitting raking leaves making bed wash dishes deliver papers take out trash feed pet, walk dog	writing reading homework watch film take test
Recreation:	"Messing Around":
play basketball TV ride bike sew read stamp collecting	talking to friends playing around watch the world go by! Living: eating sleeping bath, shower

Alternative: List categories on the board and have class as group fill in activities under each category.
Alternative: Make a checklist of activities and have students check ones that apply to them.

☐   read
☐   TV
☐   feed pet
☐   deliver papers

(2) Have students make a chart that shows how many hours each day on the average are devoted to each of the categories of activities.

(3) Have students make a pie, bar, and line graph that shows
their use of time.

Pie Graph (24 hours)

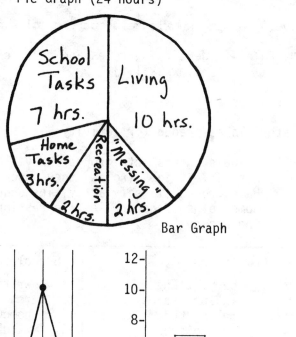

Line Graph

Bar Graph

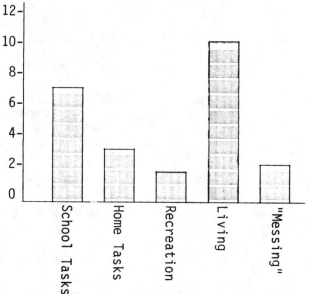

(4) Have students interview adults (relatives, neighbors) to
find out what kind of work role they had or have. Decide
on questions students should ask at interview

Interview

1. What is your work? _____
2. How did you become eligible for your work? _____
    _____
3. How would I get ready to do the same work? _____
    _____
4. If you had the chance again, would you choose the same work? ____
    _____

2.   Crafts From Pioneer Days - (identifying work roles and skills of
                              past cultures)

when: three or four periods

what: materials as needed for activity

how: Have students choose pioneer crafts they would like to try.
        They may spend several periods on one craft or use each
        period for a different craft.
        Cooking: Make cornbread, gingerbread cookies, pumpkin bars.
        Sewing: Make a sampler out of burlap. Use cardboard bar
                 from coat hanger (dry cleaner type) to hang burlap.
        Quilting Bee: Sew cotton squares together and attach to quilt
                 backing.
        Candlemaking: (Best to do with teacher or aide supervision.)
                 Tie candle wicks to narrow piece of wood.
                 Melt paraffin in deep pan (crayons add color)
                 and dip wicks in paraffin, let dry, and dip
                 again--repeat until thickness wanted is ob-
                 tained. Some parents may have candle molds
                 they would let class use.
        Wigmaking: Shape heavy paper to fit student's head like a
                 helmet. Cover paper with yarn or cotton glued
                 to stay put.
        Printing: Carve one side of styrofoam block, cover with ink
                 or paint, and press on paper. May carve cut
                 side of potato sliced in half to use as printing
                 block also. Print design on edge of paper, use
                 quill pen and ink to fill in words. Announce
                 town meeting, ship sailing dates, etc.
        Weaving: Wrap string or yarn about 21 times around a stiff
                 piece of cardboard. Use knitting needle or pop-
                 sicle stick with hole cut in end and yarn tied to
                 it to use as a shuttle. Cut strings at top and
                 bottom and tie.

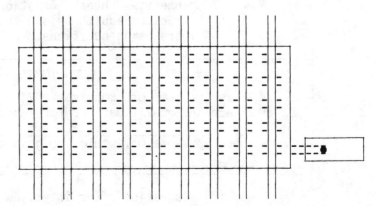

        Alternative: Have a colonial day where students dress in
           colonial clothes, eat foods eaten in colonial days, and
           play colonial games or dance as they did in colonial days.

Specific Objective: Categorizing information about cultures.

3. <u>Student Groups and Clubs</u>[2] - (identifying youth roles in present-day society)

    when: three periods

    what:

    how: (1) Have students list groups or clubs they belong to: Boy/ Girl Scouts, Brownies/Cub Scouts, choir (church), band, team sports (swimming, football, track, gymnastics, volleyball, etc.), student council.
          (2) Make a bulletin board of groups listing qualifications, goals, records or achievements, advantages of joining.
          (3) Divide students into groups. Have groups invest a club with rules for membership, an emblem, and goals. They may make posters to encourage others to join.

Remember, the purpose of this activity is to help students to note that their membership in organizations includes belonging to a grade and class in school. It is not unusual for children to conceive of society as the "society page" in the newspaper. This exercise should help students understand that their role in society includes membership in family, school, and organizations. In part, to understand society is understanding how one is bound to that society.

4. <u>Adult Groups and Clubs</u>[3] - (identify adult roles in present-day society)

    when: three periods

    what: questionnaire

    how: (1) Have students decide on questions to be included on an interview sheet. Questions should be about what groups or clubs adults belong to. Interview parents or neighbors using questionnaire.

QUESTIONNAIRE

1. What is the name of organization? _____
2. What are the qualifications for membership in this organization? _____

3. Suppose you were me, would you join the organization? _____

---

        (2) Discussion after interview: Do parents join groups for same reasons students do? Would you like to belong to any of the adult groups? Why or why not?
Have students draw emblems of youth and adult groups on board and let the other class members try to guess what club the emblem stands for.

 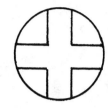 

(3) Make a bulletin board of adult <u>groups</u> under categories
    such as professional, social, political, recreational,
    civic, etc. Use art supplies to draw symbols to display
    with each <u>group</u>.

5.   <u>Suggest a Club</u> - (identify characteristics of group roles)

when: one period

what: teacher-prepared paragraphs describing cultures, but without
       naming cultures or countries

how: Have students read paragraphs and suggest groups or clubs
       that might be formed for those cultures. Would people in
       other cultures have the same reasons for joining clubs that
       students have? Sample paragraphs:

       (1) "There is a country that is flat and as low as sea level.
       The land is bisected with canals that are used much like roads
       are used in other countries. In winter the canals often
       freeze and people can skate on them. Windmills are used for
       power. The country is known for its fine cheese and for a
       certain spring flower. The bulb is exported so plants can be
       grown elsewhere."

       Suggestion on groups or clubs they might form: skating,
       cheese makers, cooperative flower export association.

       (2) "There is a group of people who live in rural communities
       in the east and midwest. Most of them farm for a living.
       They use no modern or electrical machinery, preferring a horse
       to pull a plow or pull the buggy for any traveling (trips to
       town). The adults wear mostly black. The men usually grow
       beards."

       Suggestion on groups they might form: sewing, quilting bees,
       preserving food, harvesting groups to help each other, barn
       raisings.

The point is, of course, that membership in organizations is based
on where we live, what we do for a living, and what our needs and
interests are.

Specific Objective: Identifying features of the environment for the purpose
of discriminating between similarities and differences.

6. <u>Look Around You</u> - (practicing cataloging the environment)

   when: one period (homework)

   what: checklist

   how: Have students look at features of their community and record
what they see.

____trees	____river	____fast food place
____flowers	____lake	____coffee house
____parks	____pool	____book store
____houses	____church	____drug store
____apartments	____school	____grocery store
____gas stations	____fire station	____] students'
		____ own ideas

   This activity is meant to call the students' attention to the
environment around them. It is a cataloging exercise building
toward identifying similarities and differences.

7. <u>Discriminating Between Environments</u> - (identifying characteristics of
similarities and differences)

   when: two or three periods

   what: sketches or pictures that fit activity, record form

   how: (1) Show students three sketches or pictures of natural environment (pastoral scenes--woods, prairie, seashore).
As students examine pictures, have them begin to realize
that all three pictures have something in common. Have
students answer the questions in Part I of Record Sheet
(see below).
      (2) Show students three more pictures; this time have two pic-
tures of man-made environment (Indian camp, pioneer town,
modern factory city) and one of natural (pastoral)
environment. Number the sketches 1, 2, 3. Have students
answer questions in Part II of Record Sheet.
      (3) Have students do Part III of Record Sheet.

RECORD SHEET

I. (A) Identify the similarities and differences in the three pictures.
   _____

   (B) What are the characteristics that describe the similarities in
the three pictures? _____
   _____
   _____

II.   Which picture of the second set of pictures fits the characteristics identified above? _____
_____

III. Make your own picture using the characteristics identified in Parts I and II.

Specific Objective: Identify dilemmas in solving personal social problems.

8.   Personal Social Problems - (making decisions)

when: three or four periods

what: case studies and questions below

how: Divide the class into groups and give a different case study to each group. The group may role-play the case study and then act as a panel to ask the audience selected questions. The group may role-play again using audience suggestions.

Alternative: Entire class may read same case study and discuss questions.

Case 1

My little brother does dumb things without thinking and then gets in trouble. Last week his friends dared him to throw a rock at a window, so he did. They all ran, but a man who came out of the house may have seen my brother's face. My brother came running to where I was playing football. He wanted me to say he had been with me and my friends playing football all afternoon. Promising he wouldn't do it again, he said he would do my paper route for a week if I would lie for him. What am I going to do?

Questions:

1. What are the facts?
2. What did little brother want from big brother?
3. Suppose you were the little brother, what might you have done about the broken window?
4. How would you feel about lying for someone else?

Case 2

I felt pretty good when I found the watch at the bus stop. The strap was broken so it must have dropped off of someone's wrist, but it was still running. I figured I could keep it, sell it, or trade it for something really neat. While I was waiting for the bus this strange-looking guy came by and was looking all around. He muttered something about losing his watch and asked if I had seen it or seen anyone pick it up.

Questions:

1. What are the facts?
2. What does the student want to do?
3. Suppose you found the watch, what might you have done
    with it?
4. How would you feel about keeping the watch?

Case 3

I was tagging along with a group of older kids that I
wanted to be friends with. On the way home from school they
sometimes stopped at a discount drug store. They said it was
easy to steal candy bars and if I would talk to the clerk to
keep his attention, they would take the candy bars and get
one for me. I want to be friends with them. What should I do?

Questions:

1. What are the facts?
2. What do the older boys want the younger boy to do?
3. Suppose you were the younger boy, what might you do?
4. How would you feel about eating the stolen candy?

B.   Purpose: Develop skills necessary to process information and to work
     with others

1.   Questions Are Everywhere[4]

     when: one period

     what: questionnaire (Questions Are Everywhere)

     how: This is a preliminary activity to cause students to think
            about questions. Questions are important because they are
            everywhere: What time is it? Did you get paid today? Where
            are you going? When will you be home? Did you like the show?
            What did you mean by that? Would I look better in the brown
            outfit? What will she think if I show up early? Where did I
            leave my shoes? Why am I here? Why do you treat me like you
            do? . . . Some questions are asked aloud while others are
            thought but not asked. Not much is learned without a question,
            and to process questions, one must think. Questions are,
            therefore, the catalyst of learning!

            Pass out questionnaire to students. Go over the directions
            with the students, then allow them time to write some ques-
            tions of their own.

            Have some of the students share their questions with the
            class. Read aloud the statement at the end of this activity
            as a summary of the activity.

QUESTIONS ARE EVERYWHERE!

Does it seem like someone is always asking you questions? Ones like
these below? Can you think of one or two other questions that you
have been asked in each of these places?

AT HOME: Did you pick up your room? Why did you do that? Where are
          you going?

          your questions: _____

          _____

AT SCHOOL: When . . . what. . . where. . . how much . . .? Did you
            do your lesson?

            your questions: _____

            _____

WITH FRIENDS: Whatcha doing? Did you see that TV show? Can I go,
               too? Did you like him?

               your questions: _____

               _____

WITH OTHERS: How do you feel? Where does it hurt?

              your questions: _____

              _____

That is the way the world works--by asking questions. That is the way
you work, too. It just makes sense, then, that if we learn to ask better
questions and to sort out the questions we are asked, we should be able
to get along better in the world.

Specific Objective: Students will process questions by differentiating
                     between open and closed.

2. Questioning Skills - (identifying open and closed type questions)

    when: two days training and then as regular part of activities

    what: question preference form and class textbooks

    how: Questioning is a skill. Students can learn to ask good
           questions. Asking good questions is important to many of the
           activities found in teacher's guides--but rarely are students
           taught the skill. The assumption is that students will learn
           from adults and peers through trial and error. Some do learn,
           some don't. There is a relationship between questions asked
           and creative behavior. For creativity both forms, open and
           closed, are required. The usual practice in school is for
           texts and teachers to ask mostly closed questions. The higher

the grade the more closed are the questions--so as the student proceeds through the grades less creativity is demanded. Learning about questions starts with identifying and then differentiating between open and closed type questions. Prepare a form that asks these questions. The form will help students identify their preference and strength of feeling for certain types of questions.

Teacher Key	QUESTION PREFERENCE FORM	
	I. Preference: for each group of questions below, tell which one you would most like to ask by placing a "1" in front of it, a "2" in front of the next, a "3" in front of the next, and a "4" in front of the question that you are least interested in.	II. Strength of Choice: After each of the questions below, circle how you feel about that question as follows: A = strongly like, B = like, C = neutral, D = dislike, E = strongly dislike.
closed	_____ 1. Name the . . .	A B C D E
closed	_____ 2. Compare the . . .	A B C D E
open	_____ 3. Suppose the . . .	A B C D E
open	_____ 4. Why do you think . . .	A B C D E
closed	_____ 1. Why did the . . .	A B C D E
open	_____ 2. In your opinion . . .	A B C D E
closed	_____ 3. Describe . . .	A B C D E
open	_____ 4. What would happen . . .	A B C D E

After the students have finished marking the form, discuss their preferences and choices with them: identify each question as to whether it is open or closed. The students will not know the difference at this point, but in filling out the question preference form they may have marked one type of question over the other. If students do prefer open type over closed or vice versa, ask the students why. Disclose the meaning of open and closed questions and discuss this with the class.

In brief: Open questions are those that do not have answers. Open questions require speculation such as suppose and evaluation such as opinion. Examples: "Suppose you were Washington, what might you have done?" "In your opinion, was Washington a good president?"

In brief: Closed questions have answers. Examples: "When did Washington become president?" "Explain how he became president." "Identify the name of his home." "What was his wife's name?" "What did he do that was important to the American Revolution?"

Follow-through activities:
(1) Have students look at the questions in the back of their social studies and other textbooks. Have them classify questions as to open or closed.
(2) On the social studies topic being studied, ask students to write out at least two open questions and two closed questions.
(3) When designing a test, written or oral, be sure to include both types.

NOTE: To help you continue using and developing this skill, the remainder of the activities in this book are designed to illustrate the use of both open and closed questions.

Specific Objective: Identify scale of miles on maps and globes and learn to locate places.

3. Treasure Hunt - (identifying geographic concept--direction)

    when: one period

    what:

    how: Tell students they are going to play a game of treasure hunt. Have one or two students leave the room and while they are gone the class decides on an object to be the treasure. Students are called back in and given clues by the class to tell them where the object is. Clues can only be given in terms of direction (north, south, east, west, or front of room, back, door side) or in distance (i.e., four feet from teacher's desk). Class members give directions in turn until object is located. The object is to give such accurate clues that "it" students will not have to leave their chairs to locate treasure.

4. Working With Scales - (identifying geographic concept--measurement and scales)

    when: two or three days

    what: paper, masking tape, yard stick, chalk, twist ties or pipe cleaners cut in four-inch lengths

    how: Desk: Have students measure their desks with the four-inch twist tie. Have them draw the exact size on a large piece of paper and cut it out. On a second piece of paper have students draw their desk, but first cut the twist tie in half (drawing should be one half size of desk). Cut twist tie in half again and draw desk again (drawing should be one-fourth size of desk).
    Floor: Mark the classroom floor in a yard-square grid with chalk and then cover with masking tape to make it more permanent. Have students make a grid on paper with one-inch equal to one yard (same number of squares as floor). Students can see where objects are on floor grid (desks, chairs, etc.) and then draw them in the corresponding grid on their paper.

Specific Objective: Learn to research for information from a variety of
sources, organize the information, and report it.

5.   Research "Know How" - (identifying historically important persons,
places and events, organizing and reporting)

when: three or four weeks

what: materials as needed for activity

how: (1) Have students make a list of famous Americans or people
from the state. Teacher can list names on the board and
add others that the students may not have thought of.

Names or events appropriate to early American history:	Names or events appropriate to state history:
Washington Jefferson John Adams Boston Tea Party etc.	explorer of territory territorial governor Indians--local transportation in a pioneer state etc.

(2) Have students decide on the questions they wish to answer
in a report they will write on one of the above names.
(a) Why is this person remembered?
(b) What were his/her major contributions?
(c) Suppose you had a chance to talk to this person, what
might you ask; what would he/she answer?
(d) Do you still think this person should be remembered?

(3) Have the librarian review with the students how to use
the card catalog to locate information on the subject
for their reports.

(4) Spend one period in the library for the students to use
the card catalog and check out books they find that
would help them in writing their reports.

They should be encouraged to use all types of materials:
books, encyclopedia, magazines, records, tapes, filmstrips. A simple card catalog form will help (next
page).

(5) When students have selected book, they should be encouraged
to note the important information about the book. A
simple information sheet asks for essential information
(next page).

```
┌─────────────────────────────────────────────────────────────┐
│              Information From Card Catalog                    │
│                                              Name _____ │
│  F  R  T  M  E  B     T        A      P  V  I                 │
│  i  e  a  a  n  o     i        u      a  o  s                 │
│  l  c  p  g  c  o     t        t      g  l  s                 │
│  m  o  e  a  y  k     l        h      e  u  u                 │
│  s  r     z  c        e        o      (  m  e                 │
│  t  d     i  l                 r      s  e                    │
│  r        n  o                 /      )                       │
│  i        e  p                 P                              │
│  p           e                 u                              │
│              d                 b                              │
│              i                 l                              │
│              a                 i                              │
│                                s                              │
│                                h                              │
│                                e                              │
│                                r                              │
│                                                               │
│                                Information                    │
│                                                               │
│                                                               │
│                                                               │
│                                                               │
└─────────────────────────────────────────────────────────────┘
```

Information From Card Catalog

Name _____

Filmstrip	Record	Tape	Magazine	Encyclopedia	Book	Title	Author/Publisher Information	Page(s)	Volume	Issue

```
┌─────────────────────────────────────────────────────────────┐
│                   Information Sheet                           │
│                                                               │
│                                                               │
│   Title _____      │
│                                                               │
│   Author _____      │
│                                                               │
│   Illustrator _____ Copyright _____    │
│                                                               │
│   Publisher _____      │
│                                                               │
│   Place of Publication _____     │
│                                                               │
│   Table of Contents chapter name that would be interesting:   │
│                                                               │
│   _____        │
│                                                               │
│   Use index in back of book to pick out information that is   │
│                                                               │
│   of interest: _____      │
│                                                               │
│   _____        │
│                                                               │
└─────────────────────────────────────────────────────────────┘
```

(6) Review how to use index with students using the following
    example of an index. Then have them fill out the index
    questionnaire.

INDEX

crops, 12, 13, 97, 115, 117, 180,
181, 184, 186, 192, 240, 247,
253, 255
  and air pollution, 234-235; fer-
  tilizing, 181; harvested by
  Spanish-speaking people, 170;
  historic Indiana, 24; Hopewell
  Indians, 20; in New Switzerland,
  265; Middle Missippi Indians,
  21, 23; rotating, 180
Crusades, 25, 28, 29
Cuba, 269, 271
  and slavery, 37
Cubans, 269, 271
Cumberland, 272
  Gap, 56, 82; Road, 114, 272
Czechoslovakia, 269

da Gama, Vasco, 30
  route to India map, 30
Davis, Jefferson, 159
Dawes, William, 54
Debs, Eugene V., 187, 202-203
deer, 248
Delaware Indians, 131

Democratic Party, 208, 212-214
Depression, 187, 205, 207, 223
Dutch colonies, 31

earth, changes in, 10, 12, 17
education, 67, 164
  changing world of, 172-174;
  church, 172; in Middle Ages, 26,
  27; La Salle's, 40; New Harmony,
  145
  (see schools)
Eisenhower, President, 216, 226
electric power plants,
  and air pollution, 230-231; and
  water pollution, 237-239
Ellis Island, 263-264
Emancipation Proclamation, 158,
  161, 162
England, 47, 48, 49, 50, 82, 104,
  107, 144, 151, 154, 159, 266,
  268, 269
environment, 227-244, 247, 248,
  249, 250, 252, 253, 258, 261,
  262
Europe, 15, 26, 29, 31, 34, 37,
  40, 46, 47, 117, 144, 151, 190,
  201, 205, 217, 263, 265, 266,

INDEX QUESTIONNAIRE

1. In index, do you look for a person's last name or first name?

    _____

2. If you were doing a report on Ellis Island, what page would
    you look on? _____

3. If you were doing a report on crops and wanted to know what
    historic Indians planted, what page would you look on? _____

4. If you were interested in education in the Middle Ages, what
    page would you look on? _____

5. If you wanted to know about electric power plants (and water
    pollution), what page would you look on? _____

6. If you were looking up the Cumberland Gap, what page would
    you look on? _____

(7) Students need to learn how to read to gather information and facts for their reports. The paragraph below and the questions following it should help students learn how to look for information.

Early Pioneer Transportation

The earliest transportation was on streams, rivers, and lakes where Indians used <u>canoes</u>. The waterways became the Indians' roads. Another early means of travel was by <u>horse</u> down trails cut by animals, Indians, and early pioneers. The horseback rider was soon followed by <u>wagons</u>, conestoga wagons pulled by four to six horses down the newly cut roads. Along with wagons came the <u>flatboats</u> that could only float downstream on the Ohio River.

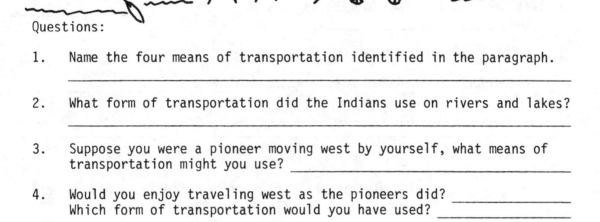

Questions:

1. Name the four means of transportation identified in the paragraph.
    _____

2. What form of transportation did the Indians use on rivers and lakes?
    _____

3. Suppose you were a pioneer moving west by yourself, what means of transportation might you use? _____

4. Would you enjoy traveling west as the pioneers did? _____
    Which form of transportation would you have used? _____

(8) Using index cards, students should have one card for each question asked (see p. 110, part (2) at beginning of activity where students decide what information is needed for their reports). Have students answer questions by using resource material in the library that they have already identified.

(9) After students have gathered their information, they must put that information in a written report form. The following is a form example that might help them write a paragraph. A paragraph writing exercise:

PRACTICE PARAGRAPH FORM

name _____

_____
Title

_____ is remembered because _____
person's name   reason

_____.

His/her major contributions were/are _____

_____.

If I had a chance I would like to talk to _____
about _____ and ask him/her _____?

I think he/she would answer _____

This person should/should not be remembered because _____
                                                              reasons

_____.

6. <u>Puzzles</u> - (identifying historically important persons, places,
    events; organizing and reporting)

    when: two or three periods

    what: puzzles to do during or following research above

    how:

Simple Crossword Puzzle

FLATBOAT
CANOE
CONESTOGA
PIONEER

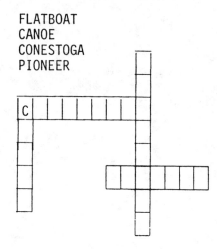

Word Search Puzzle
(find the hidden word)

F	Z	E	N	C	O	N	E	S	T	O	G	A	L	Y
C	A	N	O	E	W	R	U	I	V	M	B	S	A	T
A	B	E	L	C	D	Q	N	O	P	T	X	C	G	H
E	C	V	T	Y	H	J	F	L	A	T	B	O	A	T
O	I	W	P	I	O	N	E	E	R	M	A	Q	E	P

FLATBOAT
CANOE
CONESTOGA
PIONEER

Crossword Puzzle

ACROSS
2 Abraham _____, a backwoods lawyer who became president.
3 The _____ Gap was a way through the mountains discovered by Daniel Boone.
8 Many pioneers moved west carrying their belongings in a _____ wagon.
11 In early days the only way to cross a river was by _____.
12 Early trappers sold their furs to trading posts, many of which were _____ forts.
13 Daniel Boone made a famous trail west called the _____ Trail.

DOWN
1 George Rogers _____ was an early settler and helped fight the British during the American Revolution.
3 A _____ road is made up of logs laid side by side, one right next to another.
4 Daniel _____ was an early settler in the west.
5 Many Indians and explorers and settlers made clothes out of _____.
6 William Henry _____ was the first governor of the Indiana Territory and became President of the United States.
7 Early settlers were often called _____.
9 The _____ River was an important waterway for Indians and for settlers moving west.
10 When a territory became a _____ it became one of the United States.

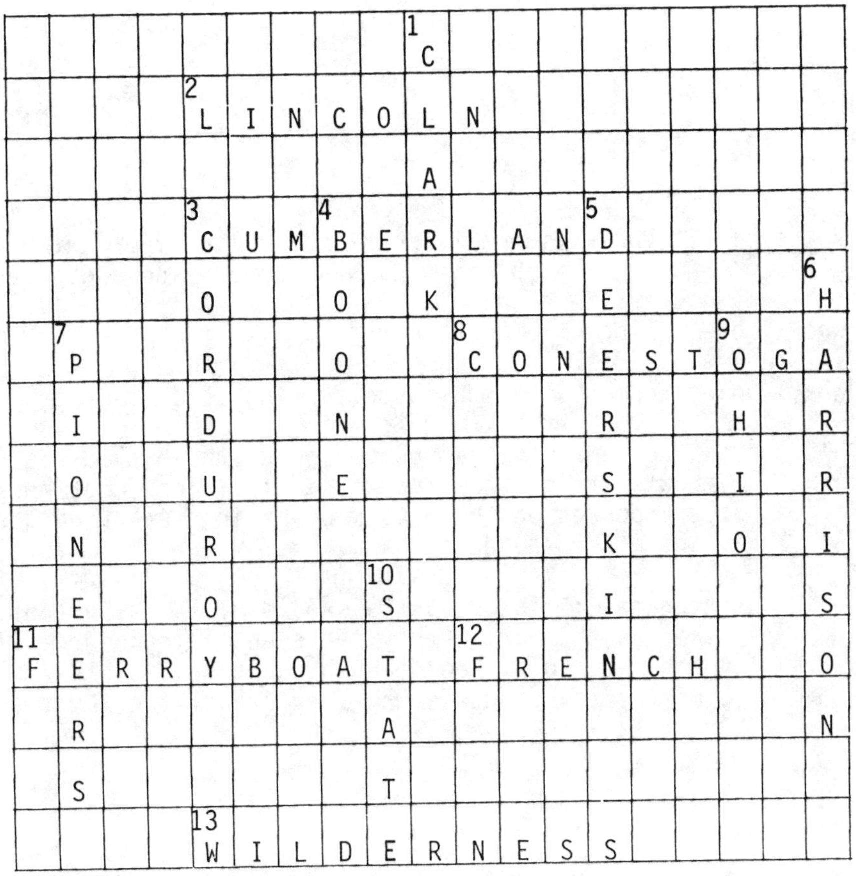

(crossword grid)

Answers shown in grid:
- 1 Down: CLARK (C-L-A-R-K)
- 2 Across: LINCOLN
- 3 Across: CUMBERLAND; 3 Down: CORDUROY
- 4 Down: BOONE
- 5 Down: DEERSKIN
- 6 Down: HARRISON
- 7 Down: PIONEERS
- 8 Across: CONESTOGA
- 9 Down: OHIO
- 10 Down: STATE
- 11 Across: FERRYBOAT
- 12 Across: FRENCH
- 13 Across: WILDERNESS

7. <u>Creating and Presenting</u> - (identifying historically important per-
   <u>a "Write-On" Filmstrip</u>   sons, places, events; organizing and
                                      reporting)

   when: one period

   what: special filmstrip kit
          (The Write-On Filmstrip),
          overhead projector

   how: Filmstrips are available that can be
          written on by the students with
          colored pencils. Students can create
          their own pictures and captions on
          the filmstrip to be shown on an over-
          head projector. These filmstrips are
          ideal for helping students organize,
          create, and present reports. The
          special filmstrips are available in a
          number of school supply catalogs.
          One supplier is Prima Educational
          Products, Irving on the Hudson, NY
          10533. The students may work up their
          presentation on a storyboard guide
          first, then transfer their pictures
          and captions to the film. The film
          can be erased and used over again.

8. <u>Personal Pin-Ups</u> - (identifying historically important persons,
                            places, events; organizing and categorizing)

   when: one period

   what: pins, names of famous people being studied written on papers

   how: Pin the name of a famous person to the back of each student
          without letting them see who it is. They must guess the name
          of the person on their back by asking yes or no questions
          of the other students.

          Alternative: The students should mill around and treat each
          other as the person they represent (King George III,
          Abraham Lincoln, George Washington, Benedict Arnold).
          Students try to guess who they are by the way they are
          treated.

9. Aiding Reports - (identifying historically important persons, places,
                       events; organizing and categorizing)

   when: one period per activity

   what: materials as needed for activity

   how: (1) Have students make a transparency about the person or
              event they researched.
          (2) Have students dress up as the person they researched if
              they wish to.
          (3) Have students locate on a map where the person they re-
              searched lived or where the event they researched took
              place. A little flag with the event or person's name
              might be pinned to a United States map.

10. Goldilocks and the Three Bears or Stereotyping

   when: one period

   what: story and questions below

   how: We all know the story of "Goldilocks and the Three Bears,"
          how Goldilocks ran all the way home hoping never to see the
          three bears again. What we did not know until now is what
          happened afterwards!

          Sometime after Goldilocks returned from her adventures with
          the bears, she came into a substantial inheritance and de-
          cided to build a new house. Her new house was not large, but
          it had several picture windows and a glassed-in patio. Soon
          after she moved in, she was visited by the three bears who
          shouted obscenities, then attacked and damaged her house.
          Goldilocks suffered shock and was physically injured by broken
          glass. The bears ran off.

          Goldilocks, feeling she was unsafe in her "glass house," de-
          cided a wooden house would be much better, so she had one
          built. Once again, soon after she moved in she was visited
          by the three bears. They set fire to the house, then ran
          away. Goldilocks called the fire department, but the house
          was a total loss. Some bears were picked up by the police,
          but they turned out to be the wrong ones. Goldilocks, in
          desperation, decided to move to a high-rent district where
          there was security protection. However, much to her dismay,
          she found that the house next to hers was rented to a bear!
          Because of her past experiences with bears, she began a
          petition to prevent bears from downgrading the neighborhood.
          She asks you to sign the anti-bear petition. What do you do?
               Is she justified in her actions, or do you feel she is
                  overreacting?
               Is she within her legal or moral rights?
               Does this story make you decide all bears are bad?
               Assume you are Goldilocks. What would your reaction be
                  to living near, knowing, or associating with bears?

C. Purpose: Develop the skill to examine <u>values</u> and beliefs

    Specific Objective: Examining one's own beliefs and values.

      1. <u>We Like . . .</u> - (identifying similarities in values and beliefs)

          when: one period

          what:

          how: Have each student pair with another student who has the same interest (model ship building). Have them touch in some way (lock elbows, hold hands). Each pair then tries to join with another pair on another shared interest or an expansion of the earlier one (model building of any kind). The four lock elbows, hold hands, or touch somehow. The foursomes try to join on a shared interest. Continue until whole class is one big circle that shares an interest.

      2. <u>Beliefs</u> - (identifying similarities in values and beliefs)

          when: three or four periods

          what: materials as needed for activity

          how: (1) Pick a TV show, a movie the whole class has seen (Wizard of Oz), or show a movie to class. Discuss one of the major characters in the movie: what the character did and why, and what beliefs or values the character might hold that would cause the character to act the way he/she did. Discuss what students would do in a similar situation. Are there similarities and differences between what they would do and what the character did and what they value as compared with what the character seems to value?

              (2) Clean the toy box: Teacher makes a list of toys and objects that might be stored in a toy box (books, baseball cards, football, skates, clay, ball and jacks, broken alarm clock, toy telephone, toy cars, trucks, dolls, etc.). Give each student a copy of the list and have them pick toys they would discard and tell why. What do the lists reveal about students' values and beliefs? Are there similar lists between students?

      3. <u>Ranking Values</u> - (identifying similarities in values and beliefs)

          when: two periods

          what: questions to rank

          how: (1) Ranking Values: rank items in questions (1 for first choice, 2 for second choice, 3 for third choice, and 4 for last choice).

1. When do you like to eat out?

    ___ breakfast   ___ lunch   ___ dinner   ___ snack time

2. How many people do you like to be (play) with?

    ___ alone   ___ two people   ___ small group or team   ___ crowd

3. What is most important to you now?

    ___ health   ___ money   ___ friendship   ___ happiness

4. What do you think will be most important to you in the future?

    ___ health   ___ money   ___ friendship   ___ happiness

5. Where would you like to vacation?

    ___ mountains   ___ seashore   ___ big city   ___ ranch

6. Which would you prefer to do?

    ___ read   ___ watch TV   ___ talk to a friend   ___ go to a movie

> Students may want to make up own questions. Teacher may wish to make up questions on topic being studied or about to be studied. Questions may be used for discussion.

These two activities, "Ranking Values" and "Personal Preference," are based upon the assumption that values determine choices between alternatives. To identify values it is sometimes important for students to identify their problems and also their needs and interests, for when a student identifies a problem, the problem leads back to a need or interest, and in turn needs and interests lead back to values. Simply, if you want to deal with values, you need to deal with those things about which people make choices.

VALUES------------>NEEDS AND INTERESTS------------>PROBLEMS

(2) Personal Preference: Have students place themselves where they think they fit. Questions may be used for discussion. Teachers and students should make up preference questions. For example:

1. How do you feel about being with people?

    Solo Sam ------------------------------------- Crowd-Seeking Chris

2. How do you like your music?

    "Rocking" Rita ------------------------------- "Classical" Cloris

3. How do you like to settle an argument?

    Talk-it-out Tom ------------------------------ Fighting Fred

4. What's your attitude about helping at home?

    Reluctant Rosie ------------------------------ Helpful Hannah

4. <u>My Values and Yours</u>[5] - (identifying similarities and differences in
values and beliefs)

    when: one period

    what: 3" x 5" file cards

    how: Give each student four file cards and have them cut them in
    halp so each student has eight cards. Discuss values, those
    things that are most important to you and that you like the
    best. List eight of the class's most important values on the
    board. Have students write values on cards (one value from
    board on one card; eight values = eight cards). Have students
    stack cards in order of importance (most important on top).
    Compare ranking with a partner. Why do your values differ?

    Value examples: making money   family
    being a leader   friends
    honesty   solo activities
    getting good grades time
    nice clothes   looking like friends
    (not conspicuous)

5. <u>Expose-Disclose</u>[6] - (identifying similarities and differences in
values and beliefs; also identifying a posi-
tive self image)

    when: one period

    what:

    how: Use words to describe yourself that have a letter the same as
    in your name.

```
     M usic lover                         i                      p
                                       t  n                      a
     I maginative                      h  t                   p  i
                                       r  e                   l  n
thin K er              capa B le       i  l   i              M  A  T  T
                                       f  l                  u  n  e  a
   s E rious             pr E tty      T  I  M                s  n  r  l
                                       y  g  p                i  e     e
                         s T udious       e  o                c  r     n
                                          n  r                i        t
                           H appy         t  t                a        e
                                             a                n        d
                                             n
                                             t
```

6. <u>And Heerreee's</u> _____! - (identifying a positive self-image)
   <u>(student's name)</u>

   when: recurring (one student at a time)

   what: materials as needed

   how: Each student plans a day when he/she can experiment and try
          new things or activities. Preparation may be done in free
          time or spare time during the day. Students should make a
          collage of pictures that describe and show things he/she
          likes. The student should collect and bring in photos of
          his/her lifestyle (as a baby and now), family, home, etc.
          Fill in a personality sheet, make sure it is correct, and
          copy it in best handwriting. Sheet should have: name,
          address, date, birthday, family members, favorite toys, TV
          shows, colors, school friends, school subject, season, outdoor
          sport or activity, indoor sport or activity, dessert. See
          teacher to set date for your special day on daily calendar.

          To the student: Fill in schedule for special day starting
          with checking in with teacher before school starts and at end
          of day. If activity involves another teacher or staff person,
          be sure to get that person's permission and initials on
          schedule. Prepare for your day by making a poster about your-
          self with your name, collage, photos, personality sheet. On
          your day, place poster in hall where everyone can see it.
          Make sure you and teacher both have a copy of your schedule.
          Your day will be a success if you plan well.

D. Purpose: Apply knowledge through active <u>participation</u> in society

   Specific Objective: Solving problems through organization.

   1. Responsibility - (participation in rule-making)

       when: one or two periods

       what: copy of school rules

       how: Have students recall that in their first three grades they
              may have had activities that examined school rules, advan-
              tages and disadvantages. Since students are now older, it is
              time to take more responsibility in defining and possibly
              proposing changes in school rules.

              Have students examine series of school rules, discuss why
              each rule was made and whether it could be modified or changed
              to make it more effective. Is the rule practical and neces-
              sary?

              Having examined the rules, class should be encouraged to reach
              a consensus on those rules that need to be discussed with
              school authorities.

The following are school rules that fourth graders might be expected to comment on:

Students are not allowed to ride bikes on school playground during school day. _____
_____

Lunch periods are one hour and fifteen minutes; would you prefer to shorten the lunch period to an hour and be excused fifteen minutes earlier in the afternoon? _____
_____

Grades kindergarten through third are released five minutes earlier than grades four through six. _____
_____

2. Getting Involved - (participation in rule-making)

   when: two or three weeks

   what: interview cards

   how: Students should find out about organizations in the school and in the community. To teach students how to get involved in rule-making, whether it be in school or perhaps community organizations, the following activities will help organize the effort.

   Have students call members or officials of organizations and set up an appointment for an interview.

Interview Questionnaire

1. What is name of organization?

2. What is purpose of organization in community (or school)?

3. Suppose fourth graders became interested in your organization, might they be welcome?

4. Are there projects that fourth graders could do to help your organization?

Have class send memos, letters, or telegrams to community or school organizations urging some action:

WESTERN UNION

Date _____   I urge your committee/organization to:

_____

_____

Sincerely _____

3. You Can Make a Difference

when: recurring

what:

how: Class members identify a service project on which they would
like to work or with which they would like to become involved.
One of the best ways to accomplish this is by field trips to
service centers for the purpose of identifying needs of the
organization and interests of the students. The following
are the types of organizations that might be considered:
community centers (working with young children); Red Cross;
YWCA/YMCA; rest homes, nursing homes, retirement villages,
county farm (working with senior citizens).

Example: Suppose the students decide to work with senior
citizens at a rest home they visited on a field trip.
(1) Contact the rest home to clarify needs of the organization and to obtain permission or approval for your proposed project.
(2) Students plan and decide on project to undertake or way
they may become involved with the senior citizens.
(3) Students might plan a play or party in order to meet
senior citizens.
(4) Adopt a senior citizen: groups of two or three students
adopt one senior citizen to visit, write to, remember on
holidays and birthdays.
(5) If senior citizens are well enough, invite them to visit
class. They might enjoy being a resource person or
"gray angel."

Notes

[1] Indiana Department of Public Instruction. 1978 Indiana textbook adoption
categories for social studies. Indianapolis: Author, 1978, p. 2.

[2] Barth, J. L., & Shermis, S. S. Teaching social studies to gifted and
talented students. Indianapolis: Indiana Department of Public Instruction,
p. 24.

[3] Ibid., p. 25.

[4] This activity was originally developed in 1980 for "Questions Social Studies
Students Ask," a Division of Innovative Education ESPA Title IV-C Research
Project of the North Montgomery School Corporation, Linden, Indiana. In
particular, the author wishes to recognize the contribution of James Spencer
and David Horney in the development of this project. The activity has been
revised for publication in this book.

[5] Barth & Shermis, p. 29.

[6] Ibid., p. 31.

INTEREST FORM

You have just completed the Chapter Fourth Grade. In an effort to have you identify activities and materials that seem most promising at this grade level to you, please fill out the following interest form.

Instructions:

Identify two activities from this chapter. Name the activities and briefly describe why these particular activities are of interest to you.

ACTIVITY 1

ACTIVITY 2

CHAPTER FIFTH GRADE

ACTIVITIES AND MATERIALS FOR FIFTH GRADE

CHAPTER FIFTH GRADE

Organization of the Chapter

Each succeeding chapter represents a particular grade level, in this case fifth grade. Each chapter consists of three parts: the first part is a brief discussion on courses, topics, and national trends in teaching fifth grade throughout the United States; the second part is an example of a state fifth grade program; the third part has activities and materials for the fifth grade categorized by the four objectives of teaching social studies--gaining knowledge, processing, valuing, and participating.

I. Topics Taught and National Trends in Teaching Fifth Grade

Recall the fourth grade curriculum trends. Three different course offerings were most frequently used. One approach emphasized historical development of the state and nation. Another stressed state as a region with comparison to other selected regions throughout the world. The third, Communities Around the World, centered on other cultures. It is useful to recall these three approaches because the fifth grade social studies curriculum may be keyed to one of the approaches in the fourth grade. In fifth grade the three most frequently offered courses are: United States History, United States History and Geography, and Geography of North America. The fifth grade, as distinct from any other elementary grade, seems to have been specifically reserved for study of American history or the North American continent. There is a reason for this, it did not just happen by accident. The recommendation that American history be taught in three cycles in fifth, eighth, and eleventh grades was proposed in 1943 by the Committee on American History in the Schools and Colleges, popularly known as the Wesley Committee. The recommendation of the Wesley Committee had a significant influence on standardizing the

teaching of American history into the three cycles that are now almost univer-
sally followed in schools throughout the United States. Your attention is
called to this recommendation because it not only identified the fifth grade
as the proper place to begin an in-depth treatment of national history but
also recommended appropriate content and the amount of time to be devoted to
certain periods of American history and geography. Recommendations of the
Wesley Committee will periodically be mentioned throughout the remainder of
the book, for they do in fact set out a curriculum structure that is recognized
and followed by text authors and most school systems.

Course, Topics, and Themes Frequently Covered in Fifth Grade: "United States History"

Objectives of the Course

Intended to provide the first chronological survey of American history.
Emphasis is on (in accordance with the Wesley Committee) discovery, colonial,
early national periods (Revolution, Constitution, establishment of the government), and growth of the United States (this is often expressed as a unit on
the movement west). The student is expected to understand the fundamental
ideas that motivated Americans (democracy, freedom), also to appreciate how
the country expanded and incorporated territory.

Basic Content of the Course

Typically the course includes these topics: European backgrounds; discovery and exploration; the colonial period, with emphasis on the founding of
the colonies and on colonial life; the winning of independence and establishment of the nation; territorial expansion and the westward movement; sectional
differences leading to the Civil War; the war and Reconstruction; the closing
of the frontier; the growth of industry and of cities; the US becomes a world
power, our nation today.

The following are illustrations of the type of topic headings that are

now found in some fifth grade American history books: The First Arrivals; The
Struggle to Build a Nation; How People Were Governed; How People Made Their
Living; How People Behaved; A Good Money System; Secession Tests the Social
System; The Chicago World's Fair of 1893; Immigration; The Status of Women;
The Great Depression; Martin Luther King and the Bus Boycott; How People Are
Governed Now; How People Behave Now; The Social System in the Year 2000.

Comment

These chapter headings and the basic content look rather traditional in
the sense that the student is treated to a survey from Christopher Columbus to
the present. However, note carefully that a large portion of the time, at
least half, is devoted to the discovery, settlement, and the colonial period
up to the end of the American Revolution in 1783. One quarter of the course
is given to the nation's growth in territory, settlement, and transportation
to about 1850. The other quarter of the time is devoted to an overview survey
of American history to the present and in some cases speculation about the
future.

Wesley Committee

To clarify and summarize, the American history course was to be an overview of the nation's history with special emphasis upon an in-depth study of
selected topics up to the Civil War. Why did the Wesley Committee make such a
recommendation? The Committee reasoned that the fifth grade would study in
depth seventeenth- and eighteenth-century American history, eighth grade
American history would study the nineteenth century, and eleventh grade American history would cover the twentieth century. If this recommendation were
followed, the teacher would not be put in the position of trying to cover all
of American history in depth in one year. The key to understanding teaching
of the three cycles of American history in school is (a) survey the entire
national history quickly and (b) study certain historical periods in depth.

Course, Topics, and Themes Frequently Covered in Fifth Grade:
"United States History and Geography"

Objectives of the Course

Develop the student's understanding of the physical, economic, and cultural geography of the United States and the influence of geographic factors on the nation's history with a detailed study of early explorations and the colonial period, and continue growth in current events, processing information through an inquiry process and the development of questioning skills.

Content of the Course

A typical arrangement of topics, according to several recent curriculum bulletins, is: geographic overview of North America; discovery and exploration; growth of English colonies, with some attention to the Spanish and French colonies; colonial life, the winning of independence and establishment of the new nation; an overview of United States history from about 1812 to the present; regional studies, heavily geographical but incorporating historical material, especially that dealing with territorial expansion and the westward movement.

United States History and Geography could just as well be called Studies of the North American Continent. History and geography are integrated, and some texts and teachers are quick to point out that geography modified the immigrant American to create a different, unique people as distinct from their European ancestry. The course also follows the Wesley Committee recommendations; the difference, of course, is the geography of the North American continent with the added dimension that Canada and sometimes Mexico are countries used to compare and contrast with the United States.

Course, Topics, and Themes Frequently Covered in Fifth Grade:
"Geography of North America"

Objectives of the Course

Develop the student's understanding of the physical, cultural, and economic geography of the United States, Canada, and Mexico; continued growth in effective use of maps, globes, and charts. Students should identify the relationship between geographic factors and the development of particular regions and nations.

Basic Content of the Course

This course frequently consists of an introductory overview unit followed by regional studies. Each regional unit includes attention to: physical features and climates of the region; natural resources; ways of making a living in the region; cities; places of special interest.

The following topic headings are illustrative of the type of content normally covered in this geography course: Questions That Need Map Answers; Regional Maps; Regions Based on Culture; Regions Inside States; Regions That Cross State Lines; Natural Resources; Using and Conserving Resources; Jobs, Wages, and Production; Sights and Sounds of Cities; The Joys and Problems of Cities; Interesting Places to Visit.

Trends in Teaching Fifth Grade Social Studies

1.   The fifth grade, as distinct from all other grades, was earmarked by the Wesley Committee as the proper grade for teaching a course in American Studies. This recommendation has been adopted nationwide. The Wesley Committee recommendation has been interpreted to mean the teaching of an in-depth study of early American history and geography leading by the end of the school year to a study of "our neighbor" Canada.

2.   The trend is to continue to follow the Wesley Committee. As in the

case of the preceding grades, there is a strong attempt by historians and social scientists to base the course on key concepts. The course, from their point of view, should not be "just a wagon train west" but should emphasize such concepts as dependence and interdependence, cultural change, social control, conflict and values. The course, in other words, should be an integration of history and geography with emphasis upon key concepts as identified by historians and social scientists.

3. There has been considerable criticism of the repetition of the three cycle study of American history in grades five, eight, and eleven. That criticism has not dislodged the cycles. They are firmly rooted in the social studies curriculum. Though many texts and other curriculum materials are designed to conform with the fifth grade concentration on the seventeenth and eighteenth centuries, the eighth grade on the nineteenth century, and the eleventh grade on the twentieth century, this is not well understood by most social studies teachers, textbook authors, or curriculum materials designers. Many continue to believe that teachers must cover all periods of American history with equal depth at all three levels. Of course, this has led to considerable criticism because students are required to cover approximately the same material three times. Efforts in the years ahead will probably be to educate teachers in their responsibility to teach in-depth specific periods and survey others rather than trying to change the cycles.

4. American history was intended to be a capstone course. Recall for a moment the expanding spiral of themes and topics from self to family, to school, to neighborhood, to city or community, to state, and now in the fifth grade to nation. The fifth grade course is intended to tie together all of the above themes and topics. After all, there were no guarantees that teachers from grade to grade would necessarily demonstrate the relationship between the themes. Fifth grade American history was assigned the task of demonstrating

how the individual, through the history of his nation, is related to all of the previous themes. In other words, the American history course was to integrate, clarify, summarize, and demonstrate the key concepts that have been taught through the first four grades.

Finally, as a clarification and summary, the one clear idea you should take from this part on trends is that of the recommendations of the Wesley Committee: (a) that United States history should be taught in the fifth grade, and (b) about two-thirds of social studies class time should be devoted to discovery, exploration, and the colonial period with emphasis on a social history overview to the present. Social history means the study of everyday life with emphasis on selected national leaders and key dates and events.

II. Illustrations of a State Fifth Grade Program

There is no one prescribed social studies program throughout the United States. However, one state's description of its fifth grade program will illustrate the content which the state expects to be taught. This illustration identifies a state's suggested social studies curriculum for the fifth grade:

> The United States is compared with other selected regions of the world. Students will examine how geography influenced the development of an area such as North America, and what impact technological development, trade, communication, transportation, economic, political, and social systems had on the historical development of the regions studied. Knowledge, process, location, valuing, and social skills should have continued development.[1]

III. Activities and Materials Categorized by Gaining Knowledge, Processing, Valuing, and Participating

A common practice is to skip specific objectives which precede the activities, but in this case the objectives are extremely important for an objective in the fifth grade will be found in succeeding grades. The following activities and materials are part of a developmental curriculum organized to build citizenship skills from one grade to another.

FIFTH GRADE ACTIVITIES AND MATERIALS

A. Purpose: Gain knowledge about the human condition which includes past, present, and future

Specific Objective: Identifying problems of exploration and colonization.

1. Claiming the New World - (practicing rule-making)

    when: two or three weeks

    what: silver spray-painted pebbles, solid spices such as cloves and cinnamon sticks cut in pieces
    We know that the early explorers, in the fifteenth and six-teenth centuries, were seeking among other things precious metals and spices. When a new continent was discovered, dis-agreement between colonial powers arose over conflicting claims. This activity is intended to suggest how the con-flicts arose over colonial claims.

    how: Suppose a new continent has been discovered and foreign countries are eager to claim land and mine its riches. Each student will represent a country and will make a claim on the new continent. Discuss with students the troubles that might arise in making claims. List the possible troubles on the board. For example:
    claims for the same area
    lack of specific boundaries
    how to know if land is already taken
    what to stake claim with
    etc.
    Divide the class into groups and have each group establish four to eight laws that they would use in claiming sections of the new continent. Each group appoints one of its members to list their laws on a chart on the board. When all groups are done, a master list is compiled, similar laws are com-bined. The class now votes by ballot for four laws that seem most important to them.

Example Ballot

_____ 1. Student may move another's claim if he wants his own claim on another's spot.
_____ 2. Student may move boundaries of another person just a little to squeeze his claim in.
_____ 3. All students must use same kind of boundary markers.
_____ 4. Claims must be registered with teacher.
_____ 5. There is a limit to how much can be claimed.
_____ 6. A claim must have a sign saying who it belongs to.

Teacher must stake out area on playground large enough to accommodate a claim for each student with room to spare. Seed (sprinkle) the ground with silver-painted pebbles and spices.

Students prepare to stake claim. They need a piece of note-book paper 8½" x 11" (represents size of claim they can stake), boundary markers, claim sign, container for pebbles and spices.

Teacher takes students out to area and allows them to stake their claims following the laws they have selected. When claims are established, they may search within their area for precious metals (silver pebbles) and spices.

Return to class: Discuss with class what real countries (Spain, France, England, etc.) did with precious metals and spices from their colonies. They used the wealth to build armies and navies to gain world power. Prepare a chart listing what can be bought by pebbles and spices and a rate of exchange. For example:

1 boat........1 pebble   1 pebble = 7 spices
3 cannons.....1 pebble
4 horses......1 pebble   (whatever ratio
suit of armor.2 spices   you wish)
sword.........1 spice
etc.

Have students decide what they can purchase with what they found at their claim. They should be allowed to trade pebbles for spices and vice versa at the ratio listed above. See which student (country) can obtain the greatest military strength.

2.   Survival Island - (practice rule-making and decision-making)

when: one period

what: map of island

how: This activity is designed to encourage students to consider the problems of establishing a colony. What factors should be taken into consideration when establishing a colony? How do you survive in an alien environment? Students, having first considered the problems of survival are more likely to identify with the problems of the early colonists at Jamestown, Plymouth, etc.

You have been elected to lead a group of 500 people to begin a new society on an uninhabited island 2,000 miles from your nearest neighbor. You want to be isolated from the rest of the world. You will take with you livestock, seed, and building materials. Among your group are people who are skilled in almost every necessary trade. As the leader you must take all conditions into consideration and choose a location for your settlement.

138 (Fifth Grade)

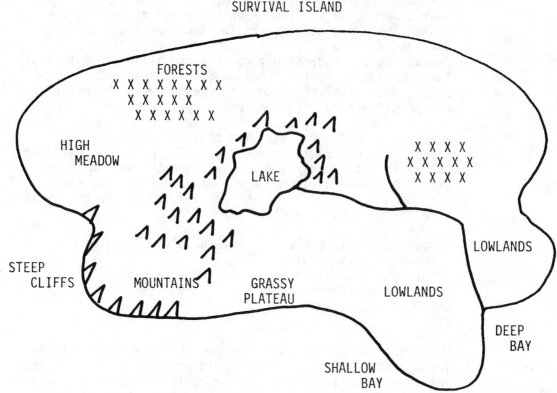

(1) Each student or group of students is to play the role of
the leader of the settlement and as leader must make a
fundamental decision on where to place the island's one
settlement. This would seem to be a rather simple decision but further consideration would suggest that a
decision on where to place the settlement involves a
number of relatively complex problems.

(2) Encourage the students to identify all of the conditions
they can think of that will be important in choosing a
location for the settlement. Consider these: ecological
problems (disposal of waste, maintenance of water quality,
power), other factors such as access to other parts of
the island, protection from storms, and finally problems
of population density and population growth, just to men-
tion a few. Of course, the problems on the island are
exactly the same as living anywhere else. The issue is
quality of life, the question is survive for what--what
will be the quality of life for which the islanders have
survived?

(3) After students have selected their spot on the island,
hold a class discussion in which the class identifies all
the conditions that should be taken into consideration
in choosing an appropriate site.

(4) Locate where each member of the class placed his/her settlement and discuss whether the locations are or are not
appropriate in terms of the considerations identified above.

Final Note: Survival on an island, at Jamestown, or on the moon is not
all that easy. Thoughtful decisions based on true knowledge
are a must for survival.

3.   Who Gets to Go? - (practicing rule-making and decision-making)

    when: one period

    what: list of individuals requesting to go to domed city on the
            moon (below)

    how: This is a contemporary problem in selection for colonizing.
            This activity involves selecting appropriate people for a
            colony, and anticipating problems that might arise in the new
            colony. Students should be made aware that problems are much
            the same whether colonizing the new world or colonizing a new
            planet.

            A domed city with controlled climate and life systems has
            been built on the moon to house a colony of settlers. A
            national selection committee has been established to deter-
            mine what people may be transported to that city.

            (1) Divide the class into groups of four to six students.
            (2) Each group should imagine that it represents the national
                committee with the responsibility of choosing seven
                people from the list below.
            (3) The list of seven the group chooses must be approved by a
                majority of the members of the group.
            (4) After the small groups have completed their lists, the
                entire class should compare and discuss the different
                groups' lists. Keep in mind that the very life (survi-
                val) of the colony may well rest on the right choice of
                people.

Individuals Requesting to Go to Domed City

1.   35-year-old carpenter who is going blind
2.   30-year-old illegal alien from Latin America who is a computer expert
3.   42-year-old tax accountant who is a professed homosexual
4.   37-year-old elementary teacher with retarded son will only go if he
     can also go
5.   68-year-old retired army officer
6.   33-year-old doctor suspected of selling illegal drug prescriptions
7.   25-year-old electrician with a history of emotional problems
8.   48-year-old dairy farmer and wife who is a special education teacher
     will only go together
9.   27-year-old lead guitarist whose rock group just split up
10. 51-year-old southern sheriff
11. 60-year-old female English Literature professor who retired to write
     poetry
12. 31-year-old female bus driver
13. 23-year-old former Black gang leader now driving a van for senior
     citizen center
14. 43-year-old ex-movie actress who now owns and operates a boutique in
     Beverly Hills
15. 32-year-old welfare mother with two children will only go if they
     can go

4. <u>Seeking the New World</u> - (practicing rule-making and decision-making)

    when: one period

    what: copies of the following story:

> The year is 1550. You along with your friends have formed a company and have bought land in the new world. On the way across the Atlantic from England your ship is hit by a big storm. The captain of the ship demands that you and your friends must throw overboard all goods and equipment brought to start the new colony, but that you and your friends may retain only personal items (clothing, money, etc.) and five other items of your company's choice. You and your friends are faced with a decision--what five items to keep. For example:

seeds to plant	rope
farm tools	weaving loom
carpentry tools	firearms and ammunition
iron and forge tools	sugar
cloth	flour
beads, etc. to trade	tea, coffee
with natives	salt

(1) Divide the class into groups. Assign each group an identifying letter, A, B, C, D, E.

(2) Distribute the story to each group and ask the students to read it.

(3) Ask the students to complete the activity in the following way:

    10 min.   groups compile original list of five items

    5 min.   groups rotate lists and make changes (see rotation plan below)

    5 min.   groups rotate lists and make changes; groups continue to rotate lists and make changes every five minutes until lists return to original group

(4) Discuss changes in lists, methods of making lists and changes in lists, and reactions to changes.

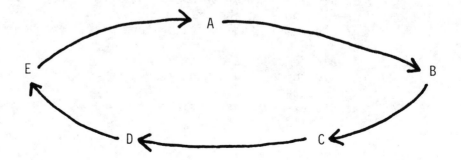

5. New World Bingo

when: two periods

what: blank BINGO cards large enough to write on

how: Pass out BINGO cards. Have students write a question dealing
      with exploration of the new world or early settlement days in
      each square and a matching answer chip, i.e., for square B,1,
      "What date did Columbus discover the new world?" Answer chip
      B,1--"1492." For square I,7, "Who led the Massachusetts Bay
      Co.?" Answer chip I,7--"John Winthrop."

      Have teacher or student collect all the answer chips. Stu-
      dents should exchange cards. Teacher or student calls out
      square number and answer. If it fits student's card, he/she
      may cover that square. First student to complete a row
      across, down, or diagonally wins.

B	I	N	G	O
1 What date did Columbus discover the new world?	6	11	16	21
2	7 Who led the Mass. Bay Co.?	12	17	22
3	8	13 FREE	18	23
4	9	14	19	24
5	10	15	20	25

Answer Chips:

B,1 1492	I,7 John Winthrop

Specific Objective: Identify roles and contributions of early colonists and events that led to changes in their society, changes that may account for how we think today.

6.   <u>Colonial Decision-Makers</u> - (identifying roles and contributions of decision-makers)

when: two weeks

what: materials as needed

how: Students make reports on famous colonial leaders or famous groups. The following is a list of possibilities for reports. The teacher should make up a list from which students can choose or have students make their choice and have it approved by teacher.

Puritans	Roger Williams
Sons of Liberty	Sam Adams
Minutemen	etc.
Mass. Bay Co.	
Salem "witches"	
etc.	

Chapter Fourth Grade has an activity that stresses what information to put in a report, how to research for the information, and how to write up a report. A fifth grader's report, however, should be more detailed and more extensive than that of a fourth grader. Reports should contain:

    a cover (perhaps picture or outline of area person was
            associated with)
    table of contents
    pictures of person or events
    researched report
    bibliography

7.   <u>Colonial People, Places, and Things</u>[2] - (identifying historically important events, people, etc.)

when: three or four periods

what: materials as needed

how: Students write a statement of several sentences describing an early American without naming the person (statements should be checked for accuracy by teacher). Put statement on an index card along with answer. Examples:

● I am the Puritan who organized the Massachusetts Bay Co. I am the first governor of that settlement and I do not like democracy. (John Winthrop)

● I am a person who is opposed to tax laws and I make speeches in the Massachusetts House of Representatives to unite the people who feel the British are not ruling us fairly. (Samuel Adams)

- I was a Puritan minister who felt that the church and state should be separated. I was forced to leave the Massachusetts Bay Colony so I started my own colony. (Roger Williams)

- I am a small town in New England where the Minutemen and British exchanged shots. The town was known for "the shot heard round the world." (Concord)

- I am a product imported to New England. There is an import duty tax on me. The king has granted a monopoly on shipping me to one English company. I was dumped in the Boston harbor as a protest. (tea)

This activity can be done by two students, small groups, or the entire class. The basic procedure is for all the cards to be placed in a box. The first student or group picks a card and reads the statement to his/her opponent or opposing group. If they can tell who is described, they get one point. The opponent reads a statement to the first student or group, and if they guess correctly they get one point. The students or groups take turns reading statements and guessing answers and the one who ends up with the highest score wins.

Alternative: Students or groups get to mark a tic-tac-toe game (X-O) when they get a correct answer.

8. <u>Historical Dioramas</u> - (identifying historically important events, people, etc.)

when: two or three periods

what: boxes and art supplies

how: Students should make dioramas depicting events connected with early American history, i.e., first Thanksgiving, Battle of Lexington and Concord, Paul Revere's ride, Salem witch trials.

Practice questioning by having one open and one closed question for each diorama. Example:

How did Paul Revere know which way the British were coming? (closed)

Suppose you were Paul Revere, what might have happened to you if you had not been caught by the British? (open)

Diorama of Old North Church Beacon Lights

9.   Private Papers - (identifying historically important events, people, etc.)

    when: one week

    what: paper (made to look old by wetting it with weak tea and allowing it to dry in sun), pen and ink

    how: Divide students into groups and have them research early Americans. The group then uses the paper to write:

- a letter a member of the Continental Congress might write home telling what is happening
- diary of one of the Sons of Liberty telling of feelings on growing rebellion of patriots
- report of British officer to his superiors in England
- a New England farmer writes to a relative in England explaining what freedom means to him

10.   Decisions Cause Change - (identifying historically important events, people, etc.)

    when: three or four periods

    what: interview sheet below

    how: After students have studied leaders who make decisions that changed early American life, the class must decide what questions should be asked to study the idea of "change" (see interview sheet below for sample questions).

Have students pick an example of change in early American life. Pair students so everyone has a partner. Give each student an interview sheet and have him/her interview partner and write down reply. After students have completed interviews, compile replies on board under heading representing each. Discuss change and how it affects our life today: free speech, religion, self-government, etc.

Interview Sheet

Name _____   date _____   interviewer _____

1.   Who brought about the change?   Reply _____
2.   What was the reason for the   Reply _____
     change?
3a. What was the decision?   Reply _____
 b. Suppose you had been this per- Reply _____
     son, would you have made the   _____
     same decision?
4a. What was the effect of the   Reply _____
     person's decision?   _____
 b. What do you think the effect   Reply _____
     would have been if he/she had   _____
     not made the decision?

Specific Objective: Identify and examine the ideas of separation of powers, democracy, republic, and federalism.

11. <u>Separation of Powers</u> - (identifying the structure of government)

    when: one period

    what: newspapers, TV news

    how: Discuss separation of powers with class. Have students bring in newspaper stories (or use old newspapers at school) or TV news stories of separation of powers in action such as Supreme Court declaring law unconstitutional, Presidential veto, or Congress overriding the veto. Pick a branch of government and list powers granted it by the Constitution. Discuss what additional powers it has acquired over the years.

12. <u>Federalism</u> - (identifying the structure of government)

    when: one period

    what: list of topics that are government responsibility; for example:

            regulating manufacturing of medicines

            inspecting hospitals, nursing homes, etc.

            regulating banks

            granting driver's license

            income tax

            building schools

            building highways

            etc.

    how: Have students establish which are functions of the state government, which are functions of the federal government, and which may be shared.

          Discuss students' findings.

13. <u>Democracy or Republic</u> - (identifying the structure of government)

    when: one period

    what:

    how: Have students agree on a definition of republic and a definition of democracy. For example:

> "Republic is a system where representatives of the people make decisions; democracy is a system where people make decisions."

Make a scale and place on the scale where certain government activities fit. Is the activity closer to democracy or republic or somewhere in between?

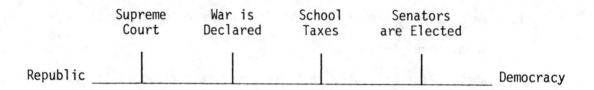

Examples of what to place on scale:

* School taxes go up (as voted by the people)

* Supreme Court judge is appointed (by the President)

* War is declared (by Congress and President)

* Senators are elected (by the people)

* Treaty is negotiated between nations (by the President)

* 55 mile speed limit (set by Congress)

* Car inspection (set by the state)

* House of Representatives are elected (by the people)

* The President is elected (by the Electoral College)

14. <u>Fill in the Capitol</u> - (identifying the structure of government)

    when: one period

    what: drawing of capitol

    how: Fill in drawing using definitions listed below.

1. A part of Congress, House of _____
2. Highest court in the land _____
3. The part of the government that makes the laws _____
4. The head of our country _____
5. The part of our government that carries out justice _____
6. The part of our government that acrries out the law _____
7. Washington is in the District of _____
8. The House of Representatives and the Senate make up _____
9. The President's assistants are his _____
10. Washington is located on the _____ river.
11. A part of Congress _____

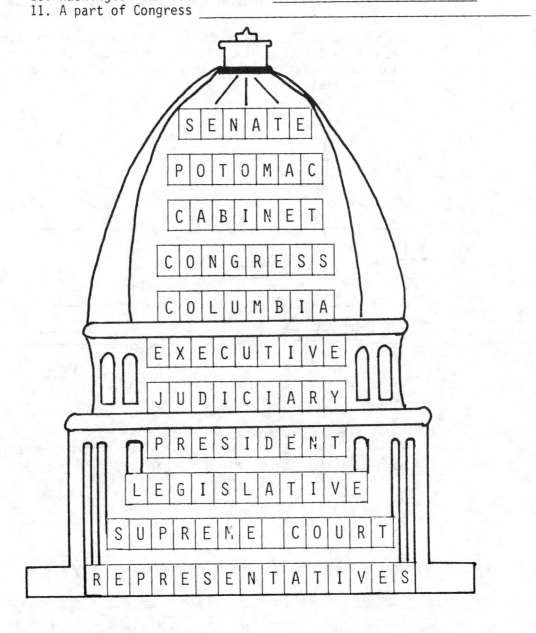

Dome contents:
SENATE
POTOMAC
CABINET
CONGRESS
COLUMBIA
EXECUTIVE
JUDICIARY
PRESIDENT
LEGISLATIVE
SUPREME COURT
REPRESENTATIVES

Specific Objective: Identify some of the ways transportation and communication helped the westward movement and the growth of
the country.

15. Transportation

when: several weeks

what: boxes, cardboard, materials as needed

how: Divide the class into two groups. One group will research
ways pioneers traveled over land and the other group will research ways pioneers traveled over water. Students should
use whatever resources are available. Each group should list
the ways:

water: canoe, flatboat, raft, keelboat, steamboat,
ferryboat, sailing ship, etc.
land: walk, horseback, conestoga wagon, stagecoach,
train, etc.

Each group should make a mobile using models of the types of
transportation they have listed. Have students use imagination and whatever supplies they need to model the parts of
their mobiles.

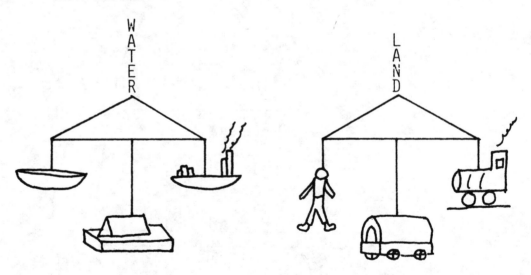

Alternative: Have students make a collage of pictures depicting water travel or land travel.

On a large map of the US have students trace some of the
famous routes west. Discuss what means of transportation
were used along each route and what present-day states the
routes passed through.

16. The Covered Wagon

when: one week

what: table, cloth materials or paper, cardboard

how: (1) Turn a table into a covered wagon by covering it with
            material or paper draped down the sides. Add big wheels
            made out of cardboard to fasten on the legs. Students
            could get under the table for quiet work such as reading.

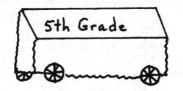

"Reading Wagon"

        (2) Pretend the covered wagon has stopped for the night.
            This is a good time to read stories and sing songs about
            pioneers, wild west heroes/heroines.
        (3) If some students would like to, they could bring in foods
            to share that are typical of what people on the trail
            might have eaten (beef jerky or dry beef sticks are
            available in supermarkets). Teacher must approve of
            foods suggested and set up a schedule.

17. Communication[3]

when: one week

what: materials as needed

how: Have students list means of communication from talking through
        letters, telephones, etc., to satellite communication. Com-
        pile lists on board. Have students list means of communica-
        tion in historical chronological order the way they personally
        think communication developed over the years. Have class
        research dates and make a timeline of means of communication.
        How does this timeline compare with their personal chrono-
        logical lists?

        Other suggestions:
          Students could pantomime means of communication for class
            to guess (telephone, Pony Express, telegraph key).
          Students could describe a type of communication without
            mentioning name and others would have to guess. For
            example: "I carried letters very quickly in leather
            pouches on horseback in the west." (Pony Express)
          Students could design a future means of communication, draw
            or model it, and write short explanation of how it would
            work.

Specific Objective: Identify factors in continental expansion and how
                       populations move.

18. How We Grow

     when: one week

     what: make a large outline of US either by tracing wall map or
            projecting transparency on paper; cut out map

     how: Have students trace outline of the following:

                    US of 1783
                    Louisiana Purchase   1803
                    Texas Annexation   1845
                    Oregon Territory   1846
                    Mexican Cession   1848
                    Gadsden Purchase   1853

            Divide students into groups and give each group a territory,
            cutting that section out of map and giving it to them. Have
            each group research their section: reasons it was acquired,
            size, states contained in it, major cities, natural character-
            istics (land forms, weather), resources, etc.

            Each group will decorate their section using as much of their
            research as possible. Starting with US of 1783, each group
            will present their section and describe it to class. As each
            section is discussed, it will be attached to the ones before
            it, eventually making a complete map and large wall display.

     NOTE: We know that in the US citizens often move. The present-day family
            moves up to six times on the average. The expansion of the US and
            the concept of movement are linked together in the notion of mani-
            fest destiny. In the following activity, "Moving," students'
            attention is directed to the reasons families move.

19. Moving

     when: three or four periods

     what: questionnaire on moving (next page)

     how: Pass out questionnaire to students and have them fill out as
            much of it as they can, then take it home to complete it with
            help from parent, grandparent, etc. Hold class discussion on
            answers and reactions.

```
┌─────────────────────────────────────────────────────────────┐
│                    Moving Questionnaire                       │
│   1.  How many places have you lived in since you were born?  │
│   2.  Check the reasons why your family has moved:            │
│                                                               │
│       ____ better job          ____ fire, flood              │
│       ____ closer to work      ____ racial or ethnic pressure│
│       ____ closer to school    ____ better housing           │
│       ____ closer to family    ____ less expensive housing   │
│       ____ climate             ____ urban renewal relocation │
│       ____ safer neighborhood  ____ other                    │
│                                                               │
│   3.  Did you have any trouble moving?                        │
│   4.  What problems did you have adjusting to new home or     │
│       neighborhood?                                           │
└─────────────────────────────────────────────────────────────┘
```

Specific Objective: Identify people and events surrounding the Civil War.

20. Your Title Is Your Point of View

    when: one or two periods

    what: list of titles for Civil War:
           War Between the States   The War for States' Rights
           Mr. Lincoln's War   The Lost Cause
           The Great Rebellion   The Yankee Invasion
           The Brothers' War   American Civil War
           The War for Southern   The Second American Revolution
             Independence

    how: Give list to students. Have students write several reasons
           why each of these titles applied to the Civil War. Have
           class discussion on possible reasons.

21. Who Am I?

    when: two periods

    what:

    how: (1) Have students write a paragraph describing someone con-
               nected with the Civil War without revealing name. Have
               student read paragraph; other students must try to guess
               identity. For example: "I planned a march across the
               south towards the end of the Civil War. Railroads and
               supplies were destroyed, as were crops and farms.
               Houses and barns were burned and Atlanta was burned to
               the ground in my march to the sea." (General Sherman)
           (2) Have students pick a person to represent. Class asks
               yes/no questions of "person" until they guess his/her
               identity.

22. <u>Letters</u>

   when: one or two periods

   what: writing materials (aged paper may be made by dipping paper in
          weak tea solution and allowing it to dry)

   how: Pair students and have them pretend to be related or be close
          friends who are on <u>opposite sides</u> in the Civil War. Have
          them write several letters expressing to each other their
          reasons for the choices they have made. For example:

   Sisters - The one from the north would write about:

          married to northern merchant

          joined Quaker faith and therefore does not believe
          in slavery or war

   The one from the south would write about:

          married to plantation owner

          house slaves are treated well

          field slaves do not want more than their primitive
          lives

          slavery is a necessary evil both for the slave
          and the economic wellbeing of the plantation

          slavery permits her to live a highly civilized
          life

          her religion recognizes slavery as a way of life

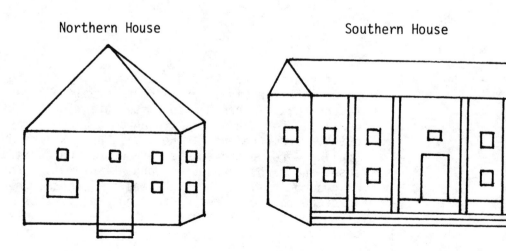

Northern House   Southern House

B. Purpose: Develop skills necessary to <u>process</u> information

Specific Objective: Students will process questions by differentiating between open and closed.

1. <u>Practicing the Writing of Closed and Open Questions</u>[4]

when: two periods

what: work sheets: "First Impressions" (10 minutes)

"Closed Questions" (15 minutes)

"O p e n Questions" (15 minutes)

"Tying It All Together" (20 minutes)

how: This is a continuation of the questioning skills introduced in Chapter Fourth Grade.

(1) Have students fill out "First Impressions" work sheet. This will prepare them for thinking about and writing questions. Have several students read some of their questions. Students will realize that there are many different kinds of questions.

(2) Hand out work sheet "Closed Questions." Read definition aloud to students. Answer any questions they may have about closed questions and then give them time to complete the work sheet. Have selected students read their questions to the class.

(3) Hand out work sheet "O p e n Questions." Again read definition aloud and answer any questions they have on understanding open questions. Have them complete the work sheet. Let some of the students share their questions with the class.

(4) Hand out work sheet "Tying It All Together." Have students complete the work sheet. Do the students understand open and closed questions? Which do they prefer?

Answers to "Tying It All Together":

1 - c, 2 - 0, 3 - c, 4 - c, 5 - c
6 - c, 7 - c, 8 - o, 9 - o, 10 - o

FIRST IMPRESSIONS

Imagine that you are Christopher Columbus and you have
just landed in the New World (America). As you are
coming ashore, you see a tall Indian named Chief Wel-Kum
step forward to greet you. What would be the first
question you would ask the Chief? Think about that and
then write your question in the blank below.

If I were Christopher Columbus, I would ask the Chief, "_____

_____

_____

Now, imagine that you are Chief Wel-Kum and you have
watched this strange man come wading ashore from a giant
ship. What would be the first question you would ask of
Christopher Columbus?

If I were Chief Wel-Kum, I would ask Columbus, "_____

_____

_____

Listen now as others read their answers.

Do you notice that there are lots of different kinds of questions?

CLOSED QUESTIONS

As you have probably noticed, we have been talking a lot about questions.
That's because it is really important to know about questions and how to use
them. Now we want to show you that there are basically two kinds of questions.

There are ones that we call CLOSED and ones that we call OPEN questions.

CLOSED QUESTIONS are ones that have
specific answers. These ask you to
either <u>remember</u> word-for-word or
<u>explain</u> something in your own words.
Either way, there is one answer and
it is your job to come up with it.

The answer to a closed question would
be the same for all of us.

Here are some CLOSED QUESTIONS about Indians.

1. Where did the early Indians live?

2. How many Indians were there when the Pilgrims came?

3. What was the name of the Indians who lived in New York?

Do you see that the answer to the first one is a place, the second is a number,
and the third one is a name? In all three cases the answer would be the same.

Choose any subject you like and complete the following sentences to make each
a <u>closed question</u>:

1. Who was the first _____?

2. What happened at _____?

3. Why did the _____?

4. What happened to _____?

O P E N   QUESTIONS

OPEN QUESTIONS are ones that have a number of possible answers. Some of these ask you to <u>imagine</u> how something could be different. Other open questions ask you to <u>judge</u> between things and decide for yourself what is better or worse or fair or unfair. You have to make up your own mind to answer an open question.

Since everyone has a different mind, they often come up with several different answers to the same questions. The answers to OPEN QUESTIONS will not be the same for everyone.

Here are some examples of open questions:

1. If you had been one of the early white settlers, how would you have felt about the Indians?

2. If you were an Indian today, how would you feel about the way the United States had treated your people?

3. Do you think it's important for all Americans to learn about Indian history?

4. When you hear the word "Indian," what picture comes to your mind?

Choose any subject and complete the following sentences to make them open questions.

1. How do you feel about _____ ?

2. What would have happened if _____

    _____ ?

3. Was it right or wrong for _____ ?

Can you tell me the difference between an open and closed question now? Let's see.

The answer to a CLOSED question is _____

_____ , but the answer to an OPEN question is

_____ .

TYING IT ALL TOGETHER

Now, let's take a test to see if you can identify the two
basic kinds of questions. Before you begin, you may want
to review the following chart:

CLOSED	REMEMBER/EXPLAIN	THERE IS A SINGLE ANSWER.
OPEN	IMAGINE/JUDGE	THERE IS A NUMBER OF POSSIBLE ANSWERS.

DIRECTIONS: Put "O" or "C" in the blank to show whether the question is OPEN
or CLOSED.

_____ 1. What is wampum?

_____ 2. If you were an Indian today, how would you feel about watching
cowboy movies?

_____ 3. Who was Sacajawea?

_____ 4. Why are there fewer Indians today than when Columbus came?

_____ 5. How were the religions of the Indians different than the religions
of today?

_____ 6. Why was dancing so important to most Indians?

_____ 7. Which tribe had totem poles?

_____ 8. What would have happened if there had never been any Indians in
America?

_____ 9. Do you think it was good or bad for Indian babies not to be allowed
to cry?

_____ 10. Which Indian tribe would you have wanted to belong to?

WRITE ONE QUESTION ABOUT INDIANS TO WHICH YOU WOULD LIKE TO KNOW THE ANSWER.

_____

_____

Is your question O P E N or CLOSED? See if your teacher can answer the question
for you.

2. Questioning Skills - (practicing the skill of asking and answering open and closed questions)

when: two class periods

what: check sheet

how: It may be necessary to review with students the definitions of open and closed questions. The following exercise is a test that should help students differentiate between open and closed questions. After marking, be sure to go over test with students. Use this as a technique for opening discussion. Mark the following questions either O for open or C for closed.

C 1. Was John Adams President?

C 2. When was the War of 1812 fought?

O 3. Suppose you were from New England, what might be your religion?

C 4. Why did the South support slavery?

O 5. How might you have felt about slavery in 1850?

C 6. What state was Henry Clay from?

O 7. How do you feel about Daniel Webster's stand on slavery?

C 8. Was John Q. Adams ever a member of the House of Representatives?

Test student skill completion exercise: Turn the following topics into one open and one closed question.

1. Leif Ericson (example)

open   Suppose you were Leif Ericson, what might your reasons be for exploring North America?

closed   What is the name of the man who some believe discovered America before Columbus?

open   _____

_____

2. Pilgrims   _____

closed   _____

_____

```
                                    open    _____
                                            _____
    3. Lexington &                          _____
       Concord                              _____
                                  closed    _____
                                            _____


                                    open    _____
                                            _____
    4. Declaration of                       _____
       Independence                         _____
                                  closed    _____
                                            _____
```

Check textbooks for study and end-of-chapter questions.

Go over some of the questions with class and classify them

as either open or closed.

Assignment: Have students read headings of both chapters
and sections of chapters, turning the headings into open and
closed questions. For example:

Heading "Indian Skills"--question might be:
   What skills did Indians have?
   Do you feel that Indian skills were useful to the colonists?

Heading "Jamestown Is Founded"--questions might be:
   What country founded Jamestown?
   In your opinion, why did the English settle a colony at
      Jamestown?

Why do this, why teach students the skill of questioning? There is a relationship between questioning and ability to learn. The two levels of thought--
lower, which refers to closed questions often associated with recall, repeat,
recite; or higher, which refers to open questions often associated with opinion,
judgment, evaluation, predicting--are both necessary for learning. As much as
thirty percent of instruction in social studies is in the form of questions
from the teacher and the text. Common sense alone suggests that to know how
to ask and answer questions would be a useful skill. The examples of questions
in this chapter are designed to illustrate open and closed type questions. If
you believe in stimulating creative behavior, then practice using both types.

Specific Objective: Learn to differentiate between fact and opinion.

3. Facts and Opinions

    when: two or three periods

    what: fact and opinion list; example story with questions

    how: Discuss with students the terms "fact" and "opinion." To check how well students can identify differences, teacher may want to give fact and opinion checklist (as a pre-test) to students.

Facts and Opinions Checklist

Mark each statement either F for fact or O for opinion.

F 1. George Washington was the first President of the United States.

F 2. The ship the Pilgrims came to New England on was called the Mayflower.

F 3. The Pilgrims learned how to grow corn from the Indians.

O 4. The British were hated by all of the colonists.

O 5. The Puritans spoke "Old English" so you would have no trouble understanding them if we could talk to them today.

O 6. The pioneers had an easy trip west after they crossed the Appalachian Mountains.

O 7. Man is basically good.

O 8. All men have natural rights of life, liberty, and property.

O 9. Alexander Hamilton was a "good" Secretary of the Treasury.

O 10. Thomas Jefferson was a "good" President.

O 11. The Boston Massacre was not a massacre.

F 12. Real American Indians did not throw tea in the "Boston Tea Party."

O 13. All Minutemen believed "Give me liberty or give me death."

F 14. The Declaration of Independence contains these words, "That all men are created equal."

O 15. Fifth graders are always good social studies students.

Teachers are encouraged to make up their own checklist as a pre-test to some of the major historical divisions, i.e., Discovery, Colonization, American Revolution.

After each child has marked his/her list, go over the fifteen items with the entire class so that each understands that there are facts and opinions. For example, teacher might ask class these questions:

    Can all communication be separated into either fact or opinion?

Can something be partly true and partly opinion?

Were you able on the checklist to identify the difference between fact and opinion?

Is everything printed in your social studies text fact?

Test their skill - Have students mark fact (F) and Opinion (O) statements at end of following story:

Pioneer Schools

You might think that pioneer children were lucky for many pioneer children did not ever go to school. Often there was no school to attend. Schools were built by parents who wanted their children to have an education, but even when there was a school most children had important chores that came before attending school. The school was usually a one-room log cabin holding up to twenty children of all ages and grades. The children sat on benches, for they had no desks, in front of a schoolmaster. The schoolmaster would call each child in turn to read outloud.

O	1. Pioneer children enjoyed attending the one-room school.
F	2. The school house was built by parents of the students.
O	3. The one-room school offered each child a good education.
F	4. The schoolmaster gave individual attention to each child.
F	5. All ages and classes were in the same room together.
O	6. Probably all pioneer children wanted to attend school.

4. ## What Really Happened?

when: one period

what: materials as needed

how: Have two students create an altercation. This can be any type of situation where there is conflict. For example: Two children run into each other, each blaming the other for carelessness; two children working on the board fight over the use of an eraser; children in a dispute over a book they are both reading together; two children in a dispute over a game.
(1) Have each student in class write a paragraph describing what happened.
(2) Divide the students into groups. Have the members of each group read each other's paragraphs.

(3) Groups must decide what was fact and what was opinion and make a list.

For example:

Altercation--Sally and Trudy were reading the same book together. Sally turned the page. Trudy grabbed the book and turned the page back. Sally shoved Trudy off her seat

FACT	OPINION
Sally and Trudy were involved	Sally and Trudy were angry
Trudy took the book	Sally was wrong to turn the page
Sally pushed Trudy	Trudy was wrong to take the book

Altercation--Randy and Jack ran into each other coming from right angles. Randy fell down and bumped his head and appeared unconscious for a few seconds, then he tripped Jack.

FACT	OPINION
Randy and Jack were coming from right angles	Neither boy was playing safely
They ran into each other	They were not looking where they were going
Randy tripped Jack	Randy was mad at Jack

The point of the activity is to demonstrate the difficulty of knowing what really happened. Would the students suppose that storytellers and historians might have the same problems of knowing what really happened in the past? Are history texts facts or opinions about history? If students were to write their own history, would they write facts, opinions, perhaps both? Be sure students know the difference.

5. Cartoon Study

when: one period

what: cartoons

how: Teacher or students bring cartoons to class. Show cartoon to entire class and have them decide what they think happened. Discuss what are facts and what are opinions and list on board.

Example on following page.

FACT	OPINION
Tea in water	Colonist accuses Indian
Boston Harbor	Indian fearful
American Indian denies participation in tea party	Colonist angry

Specific Objective: Learn to recognize propaganda, bias, and stereotypes.

6. <u>Propaganda</u>

   when: four or five periods

   what: definition of propaganda techniques listed

   how: Given the amount of advertisement that is now aimed directly
          at pre-teens and teenagers, it is important that the tech-
          niques used in these advertisements be identified so that the
          students can learn to be a bit more discriminating about what
          they are told to believe. The fifth grade is not too early
          for students to become aware of propaganda.
          (1) Hand out definitions to class and discuss with students
              these most common forms of propaganda.
          (2) Have students think of examples from TV, etc., and put
              them on the board.
          (3) Have each student bring to class at least three different
              propaganda techniques to share with class. May display
              these on bulletin board.
          (4) Have each student prepare own original propaganda example
              (a TV commercial, a magazine ad) using any one of the
              seven techniques.

Propaganda techniques can easily be related to the various war efforts in the US and abroad. Often featured in American history textbooks are posters from the Spanish-American War and the First and Second World Wars that demonstrate how feelings were generated against the "enemy."

Techniques

1. Testimonial: a famous person endorses product (credit card advertisements on TV by well-known personalities)

2. Transfer: connecting a popular or unpopular symbol or feeling to a person, event, etc. (successful general or US astronaut running for political office)

3. Plain folks: appealing to the common man as "just one of the folks" (showing presidential candidate fixing his own breakfast)

4. Glittering generalities: general ideas that promise much (glowing ads for land sales in distant states or vacation locations)

5. Name calling: putting a negative label on something (often used by politicians)

6. Card stacking: offering only favorable facts or exaggerating good facts (car selling--only mentioning favorable aspects of the car you are selling)

7. Bandwagon: urged to go along with the majority (pressuring your parents to let you stay up later because "all the kids are doing it")

7. Understanding Bias

when: one or two periods

what:

how: Along with studying the propaganda techniques by which we are persuaded, the teacher should also introduce the notion of bias. People who wish to persuade us have a bias, a preference for some product or value or action. Most written material, movies, advertisements, and other forms of media, are written and produced with a bias. The fifth grade is not too early to begin suggesting that students identify what bias is and the effect of bias.
(1) Discuss bias with students:
   What is bias?
   Do you suppose that most people are biased?
    Are you biased?
   Should we be able to recognize bias?
   How does bias affect you?

(2) Have students as a class or in groups establish ways to check for bias. Students should prepare a checklist or test that can be applied to items to check for bias.
How is item reported?
Is emotion involved?
Does the reporter have a personal interest in item?
(3) Make sure each student has a copy of checklist to test for bias. Students should begin by checking their social studies book for bias.

Sources for Bias

newspapers: editorials
  letters to editor
  movie ads
  want ads (best place to look)
  some comics

TV: Bias toward certain audience
  or product

What Biases to Look For

sex (male, female)

age (too young, too old)

size (too small, too fat, too tall)

handicapped (blind, deaf, disabled)

experience (must have extensive experience or no experience needed--
  will train on job)

8.   Stereotypes

when: one or two periods

what: materials as needed

how: (1) Divide class into two groups based on some simple differ-
      ence (i.e., boys vs. girls, those who are bussed to
      school vs. those who walk or get car-pooled, those who
      wear glasses vs. those who do not). The groups do not
      necessarily need to be evenly divided.
    (2) Give each group the same task to do. However, the task
      should be made easier for one group than for the other.
      For example, give a small test with difficult questions.
      On the test for one group just have the questions. For
      the other group give the questions and responses to
      choose from. Separate the two groups. Be sure the two
      groups do not talk to each other, but let the group with
      responses talk among themselves.

Sample test

Questions: 1. On what exact date did Christopher Columbus
              sight the new world? _____
            2. John Cabot, sailing under an English flag,
              reached the cost of North America in what
              year? _____
            3. What did Sir Walter Raleigh establish on
              Roanoke Island in 1585? _____
            4. In what year did LaSalle explore the
              lower Mississippi? _____

Responses (given to only one group)

October 12, 1492

English reached North America in 1497

first English colony

Mississippi explored in 1682

(3) The group with the answers will finish earlier than the other group; allow them some extra privileges. When the other group complains, tell them to keep working.

(4) After a short while, call a halt and start a class discussion. For example:

What were the feelings of each group? (pleasure vs. frustration)

What did one group feel about the other? (lucky vs. unlucky)

Was it easy to think of all members of one group as being fortunate or unfortunate?

This is stereotyping: thinking about a person in a particular way because he/she is part of a certain group.

(5) Can the class come up with its own definition of stereotyping? Are there examples of stereotyping that the class could identify within the school, the community, the nation, the world? For example:

Stereotypes in school

athletes are dumb

prettiest girl is brainless

those who play musical instruments are brainy

Stereotypes in community

all those living in a certain part of town are . . . (poor, wealthy)

all those going to a competing elementary school are jerks

Stereotypes nationwide

all politicians are thieves

all southern Californians are crazy

all Texans are either very rich or very poor

all Easterners are snobs

Stereotypes worldwide

all Africans live in the jungle

all Asians eat rice

all Scandinavians are blond

(6) Having identified stereotypes both near and far, the following questions might be appropriate:

Are stereotypes useful in thinking about other people?

Can stereotypes be harmful because they may mislead?

Do you have any personal stereotypes of others that you might now want to examine?

C. Purpose: Develop the skill to examine <u>values</u> and beliefs

   Specific Objective: Identify values and cultural characteristics in history
                         and contemporary society.

   1. <u>My Values, Your Values</u>

       when: three or four periods

       what: materials as needed

       how: (1) Discuss the idea of values and beliefs with students.
                  Have students examine the following list of people to
                  decide what values motivated them to carry out the
                  activity for which they are noted.

                  Columbus discovered America (wealth, prestige, discovery)

                  John Wilkes Booth shot Lincoln (the cause of the South)

                  Paul Revere rode to alert the people that the British
                  were coming (the cause of American patriots)

                  John Glenn orbited the earth (discovery, adventure)

                  Charles Lindbergh flew the Atlantic alone (adventure,
                  money)

                  Susan B. Anthony fought for women's rights (cause of
                  women's rights)

                  Harriet Tubman freed the slaves (freedom)

              (2) After students have discussed what values these people
                  had, help students arrive at a definition of "value."
                  Discuss with students what values are important to them
                  and list them on the blackboard: fairness, education,
                  money, "the future," "things." Each student should list
                  the five most important values to him/her from those
                  written on the board.
              (3) Some people say Americans share in part the following
                  values: justice, liberty, worth of the individual,
                  equality of opportunity, individual responsibility,
                  brotherhood, limited government.

                  Have students examine the <u>Mayflower Compact</u>, the <u>Declara-
                  tion of Independence</u>, and the <u>Constitution of the United
                  States</u> (found in almost every American history text) to
                  see if the above values are found in these three docu-
                  ments.

                  Fill in the following chart by writing "yes" if that
                  value is found in document and "no" if it is not. If
                  yes, then tell what line of document value is found on.
                  Do this for all three documents.

                  Have students list the five most important values from
                  the combined three documents.

(Values)	Mayflower Compact		Declaration of Independence		Constitution	
	yes/no	line	yes/no	line	yes/no	line
Justice						
Liberty						
worth of individual						
equal opportunity						
individual respons.						
brotherhood						
limited government						

2. It Was Like This

when: two or three periods

what:

how: (1) Divide students into three groups. Each group will role-play the making of a document: Mayflower Compact, Declaration of Independence, or Constitution of the US. Give them time to plan out their actions, and then they can role-play their parts.

(2) Have several students act as secretaries. Their job will be to write down all the values and beliefs they see displayed as the others are role-playing.

(3) When the three groups are finished, the secretaries will list the values and beliefs on the board.

(4) Hold a class discussion on the values. For example, these questions are appropriate:

(a) Do most of the people in the United States hold the values found in the three documents?

(b) If you believe in the values expressed in these three documents, then are those beliefs carried out in your personal life?

(c) Are there instances when we do not follow our beliefs? Do we ever say one thing and do another? Wonder why that is?

3. Decisions in the Past

    when: two periods

    what: list of historic decisions

    how: Have students examine list of decisions made by leaders in
           early American history. For example:

               crossing Atlantic to form first colonies

               dumping tea in Boston Harbor

               declaring independence to free colonists from England

               moving west for land

               moving west for gold

               leaving Massachusetts Bay Co. and separating church from
                 state

               resisting the British at Lexington and Concord

           Have students list values that must have motivated the people
           who took the actions listed above. Discuss what alternatives
           were open to the people involved in the actions above. If
           they had chosen an alternative, what values would they have
           held then?

4. Suspicion on Trial

    when: two or three periods

    what:

    how: (1) Some students always show a particular interest in the
               stories of witches and witch trials in early New England.
               Have those students research the trials to gather in-
               formation and notes that could be used for role-playing
               a classroom trial. Have students decide on a situation.
               For example:

                   "Christina likes to take a walk (on the beach, in
                   woods, etc.) early in the morning before she starts
                   the work for the day. When something strange happens
                   or goes wrong during the day, people in the town say
                   Christina had planned on those early walks with the
                   devil for it to happen."

           (2) Students must prepare for trial by selecting a judge,
               clerks, secretaries, etc. The class can act as a jury.
               From their research the students will learn (and should
               include in their role-play) that accusations against
               witches were much stronger than protestations that they
               were innocent. A person who supported a suspected witch
               often ended up being suspected himself/herself. Emo-
               tionalism also ran high in the trials and this too
               should be brought out in the mock trial.

Have students role-play the trial.
(3) When the trial is over, the class can discuss the values
and beliefs that made the participants act the way they
did, and what effect values and beliefs had on the out-
come of the trial.
(4) A culminating discussion should follow that relates the
witch trials to contemporary events. Are there still
"witch trials," that is, people who accuse others on the
suspicion that the other person might be subversive
(i.e., the McCarthy era, minority rights groups, ecology
groups, anti-war groups, in general protestors)? Would
there be anything in the newspaper, radio, TV newscast,
or in the community that would suggest suspicion on trial?

5. What Is An American?

when: two periods

what: art supplies

how: (1) Discuss with class the question, "Are Americans unique,
that is, different from all other people?" If so, how
are they different? If not, how are they similar? Are
there certain ideas, symbols, etc. that characterize or
represent an American?
(2) Have each student produce either a collage or a mobile,
filmstrip or transparency that expresses what he/she
thinks Americans look like.
(3) Let students share their projects with the class. Be
sure in summarizing that notice is taken of the like-
nesses and differences between the visual portrayals of
Americans.
(4) Discuss whether or not the class feels that values held
by Americans are different than those held by most
people around the world. Do Americans look different,
sound different, think different, feel different than
other people from other countries or cultures? What is
an American?

6. Stairway to the Stars

when: one or two days

what: copies of "Stairway to the Stars"

how: Give each student a copy of "Stairway to the Stars." Explain
that stars are rewards valued by students and that stairs are

the way to obtain rewards. Let each student fill out his own copy. Let some students fill out transparency for Stairway for use with the overhead projector. Discuss values students have marked in their stars. How do the students' values compare with the values of early Americans as listed in activity 2 under this section called "It Was Like This"?

Stairway	Stars
love	good looks
honesty	money
work hard	good family
set high goals	go places
work with others	do things
develop my talent	a nice car
	good grades

STAIRWAY TO THE STARS

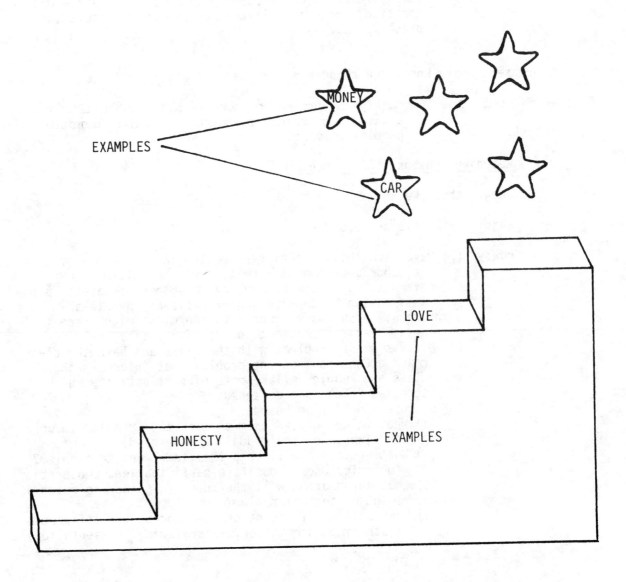

7. <u>2001 Years From Now</u> - (identifying values and cultural characteristics of contemporary society; also practice categorizing)

when: one week

what: waterproof container (time capsule)

how: (1) Discuss with students what people 2001 years from now would be interested in learning about our civilization. Have students suggest everyday items that could tell someone in the future something about how we live. Establish categories such as food, clothing, etc.
(2) Divide students into groups and give each group a category. Group members should discuss and decide on objects to bring in that fit their category and small enough to put in waterproof container.
(3) Get permission to bury the capsule (waterproof container) somewhere on school grounds or in a park. Make a map of location. Have a small ceremony to bury capsule and preserve map.

D. Purpose: Apply knowledge through active <u>participation</u>

Specific Objective: Identify the process of consensus and the skills and attitudes necessary for participation in community problem-solving.

1. <u>Reaching Consensus on a Problem</u>

when: three weeks

what: materials as needed

how: (1) Have each child identify a problem in the school or neighborhood community that should be solved. For example: problems of ecology, problems of safety, problems having to do with senior citizens, problems in school, problems a student in the class might face (illness, special treatment, needs of a family).
(2) Discuss these problems with the class and have the class reach a consensus on one problem that interests the class as a whole. (Take note of next activity which stresses reaching a consensus.)
(3) Discuss and list on board:
(a) What values caused them to pick this problem to work on? (worth of individual, brotherhood)
(b) What attitudes will help them focus on the problem? (openmindedness, positive participation, cooperation)
(c) What information will they need to gather to reach a solution to the problem?
(d) What skills will be needed to process the information? (gathering information, interviewing, presentation)

(3) Are there certain talents among class members that might help in working on the problem? (conservation skills, relatives in senior center, might have been involved in paper drives).

(4) Set out tasks based on discussion above that class must undertake to solve problem stressing the attitudes, values, information, and skills needed to successfully undertake the tasks. Divide class into groups and assign tasks. Each group should keep a list of tasks performed and the amount of time involved.

(5) After a reasonable time a solution should be reached or it should be agreed that no solution is possible at this particular time.

(6) It would be helpful to review how the students proceeded and to summarize the activity. Keep in mind that the central purpose is to encourage students to identify problems and to believe that through planning and organization they can do something about the problem, they can be effective. Participation in problem-solving is not a guarantee to success. We want students to know they can participate. Both success and failure are valuable learning experiences.

2. What Is Our Consensus?

when: one period

what: list of statements

how: (1) Divide the students in groups of five or six and give each group a copy of the list of statements.

List of Statements

Mark each statement with the number that represents your group's response to each statement:

(1) agree strongly
(2) agree
(3) no opinion
(4) disagree
(5) disagree strongly

_____ 1. The American Revolution solved the problem of British domination by freeing Americans to do what they wanted.

_____ 2. Without the Civil War America would still be suffering with slavery.

_____ 3. Protesting over the use of nuclear power and women's rights is un-American and should not be allowed.

_____ 4. Americans should be free to do absolutely anything they want.

_____ 5. Violence is necessary sometimes to achieve a citizen's rights.

_____ 6. Some citizens should have more rights than others because they contribute more.

(2) Explain to groups that they must reach a consensus on how they feel about each statement. Make sure students understand that consensus is not a majority. Consensus means that every member of the group must agree to the strength of feeling they record on their list. Tell groups they have fifteen minutes to get agreement on the list.

(3) After groups have worked only seven or eight of the fifteen minutes, stop them and tell them to leave the task. Discuss the following:

 (a) Would it help to have a group leader? If you had a leader, how did that person get the position?

 (b) Is each member of the group allowed to express his/her opinion or are some members ignored?

 (c) Did your group work out a plan on how to respond to the statements before you began?

 (d) How could the group members work together more effectively?

(4) Have the groups go back to reaching a consensus on the statements. After seven or eight minutes, again stop the groups.

(5) Discuss how each group worked and whether they were more efficient after they had considered their structure and procedure. What did the class learn about working in a group? For example, these questions might be appropriate:

 (a) What attitudes does one need to make a contribution to the group? (cooperation)

 (b) What skills are important to group work? (leadership, recording)

 (c) Is it always possible to arrive at consensus in a small group?

 (d) Does consensus require compromise? Should you always be expected to compromise? Is compromise always good?

The following is a Pupil Evaluation of Self and Group form. Students can evaluate their own participation with the group and the group's participation as a whole.

PUPIL EVALUATION OF SELF AND GROUP					
date _____	most all the time	frequently	about average	not often	did not do
SELF 1. I participated by making suggestions, arguing, discussing.					
2. I cooperated by listening to others and tried to work out difficulties (compromises).					
3. I am satisfied that I did my best to accomplish the group task.					
GROUP 4. The group made a real effort to accomplish the group task.					
5. The group worked together well by cooperating with each other.					
6. The group shared the responsibilities; no one was left out.					

Notes

[1] Indiana Department of Public Instruction. 1978 Indiana textbook adoption categories for social studies. Indianapolis: Author, 1978, p. 2.

[2] Barth, J. L., & Shermis, S. S. Teaching social studies to gifted and talented students. Indianapolis: Indiana Department of Public Instruction, p. 23.

[3] Ibid., p. 26.

[4] This activity was originally developed in 1980 for "Questions Social Studies Students Ask," a Division of Innovative Education ESPA Title IV-C Research Project of the North Montgomery School Corporation, Linden, Indiana. In particular, the author wishes to recognize the contribution of James Spencer and David Horney in the development of this project. The activity has been revised for publication in this book.

INTEREST FORM

You have just completed the Chapter Fifth Grade. In an effort to have you identify activities and materials that seem most promising at this grade level to you, please fill out the following interest form.

Instructions:

Identify two activities from this chapter. Name the activities and briefly describe why these particular activities are of interest to you.

ACTIVITY 1

ACTIVITY 2

CHAPTER SIXTH GRADE

178 (Sixth Grade)

ACTIVITIES AND MATERIALS FOR SIXTH GRADE

CHAPTER SIXTH GRADE

Organization of the Chapter

Each succeeding chapter represents a particular grade level, in this case sixth grade. Each chapter consists of three parts: the first part is a brief discussion on courses, topics, and national trends in teaching sixth grade throughout the United States; the second part is an example of a state sixth grade program; the third part has activities and materials for the sixth grade categorized by the four objectives of teaching social studies--gaining knowledge, processing, valuing, and participating.

I. Topics Taught and National Trends in Teaching Sixth Grade

To understand the course offerings in the sixth grade, it is useful to recall the most frequently offered courses in the fifth grade: United States History, United States History and Geography, and Geography of North America. It is useful to recall these three approaches because the sixth grade social studies curriculum may be keyed to the course offerings in the fifth grade. The three most frequently offered courses in the sixth grade are: American Neighbors, Western Europe and Latin America, and Eastern Hemisphere Geography and History.

Course, Topics, and Themes Frequently Covered in Sixth Grade:
"American Neighbors"

Objectives of the Course

Acquainting students with basic information about the geography and history of Canada and Latin America, or in some cases just Latin America; to extend the global view and help students develop an interest in world affairs; continuing their growth in command of basic social studies skills (processing information and valuing) and geographic concepts.

Basic Content of the Course

The course frequently opens with an overview of world geographic patterns--
continents and their physical features, oceans, climates, etc.--then emphasizes
the study of "American neighbors." If Canada is treated, the topics dealt
with usually include, though not necessarily in this sequence: geographic
overview of physical features and climates; historical development, with comparisons to United States history; resources and industries, i.e., ways of
making a living in the various regions; relationships between the United States
and other nations.

Latin America is usually treated in a similar fashion: geographic overview; historical development, with special attention to the struggle for independence; study of selected individual countries or groups of countries, with
attention to natural resources, industries and products, and daily life;
changes that are under way and current problems. Nations or groups of nations
that are frequently studied are Mexico; Central America; the Caribbean lands;
northern South America (Venezuela, Colombia, Equador); the Andean republics
(Peru, Bolivia, Chile); the Pampas countries (Argentina, Uraguay, Paraguay);
and Brazil. A final block of study treats Latin American countries in world
affairs, including their participation in the Organization of American States
and the United Nations.

Course, Topics, and Themes Frequently Covered in Sixth Grade:
"Western Europe and Latin America"

Objectives of the Course

Identify the relationship between European origins and American institutions. Though geographic concepts are stressed, the course is heavily oriented
toward the history of the old western world. Students should identify and recall the basic foundational ideas of western civilization, and should be able
to identify the differences and similarities between the settlement and growth

of Latin America and the North American continent.

Basic Content of the Course

The course places emphasis upon the geographic setting of western Europe, a brief examination of the foundations of western civilization which may include Greek, Roman, Renaissance, Reformation, Age of Reason, and the Modern States and Nations. Emphasis is placed upon Europe's contribution to American heritage with particular stress on contemporary development of western Europe.

The course also places emphasis on the geographic setting of Latin America, and the European role in exploration and discovery with special notice of Indian civilizations and their eventual conquest. The most time, however, is spent on specific Latin American countries since their independence, concentrating on their political, social, and economic problems. The popularity of this course is increasing because it does offer considerable flexibility. Teachers can point out that the American continent, though settled by Europeans, has contrasting cultures. American history in the fifth grade should provide a foundation for studying western civilization with a comparison and contrast of Latin American cultures with those of Anglo-Saxon western Europe.

Course, Topics, and Themes Frequently Covered in Sixth Grade:
"Eastern Hemisphere Geography and History"

Objectives of the Course

Extending students' global education by acquainting them with eastern hemisphere lands; continuing growth in command of geographic concepts; developing appreciation of the contributions of great civilizations of the past.

Basic Content of the Course

This course frequently devotes one-third to one-half of the year to "old world backgrounds"--i.e., ancient civilizations, including early civilizations in India, China, and Egypt; through ancient Greek and Roman civilizations up past the medieval period to the Age of Reason. The other two-thirds of the year are spent in study of Europe, Asia, and Africa, with emphasis on geography, economic life, ways of life, and modern problems of the peoples of these lands. Fairly typical are the following units: Geographic Overview (review of latitude, longitude, different types of maps, continents, oceans, important cities, general land formations); Prehistoric Times; Beginning of Civilization (Egyptian, Babylonian, Greek, Roman); Western Europe (Austria, Belgium, France, Germany, Great Britain, Greece, Ireland, Italy, Netherlands, Scandinavian countries, Switzerland); Eastern Europe (USSR and satellites); China, Japan, Southeast Asia and Australia; India, Middle East, and North Africa; Emerging Africa.

Trends in Teaching Sixth Grade Social Studies

1.   The trend continues to be toward a combined geographic and historic treatment of Europe and Latin America.

2.   The trend is away from treating all countries in the hemisphere and towards the selection of a few representative countries in specific regions. The effort is to get away from ground covering, hurrying from one state to another, towards in-depth studies that focus on economic and cultural life. Textbooks for the sixth grade used to focus on studies of population, land form, exports, and the countries' geographic location in relation to other states. Contemporary texts place emphasis on life processes, that is, how the economic, social, and political systems people work under function to meet their needs and interests.

3.   A growing trend is that of treating the Soviet Union and its satellite nations with considerably more attention than was true a decade ago. What traditionally used to be the study of separate nations is now becoming the study of certain world power blocks (Atlantic Treaty Organization versus Warsaw Pact).

4. Recent friendly relations with "mainland China," the Peoples Republic of China, along with interest in Korea and Viet Nam, as well as American interest in Japan, have led to a renewed emphasis on Asia.

II. Illustration of a State Sixth Grade Program

There is no <u>one</u> prescribed social studies program throughout the United States. However, one state's description of its sixth grade program will illustrate what content the state expects to be taught. This illustration identifies a state's suggested social studies curriculum for the sixth grade.

> In further developing the examination of regions of the world, a
> focus on either the western or eastern hemispheres may be chosen.
> Students should recognize links between the geography of the regions
> and the subsequent economic and social development which has occurred.
> The Indian cultures of the western hemisphere or European cultures
> of the eastern hemisphere provide unique links with early and modern
> world civilizations and a focus for the study of cultural influences
> on American heritage. Examine how these regions are interdependent
> and how technological development has influenced them.[1]

III. Activities and Materials Categorized by
Gaining Knowledge, Processing, Valuing, and Participating

A rather common practice is to skip purposes and specific objectives which precede the activities, but in this case the objectives are extremely important for an objective in the sixth grade will be found in succeeding grades. The following activities and materials are part of a developmental curriculum organized to build citizenship skills from one grade level to another.

SIXTH GRADE ACTIVITIES AND MATERIALS

A. Purpose: To <u>gain knowledge</u> about the human condition which includes past, present, and future

Specific Objective: Identify the explorers of the western hemisphere and
the countries they explored.

1.   Mapping Explorations

    when: three periods

    what: map of western hemisphere stressing Central and South America,
colored pencils or magic markers

    how: Have students use different colors to trace on map the ex-
ploration routes of early world explorers (Columbus, Magellan,
DeGama, Vespucci, etc.), stressing those that reached South
America. Discuss each explorer by covering the following
topics:

        Name of explorer and country he represented.

        What did the explorer find?

        What were the results of the exploration?

        Suppose you could have joined any of the explorers of South
America, which would you have joined and why?

2.   Latin Lexicon

    when: one period

    what: list of definitions

    how: Have students match up names of countries with the definitions.
It will help students become familiar with the names of Latin
American countries.

Argentina	El Salvador	Colombia
Brazil	Nicaragua	Bolivia
Venezuela	Costa Rica	Trinidad
Uraguay	Peru	Tobago
Mexico	Honduras	Panama
Haiti	Guyana	Guatemala
Cuba	Barbados	Equador
Dominican Republic	Jamaica	Chili
Paraguay		

Definitions

1. (R) + (slang term for male) + (INA) = [Argentina]
2. (what is mined for fuel) + (bump on the head) + (IA) = [Columbia]
3. (what you tie with a ribbon) + (what you do with life) + (IA) = [Bolivia]
4. (cut something just a little) + (AR) + (Spanish name for water) = [Nicaragua]
5. (L) + (nickname for Sally) + (VA) + (what you open to go from one room to another) = [El Salvador]
6. (what you say when you're cold) + (Wizard of _ _) + (L) = [Brazil]
7. (what you say when it's cold in a room. "It's _ _ _ _ _ _) = [Chili]
8. (opposite of smart) + (INI) + (what food is packaged in) + (RE) + (name for English drinking place) + (what you do to an ice cream cone) = [Dominican Republic]
9. (equal minus the 1) + (what you open to get in the house) = [Equador]
10. (nickname for Barbara) + (A) + (what you do when you take a nap) = [Barbados]
11. (box with equal sides) + (A) = [Cuba]
12. (GUA) + (favorite English drink) + (what you call your mother) + (musical note) = [Guatemala]
13. (boy) + (girl's name) = [Guyana]
14. (opposite of love) + (I) = [Haiti]
15. (what you spread on bread) + (pain) + (A) = [Jamaica]
16. (motorcycle name minus A) + (UR) + (we) = [Honduras]
17. (rhymes with Texaco) = [Mexico]
18. (what you cook in) + (A) + (name for mother) = [Panama]
19. (name for two matching things) + (A) + (waterside dock) = [Paraguay]
20. (cat sound) + (U) = [Peru]
21. (your) + (A) + (waterside dock) = [Uruguay]
22. (name of Italian city with canals) + (highway minus high) + (musical note) = [Venezuela]
23. (price) + (A) + (R) + (what you say when you see a mouse) + (A) = [Costa Rica]
24. (TR) + (not out) + (I) + (name for father) = [Trinidad]
25. (end of foot) + (sheep sound) + (opposite of come) = [Tobago]

3. Researching South American States

    when: two weeks

    what: resource materials, list of names from previous activity (or
           teacher can make up list from what class is studying)

    how: (1) Divide class into groups and give each group a different
               portion of names from the list.
           (2) Each group will research its own list of names using the
               following questions:
               (a) Where on map is country found?
               (b) Why is country important to study?
               (c) Suppose you could visit this country, what would
                   you want to see?
               (d) How would you feel about living in this country?
           (3) Each group may be requested to turn in a written report
               of its findings.
           (4) When all groups have finished they can share findings
               with entire class.

Specific Objective: Identify the effect of environment on developing
                     societies and cultures.

4. Investigating a Society

    when: two weeks

    what: materials as needed

    how: Divide the class into groups. Each group must choose a society
           or culture to study. Students research to learn about the
           land, people, customs, government, food, housing, religion,
           arts, etc. Each group must decide how to present their in-
           formation to the rest of the class. For example:
           (1) Mobile: Each thing hanging from the mobile must represent
               something in the society being reported on. Each member
               of the group will have several things hanging on the
               mobile to explain and perhaps elaborate on to the class.
           (2) Float: Make a float (as in parade) using any means for
               wheels (skateboards, wagons, etc.). Group will need to
               decorate float to represent the society researched. The
               float can be divided into sections and each member of
               the group can explain his/her section to the class.
           (3) Skit: Prepare a skit that includes costumes, scenery,
               props, singing, dancing, food, etc. that is representa-
               tive of the culture or society being studied.

5. Comparing Cultures

when: one week

what: large paper or bulletin board

how: (This can be a follow-up activity to the previous one which studied characteristics of various cultures.) Make a chart. Name the countries or civilizations being studied down the side. Across the top make columns for such items as climate, land forms, food, housing, clothing, religion, the arts, etc. Groups will fill in the columns according to the civilization they researched.

	climate	land forms	food	clothing	etc.
Ancient Greece					
Rome					
Asia					
Ancient Egypt					

Have class discussion comparing and contrasting the societies using the following questions:

How did climate and land affect what people wore, what they ate, and the type of house they lived in?

What customs arose from everyday life?

Did religion affect or give rise to any customs?

Suppose you had lived in that society, what part of living in that time would you have liked best? Liked least?

6.   "A Picture Is Worth 1000 Words"

   when: one period

   what: paper, pencil or crayons

   how: In ancient Greece, tombs were decorated with friezes of
           figures and drawings depicting the life and activities that
           surrounded the person whose tomb it was.

           Have students draw small frieze using stick figures depicting
           some everyday activity or holiday. Have students exchange
           drawings to see if they can understand each other's.

           Alternative: Have groups draw frieze of culture or society
           being studied.

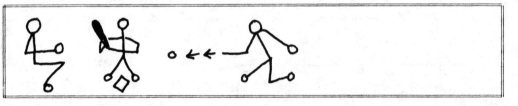

   Specific Objective: Identify the ideas of domination and freedom as they
                        are applied to people in the past and present.

7.   Are We Controlled?

   when: one period

   what: chart

   how: Have students list ten specific things they have done within
           the past twenty-four hours. Next to the activities have them
           list any rules, regulations, laws, or other controls that
           might relate to the activities. Did they do anything that
           had no control related to it? For example:

           played baseball - rules of the game

           watched TV - stations regulated by FCC

           ate apples from own tree - no controls

           etc.

Alternative: Set up chart of different areas of students' lives and have them fill in laws, rules, or regulations that affect them in everyday life.

SCHOOL	HOME	COMMUNITY	SPORTS	ETC.
tardy bell	make bed pick up clothes	traffic light	baseball (game rules)	

8. Do We Need Rules?

when: one period

what: chart

NECESSARY RULES	UNNECESSARY RULES
_____	_____
_____	_____
_____	_____

how: Have each student think of a series of rules that control his/her life. Have each student list those they think are necessary in one column and those they think are unnecessary in another column. Students should be ready to defend their positions. Hold class discussion to see if students can come to a consensus on necessary rules.

9. Government Controls

when: one week

what:

how: Have each student pick a country to study. Students should concentrate on the country's government and the amount of control in the country. Questions for consideration:

   (a) Does the country have one set of beliefs that must be believed and followed?

   (b) Are people free to contradict beliefs of the country?

   (c) Are people jailed for holding contradictory beliefs?

   (d) Are people free to hold whatever job they want?

(e) Must people join a workers' organization?

(f) Are people free to criticize political leaders?

(g) Is education compulsory?

(h) Can people own property?

After doing research on the above questions, students should write a report on the amount of freedom allowed in the country they studied. A class discussion may be held using the reports.

10. Domination and Freedom

when: three periods

what:

how: (1) Discuss with students the ideas of domination or control of people and freedom or what kind of freedom can be allowed by a society.

(2) Examine each of the following societies on the following questions:

	Egyptian	Greek/Athens	Roman Empire	Modern American Society
Who has freedom?				
Who is controlled?				
Who is doing the controlling?				
How is freedom defined?				

B. Purpose: Develop skills necessary to <u>process</u> information

Specific Objective: Identify the four levels of questions: memory, description, speculation, and evaluation.

1. <u>Questioning Skills--Sixth Grade</u>

when: two periods

what: Questioning Skills Self-Test

how: Identifying and classifying questioning skills were introduced in the fourth and fifth grades. Questions were classified into two broad categories, open and closed. Why is
knowing about the differences between questions important?
The argument is that teachers and students spend a large
portion of their time either asking or answering questions.
Educators know that good questions may produce effective
learning. Also, educators know that children ask and are
asked both open and closed questions in as well as out of
school, and that open questions are related to the act of
creativity.

Questions are such an integral part of the teaching-learning
act that it is common sense to train students in the skill of
asking and answering questions. In the fourth and fifth
grades questioning skill activities classified questions into
two categories, open and closed. This sixth grade activity
will identify two levels of open and two levels of closed
questions. Open is <u>speculation</u> and <u>evaluation</u> questions,
closed is <u>memory</u> and <u>description</u> questions.

<u>Open Questions</u>

In brief, open questions are those that do not have answers.
Open questions require <u>speculation</u> such as "suppose" and
<u>evaluation</u> such as "opinion." Speculation questions allow
for a variety of answers. This type question is often considered to be one that is thought-provoking. Teachers who
ask speculative questions are seeking original or creative
responses. This type question often confronts students with
problem situations which ask them to combine facts and ideas
in new ways in order to construct a viable solution. Examples
of speculation questions are:

(a) Suppose you had been born as a citizen of Panama rather
than the US, how might you feel about the Panama Canal?

(b) Who would you predict will be the Republican candidate
for the Presidency in the next election?

(c) How might your community be improved?

(d) What would you hypothesize about the chances for a
Third World War?

The second type of open question is evaluation which calls for judgment, values, and choices. Evaluation questions require students to reach a decision to take a position. For example:

(a) What is your opinion of the President?

(b) Why do you think the football team will win?

(c) What do you think about the weather?

Test your skill at identifying the difference between speculation and evaluation type questions. Mark S for speculation and E for evaluation.

__E__ 1. What do you think about living on the moon?

__S__ 2. Suppose you lived on the moon, how would that be different from the way you are now living?

__E__ 3. Do you believe we will ever live in another galaxy?

__S__ 4. What would you predict would happen if the earth acquired a second moon?

Closed Questions

In brief, two closed type questions, memory and description, have answers. Memory questions call for the lowest level of thinking. This type seeks answers which require students to recall factual information. Students respond to memory questions by recalling a fact, defining a term, noting something they observe, or simply giving an answer based on rote memory. For example:

(a) What is the name of your school?

(b) Are you a boy or a girl?

(c) Were you sick last year?

(d) According to the weather report, what will the weather be today?

Description type questions require students to establish a relationship between facts. They are aimed at getting students to recall one right or best answer to be put in their own words. Description questions are different from memory questions because they call for the student to explain, compare and contrast, relate or associate, whereas memory only calls for recall of a specific fact. For example:

(a) Why was the bus late today?

(b) How does the pencil sharpener work?

(c) Compare your elementary school to another.

(d) Why are you in the sixth grade?

Test your skill at identifying the difference between memory and description type questions. Mark M for memory and D for description.

__M__ 1. Name the school principal.

__D__ 2. Compare the fall weather last year with the fall weather this year.

__D__ 3. How are you different from a ninth grader?

__M__ 4. What is your zip code?

The following is a check on how well you can classify questions using the four levels of questions you have just learned.

QUESTIONING SKILLS SELF-TEST

Use the letters M (memory), D (description), S (speculation), or E (evaluation) to identify the question type.

__M__ 1. How many states make up the United States?

__D__ 2. What is a peninsula?

__S__ 3. Predict what would happen if there were heavy rains in the Mississippi Valley.

__E__ 4. What is your opinion of moving the US capitol from Washington, DC to a more central location in the nation?

__E__ 5. In your judgment, who has made the greater contributions to space travel, the US or Russia?

__D__ 6. What are the similarities and differences between the states of Maine and Florida?

__M__ 7. Was Texas one of the thirteen original colonies?

__E__ 8. Why do you feel that Summer is the best season of the year?

__S__ 9. Suppose we could control the weather, how might this affect your life?

__D__ 10. Why does time start at Greenwich, England?

Follow-through activities:
(a) As a follow-up activity, students should examine their social studies texts for examples of the four levels of questions. Questions are usually found at the end of each chapter.
(b) Be sure that evaluations (tests), written and oral, reflect all four levels of questions. Test questions reflect the real priorities of the class.

Specific Objective: Learn to measure chronologically using the correct
terms.

2. <u>Understanding Time</u>

when: three periods

what: materials as needed

how: (1) Prepare a chart of days spanning two weeks. Combine
Saturday and Sunday and call it "Weekend" between the
first week and the second week. Do first week in red
ink and second week in black ink.

Mon	Tue	Wed	Thu	Fri	WEEKEND	Mon	Tue	Wed	Thu	Fri

Explain that each day represents a century, that "red
week" will represent BW (before weekend) and that the
"black week" will represent AW (after weekend). Help
students to understand the concept. For example:

Red Tuesday is the fourth century BW.

Black Wednesday is the third century AW.

(2) Divide each day of the chart into ten sections. Each
section represents ten years or a decade. Explain to
students that you count back from BW and count forward
from AW. Check students' understanding. For example,
put an X on Red Friday (see below)--that is thirty years
BW. Place an X on Black Monday (see below)--that is
sixty years AW. Point to other sections and see if
students can tell decade and century.

(3) Explain terms BC (before Christ) and AD (anno Domini).
Draw a chart of centuries and have students mark centuries spanned by cultures or civilizations that have
been studied.

3. Personal Time Line

    when: one period

    what: personal time line chart

    how: Have each child create a personal time line. See examples below:

```
|   1960's        |    1970's         |    1980's       |
|0|1|2|3|4|5|6|7|8|9|0|1|2|3|4|5|6|7|8|9|0|1|2|3|4|5|6|7|8|9|
|             A     | BC        D      |    E           |
```

A. born

B. learned to ride bike

C. started kindergarten

D. sixth grade

E. will graduate from high school

One-Year Time Line

```
| JAN | FEB | MAR | APR | MAY | JUN | JUL | AUG | SEP | OCT | NOV | DEC |
| 1   |     |  2  |  3  | 4 5 |  6  |      7 8 |         |       9 |  10 |
```

1. New Year's Day   6. Fourth of July

2. Spring starts   7. Summer vacation ends

3. birthday   8. Labor Day

4. Memorial Day   9. Thanksgiving Day

5. Summer vacation starts   10. Christmas Day

4. Western Civilizations Time Lines

    when: recurring

    what: paper, yarn, markers

    how: (1) Long sheets of butcher paper or newsprint are fastened to
               the wall. Decide on number of time lines desired (you
               may want only one or you may want several to show the
               relationship between the political, social, and economic
               events in world history). Draw the line or lines on
               paper using a different color for each line.
           (2) As major events are studied, the students should put them
               on construction paper and fasten them to the appropriate
               line at the appropriate time (lines could have century
               or even half-century markings).
           (3) As different lines are completed, lines of matching color
               yarn can be fastened from one event to another that may
               have influenced it.

5. Time Line Rollers

    when: three periods

    what: cardboard rolls from toilet tissue or paper towels
           (Teacher should label series of rolers with a date: decade,
           year, century, etc.)

    how: Rollers are handed out to students at random. Students write
           a report or draw a picture of a preselected topic (i.e.,
           government, machines, housing, etc.) that fits the date of
           their rollers.

           Reports are rolled and placed in rollers; rollers may be
           decorated.

           Students line up rollers in chronological order.

           A long rope is attached to one wall. Each student, in order
           of dates on rollers, reads his report or shows his picture,
           rerolls it, and places it in roller and hangs it on the rope,
           making a time line.

Specific Objective: Identify the culture and values of people from items
that they have lost, buried, or left behind.

6.   <u>To Artifact or Not. That is the Question!</u>

   when: one period

   what: paper bag, small objects

   how: (1) Hold a class discussion on artifacts. Define term and
              discuss importance of finding artifacts from past cul-
              tures and civilizations. Definition: "Artifacts are
              objects such as tools, pottery, or ornaments discovered
              in ancient ruins and known to be man-made."
           (2) Teacher fills a bag with small objects such as <u>flower</u>,
              <u>stone</u>, crayon, paper clip, <u>apple</u>, nail file, penny,
              bottle cap, thimble, etc. Make sure bag has enough
              items so each student can have one. The underlined
              items are not artifacts because they are not man-made.
           (3) Students reach into bag and pick one item without looking.
              Student then places object on table in either an area
              marked "artifacts" or an area marked "not artifacts."
              Students must give reason for placement.

7.   <u>Uncovering a Lost Civilization</u>

   when: four periods

   what: materials as needed

   how: (1) Divide class into groups. The students are going to be
              archaeologists and uncover a "lost civilization." Have
              each group choose a civilization or culture that they
              would like to study. Groups must keep their culture a
              secret.
           (2) Groups should use the following form for their reports:
              (a) name of civilization
              (b) names of artifacts that would be found in that
                  civilization
              (c) bibliography of references that were used
              (d) pictures of artifacts (if possible) or careful
                  drawings
              (e) model of one artifact (use art supplies, clay, etc.)
              (f) Make a diorama of a cross section of an archaeological
                  dig showing how at least three of the named artifacts
                  might be found.
           (3) Groups should set up displays of their models and dio-
              ramas. Other groups will try to determine what culture
              was being studied. (See examples of artifacts from
              different periods on following page.)

Examples of Artifacts

Classical Rome	Medieval Europe	?
water wheel	water mill	
treadmill	stamping mill	
chariot	saddle, harness	
aquaduct	wooden plow	
stone paved roads	hand sickle	
stone bridge	windmill	
arch	castle	
stylus	lance	
	battle ax	
	armor	

8. ## School Artifacts Box

when: one period

what: grocery bag or box, articles from school's "Lost and Found"

how: (1) Teacher should go to school's "Lost and Found" and fill
bag or box with a variety of items children have lost at
school. For example: scarves, pencils (thin ones, big
kindergarten ones, stubs, chewed ones), gloves or mittens
(all sizes), boots, books, papers, T-shirts, gym shoes
(different sizes). If possible, fill box in layers
according to the seasons.
(2) The objective of this activity is to prepare students to
make accurate inferences about their culture by observing
what students in their school have either thrown away or
lost.
(3) Either teacher or designated student will select items
one by one from box in front of class. As each item is
selected it should be recorded on the board. For
example: one layer might contain boot, scarf, glove,
hanky, and heel broken off of a shoe. These things were
touching each other; is there a relationship between
these items? Yes, these are all items used in winter.
Students might hypothesize that the heel was broken off
when attempting to pull off boot. Consider the following questions:
(a) Do the items tell you anything about the season of
the year?
(b) Can you infer anything about the age and size of
people who lost items?
(c) Do the different layers of lost and found items tell
you anything about the change in seasons?
(d) Does the specific item tell you anything about who
lost it, i.e., boy or girl, rich or poor, race,
religion, or beliefs?
This is really an exercise in observation and inference. We
can learn a great deal about people or a culture by just observing what they leave behind. This is as true for finds in
Egypt as it is for the school's "Lost and Found."

9.   What Kind of Culture Was This?

    when: one period

    what: foam plastic container that "Big Mac," "Super Chef," etc.
          comes in

    how: (1) Collect trash along road, in fields, or around the neigh-
             borhood (i.e., paper, cans, etc.). A civilization is
             known by the "things" it throws away. What can you in-
             fer about a civilization from the throwaways? Discuss
             with class--we can be "known" by our trash!
        (2) Students pretend they are explorers from another planet
             and have landed on a dead Earth which is covered by dust
             and nothing else. Only one item can be found by the ex-
             plorers--the "Big Mac" container.
        (3) The class must now decide what it can infer about the
             civilization from just this one item. Have class de-
             scribe item. For example:
             (a) it has color
             (b) it has symbols or writing
             (c) it has two sections that fasten together to make a
                 container
        (4) Discuss how this item might have been used and what the
             culture might have been like that used it.
        (5) Be sure to use "What Kind of Culture Was This" to practice
             categorizing. Students should identify large categories.

Specific Objective: Use maps, charts, and tables for comparison and
                       decision-making.

10. Buried Treasure

    when: four periods

    what: teacher-prepared maps, charts, and tables (see examples)

    how: Teacher announces that there are three buried treasures and
          the students must decide which treasure they want to go for
          after studying the available information. Divide class into
          groups for this activity.

          Materials provided for study:

          (a) Maps of three different countries where the treasures
             are buried. Maps of any countries will do as long as
             the maps have a scale of miles and physical features.
             The students will need to seek the treasure by land or
             water, so the more rivers and mountains on the maps the
             better. Mark an X where the treasure is buried, and
             mark one port as the entry for the treasure seekers.

          (b) Charts of monthly climate, population, and crime rate.
             For example:

CLIMATE		Jan.	Feb.	March	April	May	etc.
Country One	Average temperature	10°	20°	35°	70°	75°	
	rainfall	11"	15"	6"	0"	0"	
Country Two	Average temperature	95°	105°	95°	75°	70°	
	rainfall	0"	0"	0"	25"	32"	
Country Three	Average temperature	65°	42°	20°	0°	-20°	
	rainfall	5"	7"	6"	0"	0"	

	Population Per Sq. Mile	Crime Rate
Country One	245	25%
Country Two	473	18%
Country Three	6	2%

(c) Tables which show what the treasure consists of (money, precious stones) and the amount in each treasure. For example:

	Money	Gold	Silver	Jewels
Country One	$1,000,000	32 bars	none	none
Country Two	50,000	none	none	$2,000,000
Country Three	none	300 bars	564 bars	none

gold bar = (set a price)   silver bar = (set a price)

Using materials provided, groups must determine:
  (a) distance to each treasure
  (b) routes and transportation
  (c) what physical features must be passed
  (d) climate--what time of year would be best to go
  (e) where to get workers to help on the trip
  (f) crime rate--where treasure might be stolen
  (g) worth of treasure

After having considered all the above factors, groups must decide which treasure they would go after.

Specific Objective: Learn to identify differences between fact and opinion
and primary and secondary sources.

11. Primary and Secondary Sources of Information

when: one period

what: list of sources and secondary reports (The best places to
find evidence of primary and secondary sources are newspapers,
popular news weeklies, textbooks.)

how: (1) Discuss with class the terms source or primary source and
secondary source or secondary report. Primary sources
are actual objects or records that tell us about the
past. Since we cannot study all primary sources, we
rely often on secondary sources. These are usually reports from someone who has examined a source or other
accounts and has put his/her own interpretation in the
report. Secondary sources can be of great help, but they
can also be misleading.
(2) The following is a list of primary and secondary sources.
Pass out list to students. Have them put P before those
they believe are primary sources and S before those they
believe are secondary sources.

Sources

_P_   1. watching Monday night football broadcast

_S_   2. listening to sportscaster description of Monday night football

_P_   3. Dead Sea Scrolls

_S_   4. history text

_S_   5. The Sword in the Stone--story of King Arthur

_P_   6. President's televised "State of the Union" address to Congress

_P_   7. satellite photo of weather condition on TV weather report

_P_   8. Sam Adams's letters to his wife Abigail before American Revolution

_P_   9. photo of the moon taken by Gemini space crew

_S_ 10. news report on interview with astronauts

_S_ 11. painting of the Mayflower arriving in New England

_S_ 12. A Thousand Days, report of President Kennedy's days in office
by A. Schlesinger, Jr.

_P_ 13. selected TV coverage of Olympic events

_S_ 14. the TV showing of Roots

12. Fact or Opinion

    when: two periods

    what: newspapers

    how: Teacher should find editorials from two papers on the same
            subject. Students should see if they can separate fact from
            opinion and give the reasons for their choices.

            Find a report on a speech or event from two newspapers. Have
            students decide what is fact and what is opinion. Compare
            the two accounts. This is particularly good with a speech if
            you can obtain the actual text of the speech. For example:

WASHINGTON, DC: President's
News Conference.
The President held his monthly
news conference this week. At
the conference he spoke about
inflation. "For the past ten
years inflation has eaten away
at the dollar to the point
where America's money is in
trouble around the world.
American money is still respected and will remain the
base for world trade."

Editorial Comment:
The President held another rather
useless, mostly ineffective news
conference this week. As usual
the President started the conference with an oft repeated, dull
and uninspiring lecture on inflation. In his lecture he said
that America's money is no longer
respected anywhere in the world
and is losing its value as the
base of world trade.

13. Bias in Media Reports

    when: two periods

    what: newspapers or school paper

    how: (1) Have students select an article about a person or event
                from any paper and pick out all the descriptive words.
                Do the words suggest approval or disapproval of the
                person or event?
            (2) Have students select articles that have a lot of descrip-
                tive words (sports reports are good for this) and for
                each positive word substitute a negative word. How does
                this change the article? For example, take the Editorial
                Comment from the previous activity. The article below
                is the same editorial with positive words substituted for
                negative words and vice versa. The words substituted
                are underlined.

                Editorial Comment:
                The President held another rather helpful, mostly effec-
                tive news conference this week. As usual the President
                started the conference with an oft repeated, stimulating
                and inspiring lecture on inflation. In his lecture he
                said that America's money is still respected anywhere in
                the world and has not lost its value as the base of world
                trade.

(3) Have each student write two of his/her own news reports of something that happened in school. Use positive descriptive words in one report and negative descriptive words in the other report. How does this change the character of the report?

14. Point of View

when: one period

what: materials included below

how: (1) Hold class discussion on patriotism. Everyone has some idea of what is right and what is wrong for the country.

(2) Have students write brief paragraphs giving their definitions of patriotism.

(3) Have students read the excerpts from a speech on patriotism given by Mr. Rafferty and excerpts from Thomas Jefferson's writings (see below).

(4) Discuss whether or not there is much difference between Mr. Rafferty's and Thomas Jefferson's feelings about patriotism. How do the students' definitions compare with those of Mr. Rafferty and Thomas Jefferson?

Excerpts from a speech, "The Passing of the Patriot," by Mr. Max Rafferty, former Superintendent of Schools, La Canada, California.

"... teach [children] every day in every necessary way to memorize and to believe and to live Decatur's great toast: 'Our country! In her intercourse with foreign nations, may she always be in the right, but our country, right or wrong!'"

"Had they been taught to love their country with the same passion that inspired other generations of American youth, they would not now be wondering what all the fuss [Viet Nam War and civil rights] is about. They would know that their country was in danger, and that would be enough today. Too many of them neither know nor care."

Excerpts from Thomas Jefferson's letters.

"A little rebellion, now and then, is a good thing, and as necessary in the political world as storms in the physical ... It is a medicine necessary for the sound health of government." (to Madison, 1787)

"The tree of liberty must be refreshed from time to time with the blood of patriots and tyrants. It is its natural manure." (to Colonel Smith, 1787)

"What country can preserve its liberties, if its rulers are not warned from time to time that this people preserve the spirit of resistance? Let them take arms." (to Colonel Smith, 1787)

15. Modifying a Stereotype

when: recurring

what: magazines and newspapers

how: (1) Discuss meaning of stereotypes and have students think of
          examples, i.e., minorities, old people, teenagers, women,
          foreigners, the poor, welfare recipients.
      (2) Have students bring in pictures of stereotypes or cut them
          out of magazines or newspapers in class. Display them on
          bulletin board.
      (3) Teacher picks one example from the display. Each student
          must obtain one example contrary to the stereotype. For
          example: Teacher picks stereotype picture of old person
          sitting in a rocking chair. Students must get pictures
          of active or involved senior citizens.

      Alternative: Have students bring in only pictures that show
      stereotypes giving way--pictures contrary to stereotypes,
      i.e., Black executive, woman telephone repairperson, etc.

16. I Am Pretending to Be a . . . Stereotype

when: one period

what: index cards with name of occupation or person that is often
       stereotyped (housewife, absent-minded professor, dentist,
       hippie, etc.)

how: Have each student draw a card and role-play the stereotype.
      Can class guess whom or what occupation is being portrayed?
      Discuss characteristics commonly used to stereotype each
      specific occupation. For example:

      (a) Are the characteristics true to life?

      (b) What are other characteristics common to this occupa-
          tion?

      (c) Suppose you worked at this occupation, would you try
          to practice a different set of characteristics?

      (d) Are stereotypes of occupations helpful or harmful when
          trying to understand the world of work?

17. Propaganda: The Art of Persuasion

when: two days

what: definitions

how: An introductory unit on propaganda was suggested for use in

the fifth grade. Propaganda techniques are now so skillfully
and persistently aimed at the general public that it is not
too early to start identifying and examining the different
types of techniques at the fifth, sixth, and seventh grade
levels. Studying propaganda techniques is an attempt to help
students gain control over a method of influencing them to
believe and act in a particular way. Propaganda is properly
used to disseminate information. However, it is important
that children begin to understand that propaganda can be used
to get them to accept questionable points of view.
(1) Hand out definitions to class and discuss with students
     these six common forms of propaganda.
(2) Have students think of examples from TV, etc. and put
     them on board.
(3) Have each student bring to class at least three different
     examples of propaganda techniques selected from the list
     to share with class.
(4) Have each student prepare one original propaganda example
     using any technique they wish--TV, magazine articles, etc.

Propaganda Techniques

1. Wishful thinking: assuming something to be true just by wishing
    that it were true.
       "I could knock out the heavyweight champion of the world; just let
       me get at him." "I know I can win, after all I'm from Texas."

2. Oversimplification: a simple or single-cause explanation for a com-
    plex event that was the result of many causes.
       "The reason the school burned down was because it was Friday the
       thirteenth."

3. Slogans: a snappy, short, catchy phrase calculated to stimulate and
    promote a particular point of view.
       "Coke adds life." "A and W root beer's got that frosty mug taste."
       "Tippecanoe and Tyler Too." "Go, fight, win, Wildcats."

4. Prejudice: reluctance to consider evidence or reasoning which is
    contrary to one's belief. A prejudgment about an event before the
    situation and facts are known.
       "All those kids over in Westside Elementary are snobs." "Look at
       him, he's just like his older brother."

5. Vagueness: the person uses a word that leaves an undefined, uncer-
    tain meaning.
       "Eat this, it's good for you." "The best things in life are free."
       "This movie is the worst." "This movie is far out, cool, tough,
       bad, and not quite with it."

6. Out of context: statement or idea taken out of its original context
    for the purpose of distorting the meaning of the statement. Suppose
    you said, "All fourth graders at Lincoln Elementary are brats," but
    were later quoted as having said, "All fourth graders are brats."
    Suppose you said, "The book I read is boring, tasteless, surprising,
    and occasionally mildly humorous," and were later quoted as saying,
    "The book was surprising and humorous."

C. Purpose: Develop the skill to examine <u>values</u> and beliefs

Specific Objective: Identify values of other cultures and compare them to each other and to one's own values and beliefs.

1. <u>Values in the Past</u>

when: recurring

what:

how: As each country, region, or culture is studied, have students compile list of values and beliefs important to those people. Students should have research to support their lists.

Alternative: Develop a master list of values and rank importance of values for each country, region, or culture being studied. For example:

Countries

Values	Brazil	Other Latin Countries	Ancient Greece	Ancient Rome or European nations during monarchies or ? whatever is being studied.
Education			1	
Future			3	
Authority			2	
Past heritage			5	
State-supported Religion			4	
Developing natural resources			6	
Etc.				

Discuss with class that these are generalizations, that there are always some people who may disagree with their society's values. (Students should discover this in their research.)

2. <u>Fly Your Own Flag</u>

    when: three periods

    what: dowel rods, construction paper, art supplies

    how: (1) Hold class discussion on beliefs valued by ourselves and
            our ancestors. Some students may have family crests
            they would like to bring in and explain to the class.
        (2) Students are now ready to construct their own pennant.
            Cut a large pennant from construction paper (two to
            three feet long) for each student. Shape depends on
            preference. For example:

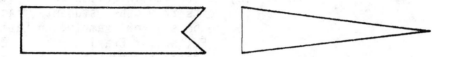

        (3) It would be best for students to plan their pennant on
            scrap paper before the art work is done on the construc-
            tion paper pennant. Students should include on their
            pennant:
          (a) Three words that describe what they value. For
              example: courage, truth, honesty, fairplay,
              equality, justice, etc.
          (b) A symbol or drawing of what they like to do now.
              For example: sewing (needle and thread or thimble),
              ball, skates, skis and poles, book for reading, etc.
          (c) A symbol that might depict something their family
              likes to do. For example: camping (tent), hiking
              figure, biking figure, fishing pole, boat, tennis
              raquet, golf club, etc.
          (d) A symbol of what they would like to be in the future.
              For example: doctor (medical bag), fireman (hat),
              teacher (torch of knowledge), etc.
        (4) Wide end of pennant is rolled around dowel rod and glued,
            taped, or stapled in place. Example of pennant:

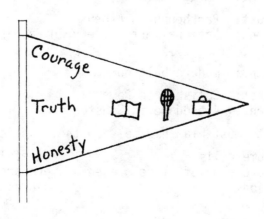

Specific Objective: Identify the meaning of beauty in other cultures and
                      compare it to one's meaning of beauty.

3.   Sixth Grade Newspaper

     when: three weeks

     what: materials as needed

     how: Students will create a newspaper using beauty as the main
             theme. Depending on what class is studying, newspaper could
             feature beauty in ancient civilization, or beauty in Latin
             American countries, or beauty in European countries, etc.

             Jobs: (a) Editors to interview, write stories, receive re-
                        ports from other students, faculty, or community
                        members. For example, on Latin America:
                        Editor for Brazil   Editor for Argentina
                        Editor for Mexico   Editor for Colombia
                        Editor for Chili   Editor for El Salvador
                        etc.
                    (b) Illustrators
                    (c) Committee to put final paper together so it can be
                        run off (on copier, mimeograph, etc.)

             A total class planning session should be held to plan news-
             paper. Jobs should be assigned or volunteered for. There
             should be a job for each member of the class. Students then
             should break up into groups for each job and plan their
             activities.

4.   In My Opinion

     when: two periods

     what: materials as needed

     how: Each student picks something that he/she believes is beautiful
             from the past and something from the present. For example:

                  past: Greek statue
               present: Calder mobile

                  past: Parthenon in Athens
               present: National Art Gallery in Washington, DC

                  past: dress from era of Louis XV
               present: modern ball gown

                  past: Coliseum in Rome
               present: Astrodome in Houston

             Students must plan how to show their choice. For example:

             costume dolls   carefully mount pictures
             prepare a brief slide presen-   prepare a clay model
               tation   diorama

D.   Purpose: Apply knowledge through active <u>participation</u>

Specific Objective: Identify one's own values and learn to participate in a group concerned with values.

1.   <u>Reaching Consensus</u>

   when: one period

   what: list of social or community problems

   how: (1) Give each student the list of problems and have him/her rank the problems in order of priority, 1 being problem he/she feels is most in need of attention, 2 being second most important, and so on.

   (2) Divide class into groups. Each group will try to reach a consensus on ranking the problems. Consensus is very difficult to reach since every member of the group must agree to the order of ranking established by the group. Suggestions for reaching group consensus:

   (a) Don't change your mind just to go along with the other members of your group, but "bend" a little if you can agree a little with the group's opinion.

   (b) Avoid easy solutions such as majority vote, compromising, etc.

   (c) Listen to all opinions and use logic.

   (d) When group reaches consensus, each member should mark group's ranking on his/her sheet and then record the difference between his/her own ranking and the group's. For example:

Individual Ranking	Social Problem	Group Ranking	Difference
6	school safety	2	4
2	women's rights	5	3

   (3) Hold class discussion on:

   (a) Reasons for differences between individual and group rankings.
   (b) Similarities and differences between group rankings.
   (c) For person in each group whose personal ranking came closest to group ranking, were there reasons for this?

> NOTE: The following activity is a technique for helping students identify problems.

PROBLEM LIST

Individual Ranking	Social or Community Problem	Group Ranking	Difference
1. _____	school safety	_____	_____
2. _____	highway safety	_____	_____
3. _____	pollution	_____	_____
4. _____	crime	_____	_____
5. _____	unemployment	_____	_____
6. _____	inflation	_____	_____
7. _____	race relations	_____	_____
8. _____	gun control	_____	_____
9. _____	women's rights	_____	_____
10. _____	alcoholism	_____	_____
11. _____	world peace	_____	_____
12. _____	cost of medical care	_____	_____

2.   Inquiry--A Citizen's Obligation in a Democratic Society

Why this concern about inquiry when our interest is in citizenship? Authorities say that the one major goal for teaching social studies is that of developing citizenship. Remember, when educators are talking about citizenship, they are not talking about some vague abstraction but about you. Social studies educators are primarily interested in your effectiveness as you participate in a democratic society.

It should be clear that an assumption is being made. Educators ask the question, "Why is it best for a citizen to inquire?" Not only do teachers assume an answer to this question, but notice that teachers also make a value judgment that there is a best citizen. "The best citizens, according to some social studies educators, should inquire in a democratic society because they can discover for themselves the most meaningful properties of their environment." In other words, the best citizen is the autonomous person who has gained the skill of checking ideas about the environment--that is, a citizen capable of making rational independent judgments.

Inquiry as a Method

Some would say that "the truth shall make you 'free.'" Others believe that it is the process of seeking truth that makes you "free." The author casts his lot with the latter belief, that it is the method of gaining knowledge (inquiry) that sets one free to be an effective citizen, an autonomous citizen. Inquiry is a method, an approach to life. Inquiry is one method by which rational decisions are made in a free, rational, democratic society.

What is Inquiry?

Some authorities suggest that one way to avoid bias, stereotypes, and prejudiced thinking is to apply the inquiry method. The method merely provides a step-by-step process by which thoughts can be verified. Inquiry implies a particular way of approaching life, for true inquirers are critical thinkers who test the information they gain through a proof process. The following six steps are part of the proof process.

(1) Experience

The process of inquiry starts with an experience.

(2) State of uncertainty and doubt

The heart of inquiry is not fact. It is uncertainty. It is not the established, symmetrical "givens" that generate inquiry, it is that which does not fit--the irregular, the confusing.

(3) Framing the problem

The sensing of the problem may lead you to frame that which you do not know, and it is that frame which becomes the statement of the problem. The statement of the problem prescribes the boundaries within which the conflict is seen and the tension created.

(4) Formulating hypotheses

When you frame a hypothesis you are literally "brainstorming the possibilities." The framing of the problem gives you the limits within which you will hypothesize.

(5) Experiencing and evidencing

The title of this stage almost explains itself. At this stage you gather and evaluate sources of evidence.

(6) Generalization

The final step in the inquiry process is generalization. The generalization is a statement about how well the hypothesis has given meaning to understanding the problem.

when: depends on problem studied

what: Inquiry Form, list of issues

how: (1) Student picks issue to investigate.
        (2) Each student uses Inquiry Form in investigation.
        (3) Individualized instruction--teacher gives help when
            needed as students work on forms.
        (4) Students' conclusions (generalizations) reported to class.

Suggested Issues

(If these issues do not spark interest, turn back to Activity
1, "Reaching Consensus," and use problems list technique.)

world hunger

birth control around the world

problems in the "Fourth World" underdeveloped nations

problems in the "Third World" underdeveloped nations

problems in the "Second World" developed nations

problems in the "First World" developed nations

China's role in the world

Middle East conflict

use of power reserves

problems of water and water usage

growing deserts

wars and the threat of wars

mining of the seas

fishing rights

space exploration

control and use of space

atomic proliferation

disease control

pollution control

United Nations

INQUIRY FORM

1. Experiencing: What experience have you had with the issue you have
    chosen from the list that has caused you to be interested in or
    curious about that issue?

    _____

    _____

2. Uncertainty and doubt: The issue can become a personal as well as a
    social problem if you feel the need to know. Express as best you
    can the uncertainty you feel about the issue. What confuses you?

    _____

    _____

3. Framing the problem: What do you know about the issue?

    _____

    _____

    What do you think you know about the issue?

    _____

    _____

    What is it you do not know about the issue?

    _____

    _____

4. Formulating hypotheses: The hypothesis is a proposed point of view
    on the issue. That view needs to be proved or disproved.

    _____

    _____

5. Exploring and evidencing: Gather and evaluate sources of evidence
    on the issue. Circle and then name the sources you will use in find-
    ing information about your hypothesis.

    books   pictures   newspapers   filmstrips   magazines

    interviews   personal observations   other

    _____

    _____

    List specific pieces of information that deal with your hypothesis.

    _____

    _____

6. <u>Generalization</u>: How does your information prove or disprove your hypothesis?

_____

_____

_____

Evaluating the inquiry: What have you learned? Has the inquiry into the issue provided you with an accurate point of view on the issue? Explain:

_____

_____

_____

_____

_____

NOTE: An important point is that the inquiry method starts with a personal concern. This method is not particularly successful if problems or issues are identified <u>for the student</u>. The motivation to complete an inquiry is intrinsic; that is, the method is one way to study and perhaps develop an appropriate response to life's problems. Inquiry offers citizens in a democratic, complex, interdependent society one method by which to rationally think through problems and issues.

<u>Notes</u>

[1] Indiana Department of Public Instruction. <u>1978 Indiana textbook adoption categories for social studies</u>. Indianapolis: Author, 1978, p. 3.

INTEREST FORM

You have just completed the Chapter Sixth Grade. In an effort to have you identify activities and materials that seem most promising at this grade level to you, please fill out the following interest form.

Instructions:

Identify two activities from this chapter. Name the activities and briefly describe why these particular activities are of interest to you.

ACTIVITY 1

ACTIVITY 2

NOTES

CHAPTER SEVENTH GRADE

ACTIVITIES AND MATERIALS FOR SEVENTH GRADE

Page

A. Gaining Knowledge

    1. World Wide News   223
    2. Inventory   224
    3. Buy American: But Don't Eat the Candy!   225
    4. "It's a Small World, After All"   225
    5. Studying Africa Through the Use of Maps and Bottle Caps . . .   226
    6. Exploring West Africa   227
    7. A Multi-Media Picture of the Culture   228
    8. The Encroaching Sahara   229
    9. Concept Wheel   230
   10. Building a Culture   231
   11. Discovery--Culture   232
   12. Ils-o-way   232
   13. Assessing the Future of Other Countries   234
   14. Proverbs   234
   15. Categorizing Cultures   236
   16. Identifying Culture   236
   17. Interdependence or Isolation   237

B. Processing

    1. Questioning Skills--Seventh Grade   237
    2. Oral Report Checklist and Teacher Evaluation   239
    3. Oral Report Evaluation Form for Students   240
    4. Papers Evaluation   240
    5. Propaganda Skills--Seventh Grade   241

C. Valuing

    1. Contrasting Cultural Values   244
    2. Foreign Film Festival   244
    3. Identifying Current Global Values   245
    4. Time Machine   245
    5. What is Said About Women and Thought About Men   246
    6. Male vs. Female   247

D. Participating

    1. Teacher-Student Contracts   248
    2. Student-Teacher Activity Evaluation   249
    3. Unit Evaluation: Student Self-Checklist   250
    4. Student-Teacher Group Procedures Evaluation   252
    5. Student Evaluation of Committee Work   253
    6. Student Evaluation of His/Her Group Participation   253

CHAPTER SEVENTH GRADE

Organization of the Chapter

Each succeeding chapter represents a particular grade level, in this case seventh grade. Each chapter consists of three parts: the first part is a brief discussion on courses, topics, and national trends in teaching seventh grade throughout the United States; the second part is an example of a state seventh grade program; the third part has activities and materials for the seventh grade categorized by the four purposes of teaching social studies-- gaining knowledge, processing, valuing, and participating.

I. Topics Taught and National Trends in Teaching Seventh Grade

In this book an examination of elementary social studies curriculum is extended to the seventh grade because in many respects what is taught in grades four through six could just as well be found in seventh grade. For example, some states and cities teach their history in the seventh grade rather than in the fourth. Some states will start American history (studies) in the seventh grade while others will wish to continue the global studies from the sixth grade through the seventh. Some states have mandated the teaching of non-western area studies in the seventh grade while requiring state history to be taught at the fourth grade level. If you have a suspicion that the alter- native directions a teacher can go with social studies increase from first grade through sixth, then you probably have sensed the trend correctly. We know for sure that the eighth grade will be American history just as we knew fifth grade would be American history, as recommended by the Wesley Committee. In a sense, seventh grade social studies is a catching up, a capstone to all of the global and comparative studies that have preceded it.

There appear to be five distinguishably different courses offered at the seventh grade level: State History; Seventh and Eighth Grade American Studies; Old World Eastern Hemisphere Geography and History; World Geography; and Global Studies (with emphasis on area studies of the non-western world).

Course, Topics, and Themes Frequently Covered in Seventh Grade:
"State History" and "Seventh and Eighth Grade American Studies"

The objectives for state history at the seventh grade level are approximately the same as those offered at the fourth grade level. If you need to recall both the objectives and the content of state history, then refer to the fourth grade course, topics, and themes.

A recent development has been the combining of seventh and eighth grade social studies into American studies. The course often resembles the following: seventh grade is state history and early national history; eighth grade is modern and contemporary national history and American government. The seventh grade portion of the course is almost exactly the same as the fourth grade course called "State and United States History."

Course, Topics, and Themes Frequently Covered in Seventh Grade:
"Old World Eastern Hemisphere Geography and History"

This course is similar in objectives and content to the course with the same general characteristics which is frequently taught and has been described in sixth grade. Those schools which teach this course in seventh grade undoubtedly devote sixth grade to a study of Latin America or American Neighbors. The historical portion of the course that deals with foundations of the western civilizations is intended to provide background for the study of United States history in eighth grade.

Course, Topics, and Themes Frequently Covered in Seventh Grade:
"Global Studies" (with emphasis on area studies of the non-western world)

With the growth of dependence on and interest in Third World nations, schools have begun to mandate area studies of the non-west. These studies

include areas such as Sub-Saharan Africa, the Middle East, South Asia, Southeast Asia, East Asia, and the Soviet Union. The course is designed in such a
way that there is an overview of the area and then one in-depth study of a
particular country: Nigeria, Egypt, India, Japan, China, etc. The emphasis
is not only upon the development of these nations but upon how the development
of these nations affects the balance of international power.

Course, Topics, and Themes Frequently Covered in Seventh Grade:
"World Geography"

World Geography has been a traditional course offered at the seventh
grade level. Because of the rather standard offering of this course, it may
be useful to view objectives and basic content as a means of contrasting this
traditional course to a similar course offered in the sixth grade and the preceding seventh grade Global Studies.

Objectives of the Course

Developing the students' world view; reinforcing and expanding their
understanding of geographic concepts and skills.

Basic Content of the Course

After an introductory unit on physical geography, selected countries and
regions of the world are studied, with attention to physical features, climate,
resources, industries and products, and the "way of life of the people." World
relationships of the various countries and regions are usually treated. The
following list of units is typical: Understanding the Physical World Around
Us; Introducing the Caribbean Countries (chief emphasis on Mexico, Canal Zone,
Guatemala, Costa Rica, Venezuela); Introducing the Countries of South America
(chief emphasis on Argentina, Brazil, and Chile); Introducing the USSR and
Eastern Europe; Introducing the Far East (emphasis on China, Japan, and India);
Introducing the Middle East and Northern Africa (emphasis on Egypt, Saudi
Arabia, and Israel); Introducing Africa South of the Sahara (emphasis on

Nigeria and South Africa); Introducing Western Europe (emphasis on Great Britain, France, and Germany).

Trends in Teaching Seventh Grade Social Studies

1.   Seventh grade social studies seems to be the catch basin for all leftover topics, themes, and key concepts which for some reason were not treated in the first six grades. It could be proper to view seventh grade social studies as the place to cap off or tie up loose ends.

2.   Some states have made an effort to coordinate seventh and eighth grades into a two-year sequence including United States history, geography, civics, and the study of the home state. This effort is an attempt to create the base for a consistent program in junior high/middle school rather than having social studies remain a tail-end course for elementary. In many states the middle schools are still unsettled as to what their systematic curriculum ought to be.

3.   As some schools devote the entire year of sixth grade to Latin America or American Neighbors, seventh grade is apparently being taken over by Eastern Hemisphere Studies, World Geography, or Global Studies.

4.   A course such as World Geography in which a large number of nations are surveyed continues to be a traditional but not necessarily a recommended approach. Courses built exclusively upon the survey tend to pressure teachers into ground covering, rushing from nation to nation in an attempt to cover the world. A contemporary approach calls for a quick survey of a region with an in-depth study of one or two illustrative countries within that region.

II.   Illustration of a State Seventh Grade Program

There is no one prescribed social studies program throughout the United States. However, one state's description of its seventh grade program will illustrate the content which the state expects to be taught. This illustration

identifies a state's suggested social studies curriculum for the seventh grade.

> Global Studies at this juncture provides an opportunity for students
> to synthesize concepts gained in prior grades while further extend-
> ing their knowledge of the world in which we live. An in-depth
> examination of areas of the world such as Europe, the Middle East,
> Africa, or Asia (depending on the emphasis in prior grades) will
> provide greater understanding of our dependence on resources avail-
> able in various geographic locations and how economic, social, and
> political institutions develop in relationship to our environment.
> Students should be provided opportunities to incorporate current
> global news into the program to emphasize how the present has been
> influenced by the past and will affect the future in a global set-
> ting.[1]

III. Activities and Materials Categorized by Gaining Knowledge, Processing, Valuing, and Participating

A common practice is to skip specific objectives which precede the acti-

vities, but in this case the objectives are extremely important for an objec-

tive in the seventh grade will be found in succeeding grades. The following

activities and materials are part of a developmental curriculum organized to

build citizenship skills from one grade level to another.

SEVENTH GRADE ACTIVITIES AND MATERIALS

A. Purpose: To gain knowledge about the human condition which includes
            past, present, and future

Specific Objective: Use current events to practice geographic skills.

1. World Wide News[2]

    when: three periods

    what: world map, thumb tacks, construction paper

    how: (1) Each student must bring in a news story (magazine or news-
              paper) about some country other than the United States.
          (2) Each student tells what his/her news story concerns, then
              he/she puts the date of the story on a small piece of
              construction paper and tacks it to the map at the place
              where the story took place.
          (3) When all students have presented a story, a list should
              be drawn up of all the places the stories represent.
              Make sure each story is listed under the continent of
              which it is a part.

(4) This activity can be extended to teach students how to measure by longitude and latitude. Have each student find the longitude and latitude of his/her particular story.

The following are sample headlines about foreign countries.

CIVIL WAR CONTINUES IN CENTRAL AMERICA

CANADA, EGYPT, AND CHINA LOOK FOR OIL

MOSLEMS PROTEST AMERICAN INTERVENTION

FARMERS STRIKE TO RESTRICT IMPORTS

ARGENTINA DENIES HUMAN RIGHTS

JERUSALEM HIT BY BOMB BLASTS

Managua, Nicaragua

Cairo, Egypt

Tehran, Iran

Sidney, Australia

Rome, Italy

Jerusalem, Israel

2. Inventory

when: three periods

what: What do students and their parents buy that is foreign-made?

how: Divide the class into four groups.

(1) Have the first group identify and list the foreign-made articles found in the classroom, including the country where they originate.

(2) Have second group identify and list the foreign-made personal articles of the students, e.g., clothes, jewelry, pens, etc., and where they are from.

(3) Have third group identify and list the country from which each of the student's ancestors come.

(4) Have the fourth group count the number of cars and bikes in the school parking lot and find out how many are foreign-made and from which country.

(5) It would be a good idea for students to have some way to display their results, e.g., pie graph, chart, flags pinned to a map, etc. Hold a class discussion on the results. From what countries do we seem to get the majority of our foreign-made products? How does this affect trade with those countries and others?

(6) Have students identify and list 5-10 (teacher decides number) foreign-made articles at their homes, e.g., cameras, TV, stereo, radio, cooking appliances. How do these lists compare with the groups' findings?

3. Buy American: But Don't Eat the Candy!

   when: one-half period

   what: What does it mean to buy American? Do students really know
          who owns or makes the products they and their families buy?
          Buy one bag of small individually wrapped candy bars (about
          30 to a bag)--Mars, Mounds, etc.

   how: Give one bar to each child. Identify with the class the in-
          gredients of the candy bar. For example, cocoa, sugar,
          flavoring, nuts, chemicals, preservatives. The point is that
          most of the ingredients are imported from other countries.
          Are you buying American if you buy candy made from ingredients
          imported from outside the country?

          Also, the same question is appropriate about American-made
          cars. In some American-made compacts, the parts are made in
          other countries. Is that compact car, then, an American-made
          car just because it is sold by Ford or General Motors?

          Does buying American mean that one should not buy ice cream
          at Baskin-Robbins or stay/eat at Howard Johnson's because
          both companies are foreign-owned?

4. "It's a Small World, After All"[3] - (identifying time and space re-
                                         lationships)

   when: two periods

   what: folders from travel agencies

   how: (1) Discuss with students the idea of the world seeming
              smaller because of modern travel--mostly by plane. Plane
              routes are planned to take the shortest distance between
              two cities. Have students look at globe from the North
              Pole. See how planes may use the polar route as a
              shorter route. For example, planes from Los Angeles fly
              over the Pole to reach England and northern Europe.

              In past years students have studied how long it took pil-
              grims to reach America, or how Forty-niners moving west
              to California had to leave early enough in the spring to
              get over the Rocky Mountains before the snows of late
              autumn trapped them. Time of year and weather are no
              longer the major concern of a traveler. Quite often we
              no longer measure how far one place is from another in
              miles, we measure it in time (Grandma lives two hours
              away).

          (2) Have students measure some distance by time. For example,
              you can travel:

```
4 miles in an hour walking
50 miles in an hour by car
25 miles in an hour by ship
500 miles in an hour by plane
```

How long would it take to get from Indianapolis to Atlanta,
Georgia 500 miles away by foot? (125 hours)
By car? (10 hours)
How long would it take to get from San Francisco to Honolulu
2050 miles away by ship? (82 hours)
By plane: (4 hours)

(3) Obtain some travel folders from a travel agency. Include
cruise folders. Have each student pick an overseas trip
he/she would like to take. Students must figure the
miles from one stop to the next and then figure the distance in hours by car, plane, and ship (or by whatever
means they would be traveling).

5. Studying Africa Through the Use of Maps and Bottle Caps

when: two periods

what: outline map of Africa; dinner plate, pie tin, or bowl with a
flat bottom; bottle cap
(If outline map of Africa is not available, draw outline on
chalkboard or cut out large paper map to use on flannelboard.)

how: Have a class discussion or question-and-answer period on what
should be put on the map of Africa. For example:

rivers and concentrations of population along the rivers
deserts and the size of them
coasts and plateaus using pie tin/dinner plate as example of
plateau and coastal region
relationship and closeness of Africa to Europe and Middle
East; Europeans in North Africa, Egypt, Middle East
isolation in some parts of Africa

Divide the class into groups and divide the map into sections
or countries and allow each group to fill in a particular
region.

Expanded activity:
Have each student bring in a quarter cup of flour and a
quarter cup of salt from home. Using the accumulated flour
and salt, have students make a salt contour map of Africa.
When it dries, they can paint and label major land forms.
Salt map: 1 cup flour   mix all ingredients
           1 cup salt   mixture can be used as
           ½ cup water   modeling clay

6. Exploring West Africa

when: one period

what:

how: Divide the class into groups. Each group has been given the
       opportunity to explore a West African country. Each group
       must plan their trip from a port or major city and travel
       across the country. As explorers they must keep a detailed
       record of the trip including land forms, weather, climate,
       vegetation, animal life, etc. Examples of trips:

       Bamako to Timbuktu in Mali

       Accra to Tamale in Ghana

       Lagos to Kano in Nigeria

       Conakry to Kankan in Guinea

       Douala to Garoua in Cameroon

       Fort Lamy to Largeau in Chad

       Example of report:

       June 1:   Disembarked at Lagos. Large city. Water unsafe

                 for drinking. Streets unsafe for walking.

                 Temperature in 90°s, high humidity, heavy late

                 afternoon rain. Official language English, but

                 most speak regional language.

       June 2:   Left Lagos to travel north. Temperature still

                 90°s with high humidity. Tropical rain forest

                 country.
       . . . .

       June 7:   Crossed Niger river at town of Jebba. Temperature

                 still high, humidity less. Country has changed

                 from rain forest to savannah.
       . . . .

       June 31: Reach Kano, city of mud-walled compounds. Dry and

                 brown. Edge of Sahara Desert lies to the north.

Specific Objective: Identify the effect of geographic factors on people and cultures.

7. A Multi-Media Picture of the Culture

   when: special projects, continuous

   what: art supplies

   how: One of the better ways to achieve some feeling for a different culture is to develop a multi-media picture of that culture. Multi-media in this activity include:

   slides   sandtable and salt map
   bulletin boards   picture
   flannelboards   diagrams, charts, and graphs
   mobiles   posters and collages
   dioramas

   (1) Offer students an opportunity to select one of the multi-media to construct either as individuals or in groups as their means of "getting into the culture."

   (2) Identify a particular day to be called "West Africa Day" or "Middle East Day," etc., when all of the media is to be displayed in a social studies fair setting. Invite other classes to see the cultural fair. Be sure the students who constructed the project are able to explain the meaning of their media.

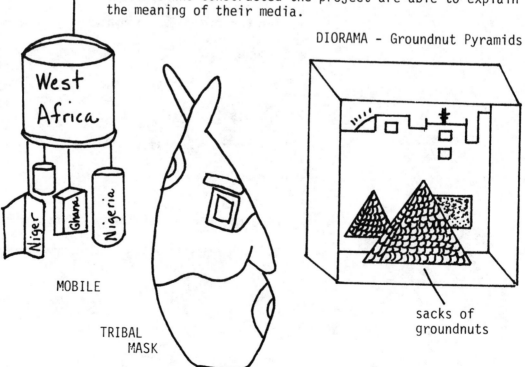

DIORAMA - Groundnut Pyramids

West Africa

Niger   Ghana   Nigeria

MOBILE

TRIBAL MASK

sacks of groundnuts

8. The Encroaching Sahara

    when: three periods

    what: story paragraph below, resource materials

    how: (1) Have students read paragraph below and perhaps some re-
                source materials that pertain to the region of West
                Africa.

            (2) Hold class discussion. Include:

                (a) geography of area

                (b) way people live

                (c) problems faced by expanding desert and improved
                    standard of living

                (d) possible alternatives for inhabitants

                (e) future predictions for area

    Jusif Tanko is a thirteen-year-old Nigerian boy. He lives in a
compound with his family near Katsina in northern Nigeria. Jusif's
family has always been able to grow enough yams and peppers to feed
themselves and to sell in the market. But in the last few years the
amount of land they could work has been shrinking. As the standard
of living improves for Jusif Tanko's family, more children live and
the family grows in number. The family needs more firewood so more
trees are cut; they own more goats which eat all of the grass at a
faster rate. As the land is stripped in this way, the Sahara Desert
advances and takes over the land. The slowing advancing Sahara is
destroying the land of the Tanko family. There is little rain and
in the winter the harmattan winds blow across the desert carrying
sand further south each year. Soon Jusif Tanko's family will be
forced from their land.

Specific Objective: Identify characteristics of a culture.

9. Concept Wheel

when: one period

what: wheel diagram

how: The following is a method to help students understand events, trends, and ideas, and their implications and consequences.

Place anything you want to understand (event, trend, idea) in the middle of a small circle in the middle of a paper. Draw lines spoke-like out from your circle. At the end of the lines write what goes with it--its implications, consequences, associations, and such. If you wish, you can then run out consequences of the consequences and so forth. This gives an orientation to the understanding you generate from your original idea in the middle of the circle. For example:

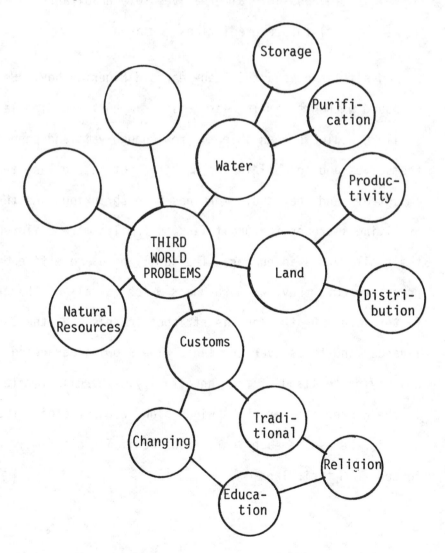

10. <u>Building a Culture</u>

   when: one period

   what: Identifying what is common to all cultures. To show how the
          common elements are related.

   how: Using what is common to all cultures, a form is built using
          triangles to show how characteristics are related. May make
          a free-form figure by placing triangles any way they fit or
          may make a specific figure. For example:

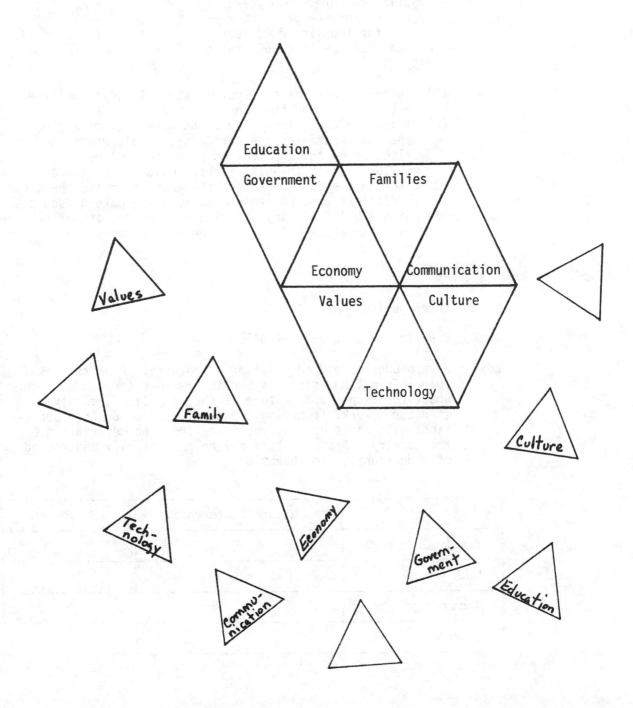

11. <u>Discovery--Culture</u>

   when: one period

   what: Artifacts or some means of learning about artifacts such as
           pictures or descriptions of a past or present-day culture un-
           known to students. Artifacts could cover long time period
           and if so they should be stated so. For example:

           pictures of Chinese culture covering all or part of 5000
              years
           Egyptian culture, 4000 years
           Japanese, for the past 200 years
           India, for the last 2000 years
           Africa, for the past 1500 years
           etc.

   how: (1) Teacher should scatter (put in several locations) the
               artifacts around the room.
           (2) Divide the class into groups and have them move around
               the room examining the artifacts and discussing and re-
               flecting on the growth (and possible decline) of the
               culture. All students' ideas should be considered.
           (3) Disclose the culture to the students after they have had
               sufficient time to study artifacts and make deductions.
               Give a brief history of culture. Compare actual culture
               with the students' speculation of artifacts.

12. <u>Ils-o-way</u>[4]

   when: three periods

   what: description of country (following)

   how: Have students read description of country. From this avail-
           able information, students should try to determine as much
           about the people and culture as they can (i.e., family
           structure, work, technology, future, etc.). Back up deduc-
           tions with facts or what you infer from the description of
           the country. A small chart may help to clarify understanding
           of deductions.   For example:

	Cultural inference	Evidence
Family Structure		
Work		
Technology		
Future		

Ils-o-way Culture

Geography:

A cold country with a short summer growing season. Surrounded on three sides by water. Low coastal area changes abruptly to hills which merge eventually with the mountains on its fourth side.

Rainfall is moderate in the summer but the winter snows drift many feet high.

The country is about the size of Arizona and has a population of about three million people, and has remained this size for the past thirty years.

The natural resources are fish and off-shore oil. There is some trade in furs and wood carving.

Effects of Geography:

Most people make a living that is in some way connected with the sea:

    fishing 42%
    ship building and trade 15%
    processing fish 9%
    off-shore oil rig 12%
    other 20%
    unemployed 2%

Housing: stone with some wood

Clothing: much use is made of animal skins for their warmth in the bitter winter cold.

Off-shore drilling has caused fishing fleets to go farther for their catch. Major harbor nearest off-shore drilling has been widened and improved.

Most people live along the coast in the major cities. There are some families who farm the coastal plains in summer and hunt and trap in the winter. Their numbers remain fairly constant. The population of the towns has begun a slow growth in the area of the off-shore oil drilling.

Goals:

Raise the standard of living for all citizens.

Become self-sufficient and independent and remain somewhat isolated from the rest of the world, for citizens do not want to experience the social change of modern industrial nations.

13. Assessing the Future of Other Countries

   when: one period

   what: information of Ils-o-way from previous activity, chart

   how: (1) Record the natural resources, goals, and the consequences
            of Ils-o-way on the chart below. Seeing the information
            on the chart makes it easy to hold a class discussion on
            following questions:

            (a) Name the country's assets and natural resources.
            (b) What are the future goals of the country?
            (c) Suppose the country were able to reach its ideal
                goal, how would that change the country?

         (2) Pick two contrasting countries. Chart them the same way.
             For example, compare Iran or Nigeria with Ils-o-way.
             How do they differ, how are they alike?

Natural resource and assets	Goals	Consequences
fish oil fur wood carving	Become independent and self-sufficient. Raise standard of living.	Stay about the same as they have been over the past 400 years.

Specific Objective: Identify the similarities and differences in different
                     cultures.

14. Proverbs[5]

   when: two periods

   what: proverbs and sayings (following)

   how: Almost every culture has "sayings" that express beliefs or
         customs of that culture. Often sayings are similar from one
         culture to another.
         (1) Have students examine the following sayings.
         (2) Have students pick African sayings that have the same
             meaning as a saying from another country. Is there a
             reason why the phrasing is different?
         (3) Have students pick out the African sayings that have no
             similar saying in another culture. Explain possible
             reasons.

By the time the fool has learned   When the horse has been stolen,
the game the players have dispersed.   the fool shuts the stable.
                      (Ashanti)   (French)

Death does not sound a trumpet.
          (Congo)

Death does not blow a trumpet.
          (Danish)

Rain does not fall on one roof
alone.   (Cameroon)

When it rains, it rains on all
alike.   (British)

There is no medicine to cure
hatred.   (Ashanti)

Hate knows no age but death.
          (British)

No matter how long the night, the
day is sure to come. (Congo)

It's always darkest before the
dawn.   (American)

Knowledge is always better than
riches.   (Ashanti)

A learned man has always riches
in himself.   (Latin)

When you follow the path of your
father, you learn to walk like him.
          (Ashanti)

Like father, like son.
          (Latin)

One camel does not make fun of the
other camel's hump.   (Guinea)

The pot does not call the kettle
black.   (British)

One falsehood spoils a thousand truths. (Ashanti)

It is the calm and silent water that drowns a man. (Ashanti)

Wood already touched by fire is not hard to set alight. (Ashanti)

If you are in hiding, don't light a fire. (Ashanti)

The ruin of a nation begins in the homes of its people. (Ashanti)

If the palm of the hand itches, it signifies the coming of great luck.
(Basutoland)

She is like a road--pretty but crooked. (Cameroon)

You do not teach the paths of the forest to an old gorilla. (Congo)

Two birds disputed about a kernel, when a third swooped down and carried
it off. (Congo)

A close friend can become a close enemy. (Ethiopia)

One who recovers from a sickness forgets about God. (Ethiopia)

Unless you call out, who will open the door? (Ethiopia)

When spider webs unite, they can tie up a lion. (Ethiopia)

You cannot build a house from last year's summer. (Ethiopia)

A blade won't cut another blade; a cheat won't cheat another cheat.
(Ethiopia)

Where there is no shame, there is no honor. (Ethiopia)

If there is no elephant in the jungle, the buffalo would be a great
animal. (Ghana)

Knowledge is like a garden: if it is not cultivated, it cannot be harvested. (Guinea)

After a foolish deed comes remorse. (Kenya)

He who is unable to dance says that the yard is stony. (Kenya)

15. <u>Categorizing Cultures</u>

> when: one period
>
> what: pictures from any source representing shelters, food, clothes, family, law, etc., in many cultures
>
> how: (1) Divide class into groups and distribute pictures.
> (2) Groups should separate pictures into categories such as shelter, food, clothes, family, law, etc., and further separate them as to whether they are representative of the past, present, or future.
> (3) Hold class discussion on results of group categorizing and observed differences between cultures.

16. <u>Identifying Culture</u>

> when: one week
>
> what: pictures of shelters, pictures of environment, designated locations, resource materials as needed.
>
> how: (1) Show students pictures of different types of shelter, preferably from a wide variety of cultures. Shelter is basic to survival. Many factors influence shelter such as environment, technology, money, etc. Have students determine where they would find these various shelters and why. Help them draw up generalizations about shelter.
>
> (2) Show students pictures of environment without shelter. Using generalization findings, have students speculate about what type of shelter would fit the environment.
>
> (3) Expand the exercise: Give students locations by longitude and latitude. Have them locate position on globe and determine what kind of shelter would be found there on the basis of research on climate, resources, land forms, etc.
>
> > Activities: construct models of shelters
> > paint mural depicting shelter and environment
> > research paper on shelter
> > invite architects or builders to visit class
> > forecast future shelter designs

Specific Objective: Identify how cultures and societies are interdependent
and interrelated.

17. Interdependence or Isolation

when: one period

what: review of regions previously studied

how: Most developed and developing countries are economically
dependent on one another to some extent. Have students come
up with examples from countries studied. Record examples on
the board. Have students answer the following questions:
(a) Are there any countries that are totally independent?
Name country and location.
(b) Are there countries that could maintain existence if
they were isolated? Explain.
(c) What are the countries that might quickly perish if
isolated? Explain.
(d) Does a higher standard of living mean a more complex
interdependence with other nations?
(e) How would your life be different if the United States
were cut off and isolated from the rest of the world?

B. Purpose: Develop skills necessary to process information

Specific Objective: Identify and practice writing the four different types
of questions.

1. Questioning Skills--Seventh Grade

when: two periods

what: practice checklist, practice writing form, textbook

how: Seventh grade questioning skills is a continuation of activities and materials started in the fourth grade. In grades
four and five categories of different levels of questions
were limited to open and closed. In the sixth grade the two
categories were extended to include speculation and evaluation
as levels of open questions and memory and description as
closed level questions. If there are questions about the
differences between the different levels of questions, see
fourth, fifth, and sixth grade materials on questioning. The
reason for emphasis on questioning skills is to encourage a
variety of levels of thinking in the classroom. Memory,
description, speculation, and evaluation are roughly the
lowest to the highest levels of thinking, all of which should
be used by both teachers and students. Have students mark
the following questions to check their mastery.

Checklist

Mark the questions with their appropriate letters: M for memory,
D for description, S for speculation, and E for evaluation.

__M__	1.	What is the population of Nigeria?
__D__	2.	Compare Nigeria with Niger.
__S__	3.	What would you predict about the future of Nigeria?
__E__	4.	Would you want to live in Nigeria?
__D__	5.	Explain how the Niger River affects Nigeria's economy.
__M__	6.	Name the largest city in Nigeria.
__D__	7.	Describe where you find the Jos highland in Nigeria.
__M__	8.	Identify Nigeria's major cash export.
__E__	9.	Do you think Nigeria is a powerful African nation?
__S__	10.	How might Nigeria improve its form of government?

If students have difficulty identifying the type of questions
in the above checklist, use the sixth grade materials on
questioning as a review. Have students practice writing the
four levels of questions at least twice over the social
studies topic the class is studying.

open
questions

1. Speculation: (for example) What would happen to Nigeria
    if its oil reserves ran out?

2. Evaluation: (for example) What, in your opinion, keeps
    Nigeria as a third world nation?

closed
questions

3. Memory: (for example) What is the name of the largest
    city in the north of Nigeria?

4. Description: (for example) Describe Nigerians' trans-
    portation problems.

open
questions

1. Speculation: _____

    _____

2. Evaluation: _____

    _____

3. Memory: _____

closed
questions

    _____

4. Description: _____

    _____

Follow-up activities:
   (a) As a follow-up activity, students should examine their
       social studies text and other supplementary materials
       for examples of the four levels of questions. Ques-
       tions are usually found at the end of each chapter.
   (b) Be sure when evaluating to include all four levels of
       questions. The four levels will assume importance if
       students find they are used in testing.

Specific Objective: Identify the criteria for good oral and written reports.

   2.   Oral Report Checklist and Teacher Evaluation

        when: time length of report determined by teacher

        what: oral report checklist

        how: (1) Students must choose topic related to what class is
                    studying.
                (2) Students must outline report and get teacher's approval
                    of outline. Students should check out anything they do
                    not understand at this time with teacher.
                (3) Students must use more than one source to obtain informa-
                    tion from more than one point of view.
                (4) Teacher should give copy of oral report form to students
                    so they can use it as a guide. Teacher will use form to
                    evaluate student while he/she is giving report and then
                    will give checklist to student after report.

Oral Report Checklist			
student's name	well done	satisfactory	needs attention
1. Approved outline			
2. Write subject on board			
3. Face class, speak slowly			
4. Identify sources			
5. State time and place of subject			
6. Relate subject to what class is studying			
7. Give report from notes (no reading)			
8. Write difficult names on board or on overhead			
9. Summarize			
10. Be ready for class questions			
11. Comments:			

3. Oral Report Evaluation Form for Students

when: at time of oral reports

what: oral report form for students

how: Students are encouraged to evaluate performance of other
       students presenting oral reports. The following form will
       allow students to evaluate an oral report and add comments.
       Have students fill out form either during or after report.

Oral Report Evaluation Form for Students					
student giving report					
evaluator	very weak	fair	good	very good	superior
1. Introduction was interesting.					
2. Student related topic to what we are studying in class.					
3. Student was able to make report interesting with personal opinions yet stuck basically to facts.					
4. Student summarized briefly.					
Comments:					

4. Papers Evaluation

when: one period or at end of writing assignment

what: evaluation form

how: This form may be used as an exercise in evaluating an essay
       selected by teacher or student may use it to self-evaluate
       his/her own paper and then check evaluation with teacher.

Papers Evaluation			
student's name		title of paper	
Content:	excellent	good	suggestions for improvement
1. Sources: number selected and quality			
2. Thoroughness of investigation			
3. Exactness of data			
4. Subject covered to extent required			
Style:			
5. Form: table of contents footnotes bibliography titles and subtitles			
6. Spelling and punctuation			
7. Student's expression of content			
8. Proofread			

Specific Objective: Identify propaganda techniques with which people attempt to influence others.

5. Propaganda Skills--Seventh Grade

  when: two days

  what: materials included

  how: We are persuaded to particular points of view and that is what propaganda is all about. Propaganda is a means by which people are influenced to make choices. In a world where media is used so frequently to teach and preach, the techniques used by that media to influence should, for the sake of the individual, be identified and understood. Activities and materials on propaganda techniques were identified in Chapter Fifth Grade and Chapter Sixth Grade. Chapter Seventh Grade will conclude the introductory activities on the propaganda techniques. Have students practice on identifying techniques studied in fifth and sixth grade as a check on their level of mastery.

Instructions: Match the propaganda techniques by writing the letter beside the name of that technique on the line by the sentence which best illustrates that technique.

__a__ 1. I call Senator Jones a liar.

__b__ 2. All politicians are crooks.

__c__ 3. You know my grandfather was a good man, so you can trust me.

__f__ 4. All the kids have one, why can't I have one, too?

__d__ 5. This is Billy Carter talking, "Drink this, it's good."

__e__ 6. "You all know me, I'm just one of the folks."

__g__ 7. Buy this used car. Look at all the wonderful things it's got, good tires, no rust, and a radio.

__h__ 8. I am the richest person in the world because I think I am.

__j__ 9. "Coke adds life."

__i__ 10. The reason I failed the test was because a black cat crossed my path.

__k__ 11. We just don't like those people, after all they are newcomers.

__l__ 12. This is really a great, wonderful product.

__m__ 13. He said, "All girls could be beautiful but many don't try." You said he said, "Most girls don't try to be beautiful."

a. name calling

b. glittering generalities

c. transfer

d. testimonial

e. plain folks

f. bandwagon

g. card stacking

h. wishful thinking

i. oversimplification

j. slogans

k. prejudice

l. vagueness

m. out of context

(1) Hand out new definitions to class and discuss with students these common forms of propaganda.
(2) Have students think of examples from TV, etc. and put them on board.
(3) Have each student bring to class at least two different propaganda techniques to share with class. May display these on bulletin board.

(4) Have each student prepare one original propaganda example using one of the four techniques learned during this activity. The example may be whatever they wish, i.e., TV, magazine ads, etc.

(5) Check students' knowledge with matching questions (see below).

Propaganda Techniques:

1. <u>Arousing feelings</u>: the attempt to persuade others for or against a particular point of view by appeal to emotion.

> "This is our big rival, so go to the game and cheer on the team." "This is the big game for our dear beloved school."

2. <u>Appeal to rank and status</u>: relating rank or status of the person or event to the object or idea which is intended to persuade.

> "The club president, who is a wealthy man, thinks this way, perhaps you should." "The greatest golfer in the world drives this make of car, perhaps you also deserve that elegance."

3. <u>Sales promotion</u>: an appeal is made on the grounds that a sale on items will save you money. The sale may or may not be real, comparative buying is the only way to know if savings are real.

> "Sale, for two days only: all items one-third off." "You'll never save more than you will right now." "Buy now, save now."

4. <u>Repetition</u>: the technique calls for repeating the idea over and over until the name or product is familiar and will be recognized at the appropriate time.

> "Vote for George. George will get the job done. George needs your support. George is the one."
> "Double your pleasure, double your fun, with double good, double good, Doublemint Gum."

Instructions: Write the letter for the appropriate propaganda technique on the line next to the most appropriate sentence.

_____ 1. All the important people have one.

_____ 2. This is our annual white sale.

_____ 3. Think pink, Dad; get pink, Dad; be pink, Dad.

_____ 4. The President has it now, do you want it too?

_____ 5. Our lives are at stake, we have to fight pollution.

a. arousing feelings

b. appeal to rank or status

c. sale promotion

d. repetition

C. Purpose: Develop the skill to examine <u>values</u> and beliefs

Specific Objective: Identify values of culture other than one's own.

1. <u>Contrasting Cultural Values</u>

when: one period

what:

how: Students will examine values of a non-west culture at the end of the study unit on that non-west culture. Divide students into groups. Have groups list values that mattered to the people during the time period studied. Compare and contrast group lists.

	JAPAN	COMMUNIST CHINA	INDIA	NIGERIA
1. EDUCATION				
2. AUTHORITY				
3. FAMILY				
4. RELIGION				
5. ETC.				

2. <u>Foreign Film Festival</u>

when: one or two periods depending on length of film

what: foreign film or film highlighting another culture

how: Show foreign film. Hold class discussion on following questions or have students answer them individually.

(a) What action did main character take?

(b) What prompted the main character to take action?

(c) What values would you imagine the main character believed in?

(d) If you (student) had been in the same situation, how would you have acted?

(e) What values would prompt you to act the way you would?

(f) Compare values and actions of main character to those of students.

3. Identifying Current Global Values

when: two periods

what: newspaper or magazine reports on a country or group of
       countries selected by teacher. For example:

TEHRAN, IRAN--Many thousands of
Moslems protested against the
United States President when
they marched through the streets
of Tehran. The Moslems were
demonstrating their objection to
Western-style democratic reforms
such as extending voting rights,
holding democratic elections and
supporting a representative
legislature. The protesting Moslems favor a return to strict
Islamic rule.

FARNBOROUGH, ENGLAND--Britain's
"air and space bazaar," which is
held every two years, opened
Monday with many fewer war planes
from the United States and none
from Russia. Emphasis is on
products manufactured in Third
World countries and on cooperation between nations on earth
and in space.

how: Examine headlines and major points of stories. What values
      are inferred? Using sample news stories above, for example:

Values Inferred	Support for Inference
Democratic values (President)	Proposed reforms
Islamic values (protestors)	Protests in the streets
Cooperation	Third World products
Peaceful use of space and land	Fewer military planes

Specific Objective: Identify how the values of national leaders affect
                     decisions in a different time and place.

4. Time Machine

when: one period

what: chart

how: Imagine that the following people have been carried through
      space and, in some cases, time. Harry Truman finds himself
      in the Germany of Adolf Hitler. He is to take the place of
      Hitler in 1932. Ghandi is to replace Churchill. Socrates is
      to replace Mao Tse-Tung in China. Attila the Hun is declared
      Pope, and the Pope is the Soviet Premier in the Kremlin. Idi
      Amin is King of the Netherlands; the list, of course, is
      endless. What would be the reaction of the above people?
      What problems would these men face if they tried to govern
      using the methods they normally practice? Use the following
      chart:

```
========================================================
```
What are the consequences of an individual applying his values and methods
in the times to which he is transported?

Name	Values & Methods	Location to which transported	Time to which transported	Consequences
Truman		Germany	1932	
Ghandi		England	1940	
Socrates		China	1977	
Attila the Hun		Italy	1975	
Pope John Paul II		Russia	1978	
Idi Amin		Netherlands	1976	

```
========================================================
```

Specific Objective: Identify values from what selected men and women say
about each other.

5. **What is Said About Women and Thought About Men**

when: one period

what: materials included

how: Every culture has values of some kind. Often the same values
are held by different cultures and often values are passed
from one generation to the next in the form of short sayings.
Below are some things that have been said about men and women.
Examine each example: Do we still hold these values?
Explain.

WOMAN

"Take my word for it, the silliest woman can manage a clever man, but it
needs a very clever woman to manage a fool."   Kipling

"Choose in marriage only a woman whom you would choose as a friend if she
were a man."   Joubert

"I will not say that women have no character; rather, they have a new one
every day."   Heine

Women better understand spending a fortune than making one." Balzac

"Being a woman is a terribly difficult trade, since it consists princi-
pally of dealing with men."   Conrad

"I would gladly raise my voice in praise of women, only they won't let me raise my voice."
                                                                    Winkle

"Talk to women as much as you can. This is the best school. This is the way to gain fluency, because you need not care what you say, and had better not be sensible."
                                                                    Disraeli

"When God saw how faulty was man He tried again and made woman. As to why He then stopped there are two opinions. One of them is woman's."
                                                                    De Gourmont

MAN

He who thinks that he never was a fool is a fool now.

Man is the only animal that can be skinned more than once.

A man who will never change his mind, may not have any mind to change.

A man is judged by the company he keeps.

A man is valued according to his own estimate of himself.

Men talk wisely but live foolishly.

He who hears forgets, he who sees remembers, he who does learns.

A lazy boy and a warm bed are difficult to part.

6. Male vs. Female

    when: two periods

    what: telephone book yellow pages (several copies)

    how: The "yellow pages" usually have groups/individuals in a like
           occupation listed under the name of that occupation. Pick
           several of these categories in advance, e.g., physicians, den-
           tists, lawyers, accountants, veterinarians, optometrists, in-
           surance agents.
           (1) Divide students into groups and give each several categor-
               ies.
           (2) Have them tally the number of men and the number of women
               in each category and identify possible reasons for the
               results.
           (3) Have groups list tallies on chart on board and briefly
               tell class why they believe there is a predominance of
               males or females in the field. Does the class agree?
           (4) List on the board a number of occupations that have tradi-
               tionally been a male or female job (nurse, fireman, tele-
               phone installer, teacher, construction worker, repairman).
               Hold a class discussion on why the jobs have been "male"
               or "female" and whether they will be in the future. Do
               children know of any examples of people in untraditional
               roles?

D.   Purpose: Apply knowledge through active <u>participation</u>

Specific Objective: Identify the relationship between quality and quantity
of work and grade achievement.

1.   <u>Teacher-Student Contracts</u>

when: recurring

what: contract form

how: Student participates by entering into a contract with teacher.

CONTRACT

_____ is contracting for a grade of _____ .
(student's name)

_____ may contract for a higher grade at any
(student's name)   time but never for a lower grade.

_____ (Twenty points will be subtracted for each
(due date)   day work is overdue.)

_____   _____
(teacher's name)   (date)

Activities selected from list below to fulfill contract obligations:

Activity selected (describe)   possible points   grade

Contract Activities for Africa
(example)
possible points
 50 1. Prepare a chart naming countries in Africa and date they won inde-
         pendence. Include whether independence was gained peacefully or
         with violence.
 30 2. Do map of colonial Africa in 1920's.
100 3. Write essay on slave trade in West Africa.
100 4. Write essay on early native government including powers of sultans
         and emirs in Nigeria.
 60 5. Make a chart of resources of West Africa that attracted foreign
         nations.
 50 6. Write essay on how Great Britain could claim Gold Coast and force
         Africans to follow their rule.
 75 7. Read text _____ pages _____ to _____ .
         Answer questions numbers _____ on page _____ .
 75 8. Read text _____ pages _____ to _____ .
         Answer questions numbers _____ on page _____ .
 75 9. Read text _____ pages _____ to _____ .
         Answer questions numbers _____ on page _____ .
200 10. Do a biography of an African dictator. Include bibliography.
 90 11. Make a chart of ten African tribes giving name, way of life, and
         location.
 60 12. Make a chart of wildlife native to West Africa.

<u>25</u> 13. Prepare native African food and serve to class.
<u>30</u> 14. Summarize (one page) movie seen in class.
<u>100</u> 15. Write essay on Moslem religion and customs.
<u>50</u> 16. Make chart with drawings of native shelter in various parts of Africa.
<u>?</u> 17. Student-identified activity with teacher approval. Teacher sets possible points.

_____ points = A _____ points = B _____ points = C

Specific Objective: Student and teacher identify their roles in evaluating achievement.

   2. <u>Student-Teacher Activity Evaluation</u>

      when: three periods

      what: joint evaluation form

      how: This activity is one way to involve students in self-evalua-tion. How to use:
         (1) Pass out form and have students complete I and II before activity is begun.
         (2) Have students complete III, IV, V, and VI after activity is finished, and turn it in to teacher.
         (3) Teacher completes VII and gives it back to student, <u>OR</u> teacher and student complete VII together during a con-ference.

Student-Teacher Activity Evaluation

_____
   (student's name)

   I. Issue being studied _____

      _____

  II. My activity _____

      _____

 III. What I have accomplished specifically _____

      _____

      _____

      _____

IV. Research materials used:

   titles   authors

   _____   _____

   _____   _____

   _____   _____

   _____   _____

V. What I learned _____

   _____

VI. Student's self-evaluation:

   I deserve the following grade _____ because _____

   _____

   My suggestions for changes in this activity: _____

   _____

   _____

VII. Teacher's Evaluation: Grade _____

   Ranking: from 4 representing
   excellent to 0 representing   Comments: _____
   poor work.

                                      _____
   4 3 2 1 0 class work
   4 3 2 1 0 self-control   _____
   4 3 2 1 0 use of time
   4 3 2 1 0 research   _____
   4 3 2 1 0 cooperation
                   with others   _____

3. Unit Evaluation: Student Self-Checklist

   when: one period

   what: checklist form

   how: At the end of a unit of study, have each student fill out the
          self-checklist. This activity will help student to evaluate
          his/her own participation and provide the teacher with neces-
          sary feedback from the student.

Unit Evaluation: Student Self-Checklist

Name _____ Unit Title _____

Date _____

1. I understood the purpose of the unit . . .
    (check those words that best represent your feelings)
    ____ right from the start of the unit
    ____ not during any part of the unit
    ____ got some understanding, but not much
    ____ confused most of the time
    ____ knew what I was doing
    ____ don't really know what the unit was all about
    ____ just never made sense to me
    ____ (your own words) _____

2. I spent most of my time during the unit . . .
    (check those words that best represent your feelings)
    ____ reading
    ____ talking
    ____ listening
    ____ doing very little
    ____ working hard most of the time
    ____ playing around
    ____ with a small group project
    ____ learning something
    ____ learning a lot of things
    ____ just kind of messing around
    ____ (your own words) _____

3. The best part of the unit for me was . . .
    (check those words that best represent your feelings)
    ____ working with others
    ____ working by myself
    ____ finding resources
    ____ just sitting around
    ____ the class presentations
    ____ the small groups
    ____ talking with the teacher
    ____ learning things that were important to me
    ____ (your own words) _____

4. If I had a chance to do the unit over I would . . .
    (check those words that best represent your feelings)
    ____ work a little harder
    ____ work about the same
    ____ discourage the teacher from teaching this unit
    ____ read more
    ____ write more
    ____ play around more
    ____ participate in small groups more
    ____ try to get more out of the unit
    ____ (your own words) _____

4. <u>Student-Teacher Group Procedures Evaluation</u>

when: one period

what:

how: (1) Divide students into groups of four or five. Leave
            enough students so each group has an "observer."

      (2) Observers must listen to statements made by group members
            and categorize them:

            (a) statements related to activity: "Explain what you
                  mean."
            (b) positive statements: "Good idea!"
            (c) negative statements: "That's dumb!"

            Observers can just make a checklist and mark it off as
            they listen to the group. For example:

            +---+
            | |
            | a: statements related to activity √√√ |
            | |
            | b: positive statements   √√√√√ |
            | |
            | c: negative statements   √√ |
            | |
            +---+

            If possible, observers might want to write some statements
            down if they have time.

      (3) Give groups a topic to discuss. For example:

                  providing more electrical power for African nations

                  using the natural resources of African nations

                  human rights in African nations

                  selling arms to African nations

      (4) After a short group discussion, have observers report on
            their own checklist or on combined checklists to the
            teacher and then to the class.

      (5) Discuss checklists with class, stressing how related
            statements and positive statements achieve more than
            negative statements.

      (6) Let each group give brief report on their discussion.

5. Student Evaluation of Committee Work

    when: one period

    what: evaluation form

    how: At the end of committee or group work, have each student
           evaluate how well his/her own committee functioned. The
           form will help students summarize their participation and
           provide teacher with necessary feedback.

Student Evaluation of Committee Work					
Check the box that tells how the committee worked.					
Evaluation Sentence	most all the time	frequently	above average	not often	did not do it
1. The committee members contributed ideas and suggestions.					
2. The committee shared materials.					
3. The committee did the job assigned to it.					
4. The committee members listened courteously when others were talking.					
5. The committee works well together.					
6. This committee should work together again.					

6. Student Evaluation of His/Her Group Participation

    when: one period

    what: evaluation form

    how: At the end of group work, have each student evaluate his/her
           participation as a member of the group. This form will help
           students identify their own particular contribution to the
           group effort. Suggest these forms be used by students at
           least once a week, collected over the period of the grouping,
           and passed back to student for analysis and evaluation at the
           end of a marking period.

```
+------------------------------------------------------------------+
|          Student Evaluation of His/Her Group Participation        |
|   name _____  date _____  |
|   Place check over the word that best expresses your feelings.    |
|                                                                    |
|   1.  The group discussion helped me learn                        |
|   |____|____|____|____|____|____|____|____|____|____|             |
|      VERY MUCH   QUITE A BIT   AVERAGE    LITTLE    NOT AT ALL     |
|                                                                    |
|   2.  My participation was                                        |
|   |____|____|____|____|____|____|____|____|____|____|             |
|      VERY GOOD    GOOD    AVERAGE   NOT VERY GOOD   BAD            |
|                                                                    |
|   3.  The group as a whole was                                    |
|   |____|____|____|____|____|____|____|____|____|____|             |
|      EXCELLENT   GOOD    AVERAGE   NOT VERY GOOD    BAD            |
|                                                                    |
|   4.  In summary my experience in the group today was             |
|   |____|____|____|____|____|____|____|____|____|____|             |
|      VERY      PLEASANT   AVERAGE   UNPLEASANT   QUITE            |
|      ENJOYABLE                                   UNPLEASANT       |
|                                                                    |
|   5.  Comment:                                                    |
+------------------------------------------------------------------+
```

Notes

[1] Indiana Department of Public Instruction. 1978 Indiana textbook adoption categories for social studies. Indianapolis: Author, 1978, p. 3.

[2] Barth, J. L., & Shermis, S. S. Teaching social studies to gifted and talented students. Indianapolis: Indiana Department of Public Instruction, p. 33.

[3] Ibid., p. 33.

[4] Ibid., p. 35.

[5] Ibid., p. 37.

INTEREST FORM

You have just completed the Chapter Seventh Grade. In an effort to have you identify activities and materials that seem most promising at this grade level to you, please fill out the following interest form.

Instructions:

Identify two activities from this chapter. Name the activities and briefly describe why these particular activities are of interest to you.

ACTIVITY 1

ACTIVITY 2

NOTES

CHAPTER EIGHTH GRADE

ACTIVITIES AND MATERIALS FOR EIGHTH GRADE

CHAPTER EIGHTH GRADE

Organization of the Chapter

Each chapter represents a particular grade level, in this case eighth grade. Each chapter consists of three parts: the first part is a brief discussion on courses, topics, and national trends in teaching eighth grade throughout the United States; the second part is an example of a state eighth grade program; the third part has activities and materials for the eighth grade categorized by the four objectives of teaching social studies--gaining knowledge, processing, valuing, and participating.

I. Topics Taught and National Trends
in Teaching Eighth Grade

Eighth grade social studies, much like the fifth grade, as distinct from other grade levels is "reserved" for American history. Again this did not just happen, it was planned as part of a fifth grade, eighth grade, and senior high American history cycle by the 1943 Committee on American History in the Schools and Colleges commonly known as the Wesley Committee. The Wesley Committee is important to the social studies curriculum because school systems by and large have followed the recommendation of the Committee. The Committee not only established the three cycles but also recommended appropriate historical periods and topics to be taught in each cycle. The fifth grade was to emphasize discovery, colonization, colonial period, becoming a nation, and the movement west, with in-depth study up to the 1850's followed by a rapid survey to the present. The intention was that history and geography were to be integrated into telling the story of the development of the North American continent in the seventeenth, eighteenth, and early part of the nineteenth centuries, with special emphasis on the United States and often Canada.

Eighth grade American history, according to the Wesley Committee, was to be concerned essentially with the nineteenth century with special emphasis upon the Constitution, development of the nation, sectionalism, slavery, Civil War, industrialization, immigration, and America's emergence as a world power. This was to be followed by a rapid survey of contemporary American history. The third and final cycle, senior high American history, offered usually in eleventh grade, was to emphasize the twentieth century, stressing the World Wars, economic problems, and social movements with at least one-third of the time devoted to today's contemporary problems. The general recommendation was that: (a) all three cycles (grades five, eight, eleven) should offer rapid surveys and (b) would emphasize a particular historical period. The intention of the recommendation was to discourage teachers from attempting to cover (in depth) all of American history in each cycle. Teachers who have attempted the in-depth approach from discovery to the present in one year found that the school year runs out somewhere around the Depression and the Second World War. If one assumes that the study of history was intended to help students identify appropriate lessons from the past to help understand contemporary events, then the study was not achieving the desired goal, because instruction rarely reached contemporary times. The course, in practice, remains a survey from discovery to modern times with little or no class time devoted to contemporary problems or to the application of historical understanding to real social problems. Hence the question: "Why do we [students] have to take history? What is it for?"

Course, Topics, and Themes Frequently Covered in Eighth Grade: "United States History"

Objectives of the Course

Students will identify significant historical events which led to the development of the nation's traditions and its territory. Will develop a critical (reflective) attitude when examining concepts such as freedom and

democracy. Will continue to develop skills in decision-making through an inquiry process.

Basic Content of the Course

A chronological survey of American history with special emphasis (perhaps
three-quarters of the time) on the nineteenth century. Such topics as European
origins, discovery, colonization, and independence are rapidly surveyed. In-
depth attention to fundamental documents (Declaration of Independence and Constitution) and topics: slavery, Civil War, Reconstruction, Industrialization,
and America as a world power. The final weeks of the course should emphasize
contemporary problems with special attention on using history (concepts,
generalizations) to understand the present and the future. Simply, what did
we learn from past experience about ourselves, about others, about the present,
and about the future?

Course, Topics, and Themes Frequently Covered in Eighth Grade:
"United States History and Government"

This course is not unlike "United States History." However, it is usually
part of a seventh-eighth grade block that seems to be finding favor in junior
high/middle schools. Emphasis in the seventh grade is on United States history
and in the eighth grade upon United States government. The seventh-eighth
grade block usually contains such units (in addition to history and government)
as law, career units with special emphasis on jobs and work, and future
studies. In some cases states mandate that state and local history be integrated into the American history course. Given the demands on the middle
school to cover additional topics such as those mentioned above, curriculum
committees are turning to greater coordination between seventh and eighth
grade social studies.

Trends in Teaching Eighth Grade Social Studies

1.   The middle school organization, sixth, seventh, and eighth grades, has helped teachers who are traditionally separated from each other to coordinate their programs. Given the pressures from the federal government to teach units on careers and consumer education, public interest groups such as economics education, law-related studies, multi-ethnic studies, economics education, and environmental studies, along with the traditional historical events and structures of government, have encouraged middle school teachers to consider coordinating their programs. It is perfectly obvious that no one teacher can cover all the topics above in one course.

2.   Curriculum planners will continue to follow the Wesley Committee recommendations. Emphasis will remain on nineteenth century history for eighth grade American history but will be modified by some of the special interests noted in the first trend.

3.   The American history course as taught in the three cycles will continue to be considered a capstone course, capstone in the sense that the course is a summarizing of social studies up to that cycle. As for example: fifth grade is the capstone for grades one through four summarizing self, family, school, neighborhood, community, region, and state, with the fifth grade American history course capstoning, summarizing the first five years of social studies. Eighth grade American history is the capstone for sixth and seventh grades, providing a content to which all world and global studies are related.

4.   Social studies teachers will probably continue to ignore efforts of the curriculum planners to limit eighth grade American history to an in-depth study of the nineteenth century and a rapid survey of the rest. In-depth ground covering of "all significant" events will continue to prevail even though that organization continues to receive considerable criticism from both teachers and students.

II. Illustrations of a State Eighth Grade Program

There is no <u>one</u> prescribed social studies program throughout the United States. However, one state's description of its eighth grade program will illustrate the content which the state expects to be taught. This illustration identifies a state's suggested social studies curriculum for the eighth grade.

> This is to be a general overview of American history with the emphasis on pre-twentieth century America. The course should examine the nature and development of forms of government and law, colonialism, democracy, revolution, land acquisition, immigration and assimilation, technological development and urbanization. A focus on the state's current development during the development of the United States will help students relate history to their own lives and location.[1]

III. Activities and Materials Categorized by
Gaining Knowledge, Processing, Valuing, and Participating

A common practice is to skip specific objectives which precede the activities, but in this case the objectives are extremely important for an objective in the eighth grade will be found in succeeding grades. The following activities and materials are part of a developmental curriculum organized to build citizenship skills from one grade level to another.

EIGHTH GRADE ACTIVITIES AND MATERIALS

A. Purpose: To <u>gain knowledge</u> about the human condition which includes past, present, and future

Specific Objective: Identify the geography of the United States, stressing westward expansion and sectionalism.

1. <u>Comparing and Inferring from Sectional Population</u>

   when: two periods

   what: population percentage figures for 1810, 1830, 1860; outline map of US

   how: (1) Have students divide the outline map into three sections: northeast, southeast, and west. Make sure students understand what states or territories are contained in each of the sections.

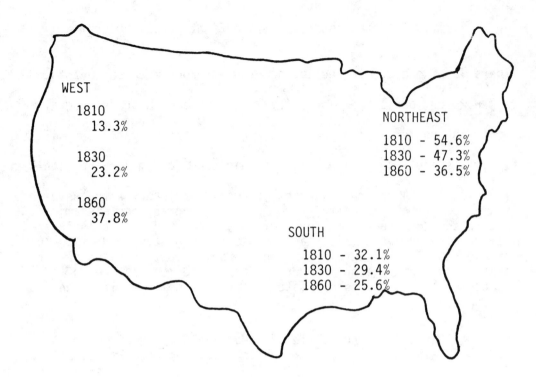

WEST

1810
13.3%

1830
23.2%

1860
37.8%

NORTHEAST

1810 - 54.6%
1830 - 47.3%
1860 - 36.5%

SOUTH

1810 - 32.1%
1830 - 29.4%
1860 - 25.6%

(2) In each section write the date and population percentage figures. Use a different color for each of the three sections.

(3) Have the students write questions on what they infer about population shifts from the figures on the map.

(a) Why did people move from one section to another?

(b) Suppose one of the sections wanted to secede from the Union, which section would have had the best chance to fight off the other two? Which section would have had the most difficulty?

(4) Use students' questions as basis for class discussion. Encourage the use of different levels of questions-- not only "What do the percentages say about population distribution" but also questions such as "What would one speculate about future distribution?" "Where might the population shift to in the twentieth century?"

2. Acquiring and Sectioning America

when: one week

what: large outline map of US (This can be done by throwing a transparency outline map onto a large sheet of paper and having students trace the outline and cut it out.) The map should have the outline of the following:

US of 1783
Louisiana Purchase of 1803
Texas Annexation in 1845

Oregon Territory in 1846
Mexican Cession in 1848
Gadsden Purchase in 1853

how: (1) Divide class into six groups.
      (2) Cut map into the six sections listed above and give each
          group a section.
      (3) Each group will cut its section into the states contained
          in its section. Divide the states among the members of
          the group. (Be aware that the sizes of the groups will
          have to vary according to the number of states in the
          section being researched.)
      (4) Students should research the following information for
          each state:

              when it became a state
              size and current population
              capital and major cities
              natural resources
              well-known land forms and rivers that run through
                state or border it
              unusual history

      (5) Starting with the first thirteen states, have each group
          tell about its states and put map together like jigsaw
          puzzle.

      Alternative: Forget about land purchases and acquisitions
      and just divide the states among the students and have them
      work on them individually.

(NOTE: Save completed map for display during Social Studies Fair;
        see last activity in this chapter.)

3. <u>Nineteenth Century in Review</u>

    when: two weeks or time established by teacher

    what: materials as needed

    how: (1) Students are going to produce a newspaper on the nine-
              teenth century. News magazines usually put out an issue
              at the end of each year called something like "Year in
              Review" or "Highlights of the Past Year." The students
              could name their paper along the same lines: "Nineteenth
              Century in Review" or "Highlights of the Nineteenth Cen-
              tury."
          (2) Divide class into groups (or each student could work
              individually). Each group will develop its own news-
              paper.
          (3) Have students look at index of local newspaper and go
              through the paper to get a feel for the various sections.
              For example: news stories, editorials, pictures, human
              interest stories, interviews, ads, cartoons, birth and
              death announcements, advice columns, women's fashions,
              and homemaking tips such as recipes.
          (4) Groups should develop their papers along the lines studied
              above, confining their news, of course, to the nineteenth
              century on such topics as the Monroe Doctrine, the Forty-

niners, Civil War, Gay 90's.
(5) Have groups compete and get someone in the school to judge the papers. Display all papers but give most prominent display to the one judged best.

(NOTE: Save newspapers for display during Social Studies Fair; see last activity in this chapter.)

4. Nineteenth Century Bingo

when: two periods

what: blank bingo cards (see Chapter Fifth Grade for example)

how: (1) Have each student write a question and answer for each square of the bingo card. Confine questions to nineteenth century.
(2) Have students write each question on a card and write the answer on a bingo card being sure to mark each space on both card and bingo card with square letter and number. For example: B,5 When did Civil War start? Square B,5 1960. N,15 Where was gold discovered in California? Square N,15 has Sutter's Mill.
(3) Teacher collects question cards from students and mixes them up. Collect bingo answer cards and pass them out making sure students do not have their own cards.
(4) Teacher reads square letter and number and then reads question. The student with the correct answer in the correct square puts a marker on the square.
(5) Winner is the first one to get a straight line completed across, down, or horizontal.

(NOTE: Save bingo cards and questions for display during Social Studies Fair; see last activity in this chapter.)

5. Eighteenth and Nineteenth Centuries Review of Eras

when: three periods

what: list of eras

ERAS	
a. Progressive Era	g. Age of Sectionalism
b. Age of World Power	h. Era of Good Feeling
c. Age of Imperialism	i. Federal Period
d. Gay Nineties	j. Era of Revolution
e. Period of Industrialism	k. Period of Salutory Neglect
f. Age of Manifest Destiny	

how: (1) American history has been divided into general areas. Give each student a list of eras.
(2) Each student must establish the years contained by each era (or this could be supplied by teacher) and one event that supports the title for each era and one event that seems to prove the title wrong.
(3) List eras and years covered by era on board. Under each era list supportive events chosen by students, then list events that seem to prove the title wrong. For example:

1815-1824 Era of Good Feeling

Support	Prove it wrong
1. East coast prospered	1. Frontier had hard times
2. Nationalism	2. Sectionalism

Count those with similar answers and put number beside event.
(4) Hold class discussion on whether the time period deserves the title it has or whether students think another name would be more appropriate.

Specific Objective: Identify cause and effect relationships.

6. Cause and Effect Concept Wheel

when: several periods

what: list of events, concept wheel (see next page)

how: Establishing cause and effect relationships is important because it helps to promote the notion that an event may be part of a number of causes. A cause is usually an event that contributes to or determines a particular effect. For example: the causes of the First World War, the cause for liberty, causes of the fall of the Roman Empire. Effect usually means the result of a cause or a set of causes. For example: causes are sectionalism, slavery, election of Lincoln; effect is the Civil War. A cause is Manifest Destiny and the effect is westward expansion.
(1) To illustrate that complex events have multiple causes and effects, have students consider the following events of the nineteenth and twentieth centuries, recalling cause and effect relationships of each:

Independence	Sectionalism	Industrialization
Confederation	The Great Compromises	Urbanization
Constitution	Civil War	Immigration
National Expansion	Reconstruction	World Power

(2) Have each student select one of the events listed above and construct a concept wheel visually demonstrating cause and effect relationships. For example, the Industrial Revolution:

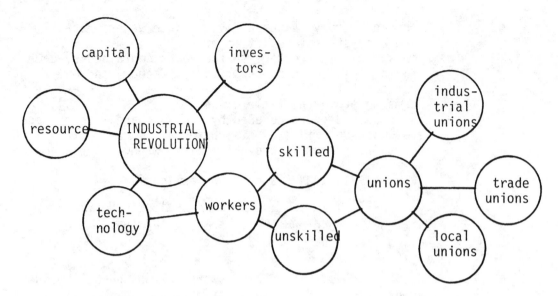

7.   Tracking Cause and Effect

     when: recurring

     what: construction paper

     how: (1) Draw four sets of train tracks, one above the other, on
                 large paper attached to wall or bulletin board. Mark
                 sections of rails off into years or decades or half
                 centuries (whatever will work best with what students
                 will be studying). Mark top set of tracks social,
                 second set of tracks political, third set of tracks
                 economics, and bottom set of tracks foreign affairs.
             (2) As tracks are being completed, students may wish to make
                 small "spur" railroad tracks from one track to another
                 connecting events that may have cause and effect rela-
                 tionships.

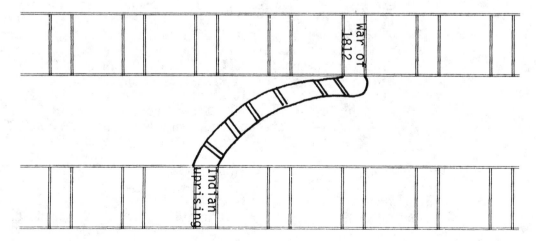

     (NOTE: Save these tracks to display at Social Studies Fair; see
             last activity in this chapter.)

Specific Objective: Identify status of blacks during the nineteenth century.

8. <u>What Do You Know About Africa?</u>[2]

   when: one period

   what: pictures and maps of Africa, list of words (below)

   how: (1) Have each student select five words that he/she thinks
            best describe Africa, i.e., hot, jungle, poverty, hunger,
            wild animals, primitive people, native villages. OR
            Have students check words they think best apply to Africa
            from list below.

   ____ 1. beautiful people   ____ 8. poverty

   ____ 2. change   ____ 9. mineral wealth

   ____ 3. developed   ____ 10. revolution

   ____ 4. enemy   ____ 11. stable

   ____ 5. exotic   ____ 12. technically advanced

   ____ 6. hunger   ____ 13. underdeveloped

   ____ 7. peaceful   ____ 14. unfriendly

   (2) List students' words on board under headings (work on
       categorizing) such as climate, shelter, animal life,
       vegetation, food, people, technology, etc.

   (3) Have students examine pictures and maps to check their
       words for accuracy.

   (4) Hold class discussion on reasons for any ideas about
       Africa that have no basis in fact. For example, ask
       such questions as:

       (a) Are there old established universities in African
           nations?

       (b) Are there metropolitan cities?

       (c) Do Africans manufacture such products as steel,
           automobiles, refined oil?

       (d) Are all African nations alike?

9. <u>To Be a Slave</u>

    when: two periods

    what: resource material on slavery, chart (below)

    how: (1) Discuss with students or have them read about the reaction of slaves to the conditions of slavery.
          (2) Have students fill out chart on slaves' reactions and reasons for their reactions and the consequences of whatever actions the slaves took.
          (3) Have students rank what their choice of reactions would have been (see chart).
          (4) Hold class discussion:
              (a) What action did slaves take most often?
              (b) Explain consequences of different slave reactions.
              (c) Suppose you had been a slave, what would you have done?
              (d) Is it ever right to own another person as a slave?

	first choice of slaves	second choice of slaves	third choice of slaves	etc.
Actions taken by slaves	(example) Acceptance			
Why slaves took action listed above	well-treated by owner afraid of being caught while escaping			
Results of actions taken above	remain well-treated remain with family			
student ranking of their choice				

Instructions: Below is a list of possible actions taken by slaves toward their condition of slavery. On the chart above, list the actions from most frequently taken to least frequently taken. Then fill in the rest of the chart. On the bottom line place your choice of actions from 1 representing what you would have most likely done to 5 which would be least likely done.

acceptance
hindering work (passive resistance)
  on plantation by doing work slowly
escape

revolt
hindering work (sabotage) by
  doing work badly or being
  destructive

10. <u>Civil Rights Time Line</u>[3]

   when: four periods

   what: resource materials on laws pertaining to blacks: slave codes,
          Black codes (Jim Crow), voting laws, Supreme Court decisions,
          national legislation

   how: (1) Have students look at laws that have affected Blacks.
              Through research students, individually or in groups,
              can learn the reasons why these laws came to be passed
              and the dates of such laws.
          (2) Have students find illustrations or make their own
              (either written descriptions or drawings) of the laws in
              practice.
          (3) Have students make a time line on bulletin board of their
              illustrations making sure illustrations are in the order
              that the laws were passed.
          (4) Hold class discussion on the results of the legislation
              and any conclusions the students may have arrived at.

11. <u>Are You Free If . . .?</u>

   when: one week

   what: Jim Crow laws, chart

          Jim Crow laws referred to laws that restricted Blacks such as:
            Blacks had separate waiting rooms at depots.
            Blacks were required to sit in special Jim Crow sections at
              the back of trains and street cars.
            Blacks were not allowed in white theaters, hotels, restau-
              rants, or barber shops.
            Schools were segregated.
            Race etiquette: act inferior to whites, doff hat and get
              off sidewalk in presence of white people, say "Sir" and
              respond to term "Boy!".

   how: Have each student keep a record of all his/her activities
          during a given week, then fill out following chart.

Activities	Those activities pro-hibited by Jim Crow laws for Blacks	Those activities allowed for Blacks but restrict-ed by Jim Crow laws.
example: ride bus to school example: ate dinner at restaurant other examples: went to movie drink from public fountain get hair cut walk down street	white only restaurant	must sit in back of bus

Specific Objective: Identify present attitudes, opportunities, and re-
strictions on immigration.

12. <u>Immigration: A Right or a Privilege</u>

when: one period

what: statements below

how: (1) Have students mark strength of feeling about following
statements.

1. The legend on the Statue of Liberty is right for America: "Give
me your tired, your poor, your huddled masses yearning to breathe
free . . ."

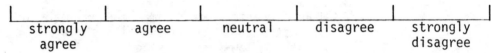

2. I like a lot of mixtures of different races, religions, and in
general people who don't look like me.

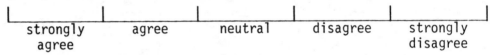

3. The fact is . . . if you are an American you should adopt American
ways, leaving behind the culture of your native land.

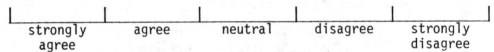

4. Idealistically, let everyone who wants to come live in America;
but that's not realistic. There are some people more valuable
than others. We can't admit everyone, so admit the valuable people.

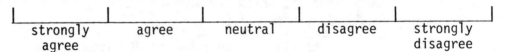

5. Keeping your foreign cultural heritage is important even though
you are an American citizen.

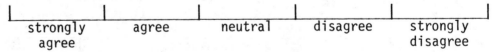

6. Yes, America is a multi-cultural, multi-ethnic, and pluralistic
society, but there are basic ideas that all citizens should accept
if they really want to be real Americans.

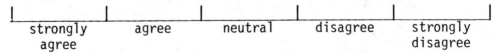

7. My relations immigrated to this country to gain greater opportunity. However, if immigration continues to be open to every
foreigner, that opportunity will be lost.

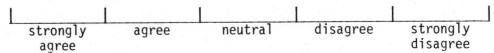

(2) It is well known that immigrant groups, once settled and established, tend to wish immigration restricted to a qualified few. Do students follow that wish or do they idealistically propose to open the door to all who would enter?

(3) Determine where class as a whole falls on the scale.

As a final note: When studying unit on immigration, refer back to students' attitudes as expressed above.

13. When Immigration Became a Privilege

when: two days

what: readings on immigration laws

how: (1) Have students read immigration laws and make a brief outline giving date and law. For example:

1882 prohibited Chinese workers, insane, diseased criminals, paupers
1907 prohibited Japanese workers
1917 literacy test demanded
1921 quota system based on national origins
1924 quota revised to 2% of number of people from that nation living in the US in 1890 (mostly northern Europeans) except for Canadians and Latin Americans who were not limited
1933 Displaced Persons Act
1952 allowed small quota for Chinese and Japanese
1953 Refugee Relief Act
1967 set limit of 170,000 with no more than 20,000 allowed from each country. Parents, spouses, and children not part of quota. Preference given those with skills or those who have relatives in US.

(2) Discuss laws with students:

(a) What were the reasons for the laws?

(b) Do you think the present law is fair? If not, what would be fair? Be sure to refer students to the attitudes expressed in the above activity. Our concept of fairness is based on our attitudes, our values.

(3) When would the following people be allowed to immigrate?

(a) nurse from Chile

(b) Chinese laborer from mainland

(c) baker from Germany

(d) Hungarian anti-Communist

(e) dental hygienist from Japan

(f) gem cutter from Colombia

14. Who Is Acceptable, You Decide

   when: one period

   what: descriptions of immigrants prepared by teacher (see samples
          below)

   how: (1) Divide class into groups. Supply each group with the
              sample descriptions of immigrants.
          (2) The group is to play the role of the US Immigration
              Bureau and decide who may enter the US. Five out of the
              eight immigrants should be allowed to enter.
          (3) Groups discuss and make decisions.
          (4) Compile groups' choices on board. Hold class discussion
              on reasons for choices. Examine quotas and criteria
              government uses for admitting immigrants.

   Sample Descriptions:

   1. Young university student who has taken part in demonstrations
       against his government, but wants both American university edu-
       cation and a good job.

   2. Daughter of a minor party official in her native land.

   3. Musician who has lost his hand in an accident.

   4. Pregnant woman from underdeveloped nation who wants her baby to
       be born and raised in America.

   5. Medical doctor who speaks no English.

   6. Farmer and family who have always been poor for his ancestors,
       as he, worked marginal lands.

   7. Military officer who took part in an attempted overthrow of his
       country's government.

   8. A child who lost both parents in a civil war in which the US
       played some role by backing one of the warring parties.

15. Is America Stealing the World's Children?

   when: one period

   what: current events articles on refugee children from Korea, Viet
          Nam, Cambodia, Laos, Central America

   how: (1) How do the students feel about "saving the children" from
              civil wars in other countries where the US has backed
              one of the warring parties? Survey opinions; identify a
              consensus if possible.
          (2) Ask this question: How do you think other people in the
              world view American concern for the children, that is,
              bringing other nations' children to America to become
              Americans? Have students speculate on how Asians and
              Africans might view the "taking of children." Recall
              the dramatic stories of American relief agencies flying

children out of their native countries to America. From the American point of view, "saving the children is an act of humanity"; from some other nation's point of view it is an act of "stealing the world's children."

(3) Ask the class: Why do you think other nations question American effort at saving the children? Some nations, particularly Third World nations, accuse America of encouraging a declining birthrate among American families, but then make much of their humanitarian efforts to save the foreign children for American families.

(4) This activity is intended to demonstrate that certain peoples around the world, in particular children, are acceptable. Though this is viewed as a <u>positive</u> sign of American goodness by most Americans (go back to consensus at beginning of class), this type of immigration is viewed in some other nations as <u>negative</u> and a sign of American inhumanity to oppressed people. The point is, "Even that which seems clear cut from one nation's point of view is not at all clear from another nation's point of view."

16. <u>Are You Eligible?</u>

when: one period

what: personal history card, "help wanted" ads

how: (1) Have students fill out personal history cards. (Do not tell them what it is for!) After students have filled out cards give them classified "help wanted" ads to see if there are any jobs they could apply for (see below).

PERSONAL HISTORY CARD

_____ (name)   _____ (age)

          ○ male

_____ (nationality)   _____ (height)

          ○ female

_____ (race)   _____ (weight)

_____ (religion)   _____ (schooling)

_____ (languages spoken)

_____ (languages read)

_____ (skills)

                                          _____ (job in native country)

(2) Teacher selects from newspaper "help wanted" ads (no more than 10) with specific skills and/or make up your own. Make sure each ad has a restriction such as age (no one over 25), religion, language, etc. Run off copies of ads and give a copy to each student.
    (a) How many jobs, given his/her personal history card, would each student be qualified to apply for?
    (b) Do some immigrants have a better chance for finding a job than others?
    (c) Suppose you were an employer, what type people would you want to hire?
    (d) Should getting a job depend on "who you are" rather than on your work record?

Sample want ads:

We have openings for dishwashers and bus boys. Must be 18 years or older. Also looking for waitresses or waiters, must be 21 or older. Apply in person.	Mature woman wanted to babysit one infant in my home, five days per week. Must be white and Catholic.

17. What's in a Name?[4]

when: two periods

what: list of names

how: (1) Discuss with students the fact that Americans have often modified or changed their names for one reason or another. The very name America comes from the name of the Italian explorer Amerigo Vespucci. Foreign students studying in the US often pick a nickname or shorten their first names for easier pronunciation. Movie stars often change their names.
        (2) Below is a list of original names and new names. Give list to students to see if students can match them up.

Original Names	New Names
Krikor Ohanian	Mike Connors
Suzanne Mahoney	Suzanne Somers
Samuel Godfish	Sam Goldwyn
Norma Jean Mortenson	Marilyn Monroe
Monir Amin-Sichani	Mona Ames
Sopapim Sresthputr Hatayodom	Sophia Hata
Presyanch Apibunyopas	Pat Abby

(3) After names have been matched correctly, discuss with students the following questions:
    (a) What countries might these people come from?
    (b) Why do you think they changed their names?

(c) Are immigrants from certain parts of the world more apt to change their names than others?

(d) Do you think immigrants will continue to change their names, or do you think it is a trend that has weakened and why?

(e) If you changed your name from Giuseppe Marfussgo to George Mar, then might you have more opportunity in the US?

18. <u>Geneology Roots</u>

when: one week

what: geneology chart below

how: Have students research their own family history. Student may trace both or only one side of his/her family back to time of immigration. Student may write up the reasons for immigration, where ancestor settled, and what work he did, etc. OR Student may trace family back to an ancestor who was perhaps the first to move west, or the first to move to the city, etc. Student may write up what life ancestor would have witnessed in his day.

The point of this activity is to have students see these ancestors as real people, not just names on a chart. If a student has an idea for his/her project other than the two suggested above, he/she should discuss it with the teacher and get approval. This should be a flexible activity.

Sample Family Chart

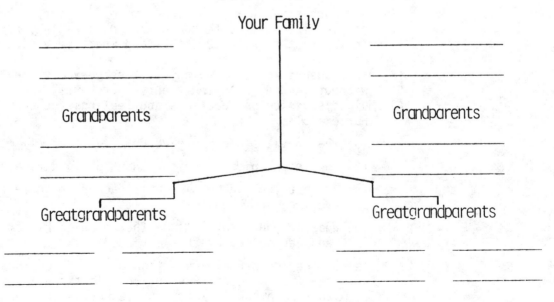

(NOTE: Save family geneology charts to display at the Social Studies Fair; see last activity in this chapter.)

19. American Symbols[5]

    when: two periods

    what: poster board, art supplies, materials suggested below

    how:
      (1) Discuss with class what symbols, phrases, etc. are used to describe Americans. What distinguishes an American from other nationalities, such as language, dress, heritage, needs, etc.? List suggestions on board.
      (2) Have each student pick one or more of the suggestions listed on the board as a theme around which he/she will build a poster. For example, students may find songs, poems, paintings, cartoons, photos, materials from magazines or newspapers, or create materials of their own. Students use collected materials to decorate their own poster.
      (3) Display posters around room.

    (NOTE: Save the posters to display at the Social Studies Fair; see last activity in this chapter.)

Specific Objective: Identify the technological effect of the Industrial Revolution on everyday life.

20. Technological Dependence

    when: two days

    what: Tech Use form

    how:
      (1) Give each student a Tech Use form to fill out. They should list all the technological devices they have used in the last twenty-four hours and what the device was used for.
      (2) Ask students to see how many of these devices they can do without in the following twenty-four hours.
      (3) Hold discussion on reactions and feelings the next day. For example:

        (a) What devices did you give up?

        (b) How inconvenient was it without using device?

        (c) Suppose you had to give up (teacher can name certain device), how would you react?

        (d) What do you think will be the relationship of man and technology by the year 2000?

        (e) Is the Industrial Revolution going to continue as the Technological Revolution? Is there any sign that people will want less technological dependence in the future? Will your children be more or less dependent?

Tech Use Form Last 24 hours:		
where used	name of device	what device used for
(examples) home	blow dryer stereo	dry hair enjoy listening to music
school	projector	see movie on technology
other	bus	transportation to and from school

21. Does Technology Own Us?

   when: one or two periods

   what: magazines, art supplies

   how: (1) Have each student write down any ten technological inventions. For example: radio, TV, lights, bike, etc.
   (2) Have students cut out a magazine picture or make a drawing to illustrate each of the ten inventions they have named.
   (3) List inventions from most useful invention to least useful, including a reason beside each invention.
   (4) Discuss choices and rankings. Some questions to ask:
   (a) Are there gains and losses when we depend on technology?
   (b) Does technology own us or do we own technology?

22. Conserving Power

   when: two weeks

   what:

   how: (1) Students should list and categorize all electrical equipment used by their families. Or teacher can make up a checklist of typical electrical appliances found in home for students to check off.

   (2) Students should see what they personally can do to cut down on their own use of electricity for one week. For example: turning off lights when not used, going without radio, stereo, TV, etc. when possible.

   (3) Have students make a written report on how they cut down and their reactions.

   (4) Students or their parents or relatives may have experienced "brown-outs" or cutbacks or shortages of electricity or natural gas in recent years. Students might report on how family coped with problem and reactions to power cutback.

23. A Campaign for Technology

    when: four days

    what: materials as needed

    how: (1) Divide class into groups. Have each group select a tech-
               nological device (invented since 1800). Make sure each
               group has different device.
          (2) Groups are to research their technological devices and
               prepare an oral presentation on what the device has done
               for man. Groups may use any means available to persuade
               others that their device is the most important one.
          (3) Hold class vote for most persuasive presentation.

24. Which Technology Projects Get Funded?

    when: two periods

    what: list of funding requests

    how: (1) The needs of today's society are many and varied and all
               seem urgent. There are social problems, medical problems,
               environmental problems; all need funds for research and
               development. Hold brief class discussion on above
               issues.
          (2) Divide class into groups. Each group must act as a
               federal government funding agency. Give each group the
               list of technology projects.

Each of the ten projects proposed in the President's Budget was to
receive 10 million dollars, so all projects together received a
total of 100 million dollars. Congress cut the 100 million to 50
million. You must decide from which of the ten projects the 50
million will be cut. List the amount you propose to fund each project; no project should receive more than 10 million.

_____ 1. Project on "wave power" to see if action of the sea can
          generate power.
_____ 2. Project on "test tube" babies.
_____ 3. Project on car safety.
_____ 4. Project on space flight equipment.
_____ 5. Project on weather control.
_____ 6. Project on new weapons system.
_____ 7. Project on retarding old age.
_____ 8. Project on turning sea water into good drinking water.
_____ 9. Project on producing abundant quantities of enriched food.
_____ 10. Project on rat control.
$50 million total

         (3) By majority vote group must decide the distribution of
               funds.
         (4) Hold class discussion and compare groups' decisions. The
               following questions might be appropriate:

(a) To what category of projects, people or things, did you fund the most money?
(b) Does your funding tell you anything about what you value?
(c) Are there projects not listed here that should be funded?

25. Technology Mural

    when: time set by teacher

    what: large piece of long paper for mural

    how: The students will make a mural on the theme of technology and how it has affected our lives and our environment.
    (1) Hold class discussion to plan the mural. Possibilities:
        (a) Section it off into time periods.
        (b) Section it off into categories such as land, water, air; or rural and urban; or transportation, communication, etc.
        (c) Class may want to have no predetermined organization.
        (d) Some students who do not like to draw may want to bring in pictures or do lettering, perhaps using a stencil.
    (2) Students might like to post unfinished mural in hall and invite other students to offer drawings that could help complete the mural.
    (3) Hold informal discussions on facets of technology as they are incorporated into mural.

    (NOTE: Save mural for display at Social Studies Fair; see last activity in this chapter.)

26. Lost on the Moon

    when: one period

    what: materials included

    how: You are in a space crew originally scheduled to rendezvous with a mother ship on the lighted surface of the moon. Mechanical difficulties, however, have forced your ship to crash land at a spot some 200 miles from the rendezvous point. The rough landing damaged much of the equipment aboard. Since survival depends on reaching the mother ship, the most critical items available must be chosen for the 200-mile trip. The thirteen items left intact after landing are listed below. Your task is to rank them in terms of their importance to your crew in its attempt to reach the rendezvous point. Place number 1 by the most important item, number 2 by the second most important, and so on through the least important, number 13.

_____ Box of matches
_____ Food concentrates
_____ 50 feet of nylon rope
_____ Parachute silk
_____ Portable heating unit
_____ Two .45 caliber pistols
_____ Case dehydrated milk
_____ Signal flares

_____ Two 100 lb. tanks of oxygen
_____ Stellar map of the moon's constellation
_____ Life raft containing CO_2 bottles
_____ Magnetic compass
_____ 5 gallons of water

The game can be played in several different ways, depending on the amount of time the teacher wishes to devote to it or on what special needs the group has. The quickest, simplest use of the game is for the group to set to work immediately trying to arrive at consensus as to how the items should be ranked. Students should be reminded that their rankings must represent agreement by all members of the group and may not be arrived at by simply taking a majority vote. For this simpler use of the game, give the following instructions:

(1) Read the problem explained on the distributed sheets.
(2) Your task is to solve the problem as a group.
(3) The only "catch" is that your answers must be agreed to by every member of the group. This will require that you spend a fairly long time talking over your ideas about each of the items, sharing any information you have that could help the group. While you should not be unduly stubborn, neither should you give in simply to speed the work of the group. Often one hard-headed member can save an entire group from making a serious error.
(4) When you have made a final decision, record your group answer on a fresh copy of the problem and compare it to the answers prepared by NASA.

Below are the correct rankings for the items, as determined by the space-survival unit of NASA:

13 Box of matches (little or no use on the moon)
 4 Food concentrate (supply daily food required)
 5 50 feet of nylon rope (useful in tying injured, help in climbing)
 6 Parachute silk (shelter against sun's rays)
11 Portable heating unit (useful only if party landed on dark side)
 9 Two .45 caliber pistols (self-propulsion devices could be made from them)
10 One case dehydrated milk (food, mixed with water for drinking)
 8 Signal flares (distress call within line of sight)
 1 Two 100 lb. tanks of oxygen (fills respiration requirement)
 3 Stellar map of the moon's constellation (one of the principal means of finding directions)
 7 Life raft (CO_2 bottles for self-propulsion across chasms, etc.)
12 Magnetic compass (probably no magnetized poles, thus, useless)
 2 Five gallons of water (replenishes loss by sweating, etc.)

Specific Objective: Identify the cause and effect of America's involvement and growth as a world power.

27. Take Care of Number One!

when: one period

what: see statements below

how: (1) Have students rank feelings about statements. Compile lists and record results.
(2) Discuss with class the fact that there are always some things people seem to agree on just as there are things people cannot agree on.
(3) Save the findings to see if they hold true when class studies foreign policy.

Rank statements by marking them: 1 for strongly approve, 2 for approve, 3 for undecided, 4 for disapprove, and 5 for strongly disapprove.

_____ 1. It is a nation's duty to take over a neighbor that is doing things that might threaten the peace and safety of the nation.

_____ 2. A nation should give aid and assistance to whichever side they think will win when countries are at war.

_____ 3. I always say, "Take care of number one first because no one is going to come to our aid."

_____ 4. One should learn to help others without thinking, "What's in it for me?"

_____ 5. Underdeveloped nations should receive only the aid and assistance they request.

_____ 6. When someone doesn't want to do something he should do, our duty is to see that he does it.

_____ 7. If we have defeated another nation in a war, we should help that defeated nation with foreign aid. Turn an enemy into a friend.

_____ 8. A nation should be ready to aid disaster victims in other countries without first thinking how it will be reimbursed.

28. Going it Alone or Together

when: two periods

what: newspapers, magazines

how: (1) Discuss with class things people do to stay apart or alone and things people do when they want to share and be with other people. List students' suggestions on board. For example:

Separate	Together
eat alone at lunch	sit with friends
keep to oneself	take part in discussions
don't participate	go places together

(2) Broaden discussion to what nations do to stay isolated
or to become involved and list these on board. For
example:

Separate	Together
Make it difficult to enter or leave country.	Send military hardware to country under attack.
Close countries' borders.	Join international organizations, trade agreements.

(3) Have students look for examples of America remaining
separate (going its own way) or working together with
other countries. For example:
  (a) Is the Berlin Wall an attempt at separation and
      isolation?
  (b) What about the United Nations and the Olympics, are
      these examples of separation or togetherness?
  (c) Are there countries that seem to wish to remain
      separate from all other nations?

29. A Question of Personal and National Values

   when: two periods

   what: charts (see below)

   how: (1) Have students fill out the chart using their own recent
              actions.
          (2) Hold class discussion on what students have cited as
              examples. Which are people most strongly controlled by,
              the attitude of "take care of number one first," or an
              idealistic sense of duty, or are both fairly equal?
          (3) Have students prepare a similar chart on a country.

Examples: Myself

What I do for others	What I do for #1	What I do for both
1. Clean up after art work	1. Scrounge food in lunchroom	1. Make batch of popcorn
2. Share class notes	2. Study for test	2. Team sport
3. Give classmate a ride home		

Country

What country does for others	What country does for itself	What country does for both
1. send medical supplies to earthquake victims 2. prevent instability among second and third world nations	1. restrict imported goods 2. need to sell finished goods and gain raw material to support standard of living	1. get rid of surplus wheat by sending it to starving countries 2. sale of arms and training armies to prevent invasion and civil war to encourage orderly growth

30. **Do National Values Determine Military Aid?**

   when: two periods

   what: foreign aid chart

   how: (1) Discuss with students the meaning of foreign aid and possible reasons for foreign aid.
   (2) Have students examine the chart on military aid.
   (3) Hold class discussion:
   (a) What area in the world received the least military aid from 1945-55? from 1966-75?
   (b) What area in the world has received the most military aid from 1945-55?
   (c) What area has received the most military aid from 1966-75? Possible reason for this?
   (d) From total figures on foreign military aid, where would you say America's interests lie around the world?
   (e) Some say Manifest Destiny did not stop at the Pacific coast but continued across the Pacific; does the chart bear this out?
   (f) Is military aid provided for countries because it helps the country or because it will benefit the US or both?
   (g) What do you think the policy of military aid should be in the future? Does our aid follow the areas of the world that we most value? Do you think the US is likely to value different parts of the world than it has valued in the past?

Where	Military Aid Amounts			
	1945-55	1956-65	1966-75	Total
Western Hemisphere	1/4 billion	3/4 billion	1/3 billion	1 1/3 billion
Western Europe	9 1/2 billion	6 1/2 billion	4/5 billion	17 billion
Africa	7 million	166 million	1/4 billion	393 million
Near East	2 billion	3 4/5 billion	4 billion	10 billion
Far East	4 2/5 billion	7 2/3 billion	23 billion	35 billion

31. A Foreign Policy Study

    when: five periods

    what: list of foreign policies followed or promoted by US

    how: (1) Hold class discussion on what policy means.

            (2) Divide students into groups. Each group must research one policy (groups must each pick a different policy). Hopefully all policies on the list can be covered.

            (3) Each group must make a list of events connected with the policy they are researching.

            (4) Have each group give a brief presentation on the meaning of their policy and events connected with it, and effectiveness of policy.

            (5) Activities:

                (a) policy time line

                (b) world map with flags marking locations where events took place

                (c) posters, graphs, charts (depending on policy and group's imagination and research information)

Suggested policies:		
Manifest Destiny	Monroe Doctrine	World Policeman
Detente	Domino Theory	Isolation
Shuttle Diplomacy	Good Neighbor Policy	Make World Safe for Democracy
Camp David Middle East meeting (Spirit of Camp David)	Arms Limitation	
	Containment	

Specific Objective: Identify social, economical, and political values of the past, compare them with the present, and make predictions about the future.

32. Values Past, Present, and Future

    when: two periods

    what: student-prepared questionnaire

    how: (1) Discuss with class the issues that seem important today. List these on the board under the three categories of social, political, and economic.

(2) Divide the class into three groups, one for each of the categories. It will be the task of each group to write five questions on the issues listed under their category on the board.

(3) When the groups have finished the questions, combine them in a questionnaire.

(4) Give each student three copies of the questionnaire. Students should administer the questionnaire to someone their own age, their parents or someone of their parents' generation, and a grandparent or someone of their grandparents' generation.

(5) Tally results and discuss:

    (a) Are all the answers from one age group similar? How about the other age groups?

    (b) What events do you think influenced the answers in each age group?

    (c) Suppose you had lived in your grandparents' day, do you think you would have answered the questions as they did?

    (d) What values seem to be expressed in the answers for each age group?

    (e) How do you think the questions will be answered thirty years from now? What values will dictate the answers?

33. Predicting the Future

when: two periods

what: Futures Checklist (below)

how: (1) Have students examine predictions of future on checklist. Have them put a check (√) beside those they believe will happen, a plus (+) if they believe it will be a good change, and a minus (-) if they think it will be a bad change. They may wish to add predictions of their own. This will give students a chance to examine their own values.

    (2) Tally results of checklist on board. Discuss those statements over which there seems to be strong disagreement.

    (3) Possibility: Have students make own predictions and survey a group of students, tally results.

Predictions of Change by the Year 2001

√   ±

___|___ 1. Nuclear power and solar power will be the main sources of energy.

___|___ 2. Marriages will be by contract only, renewable every five years.

___|___ 3. Daycare centers will be provided for all preschool children because most mothers will be working.

```
√   ±
___|___  4. All medical care will be paid for by the government.

___|___  5. No public school buildings; all instruction is individualized
            and carried on in student's home.

___|___  6. Israel and the Arab countries will have united to become the
            United States of the Middle East.

___|___  7. Because of medical advances the average life span will be 95
            and the majority of the population will be over 50.

___|___  8. No more private homes; only housing built will be 100-story
            high-rise apartments with all necessities of life built into
            each of the high-rise complexes.

___|___  9. (Student Prediction)

___|___ 10. (Student Prediction)

___|___ 11. (Student Prediction)
```

34. The Year 2025

    when: three periods

    what:

    how: (1) Have students pretend their family is transported to the
             year 2025. Have them write what life would be like in
             the areas of homes, furnishings, transportation, clothes,
             school, jobs, environment (climate control), etc.
         (2) Pick ideas from student essays and list on board. Hold
             class discussion on validity and probability of projected
             ideas.
             (a) Do the changes suggested by the year 2025 reflect
                 different values and beliefs than we now hold?
             (b) Do technological changes affect a society's values?

B. Purpose: Develop skills necessary to process information

   Specific Objective: Identify and apply the four different levels of ques-
                       tioning.

   1. Questioning Skills--Eighth Grade[6]

      when: two days

      what: materials included

      how: Questions are such a vital part of social studies that acti-
           vities and materials have been offered on that skill in this

book at all grade levels since the fourth grade. The skill of questioning, we have argued, is not the exclusive domain of the teacher. Students can learn to ask and answer a full range of questions. Questioning is a skill that can be learned, that can be applied. Classroom teachers know that good questions from students stimulate class discussion. What kills discussion and discourages teachers are students who have no questions. Obviously the skill of asking and answering different levels of questions does not guarantee stimulating useful discussion, but it is a step in the right direction.

Learning happens when there is give and take between a teacher and his/her students. Questions are asked and answers are given. The answers are the same for everyone in the group. Learning also happens when there is exchange between and among students dealing with questions that have individual answers and are not the same for every student. Learning also happens when students individually process all kinds of questions by themselves. If you agree with the author that questions are an important part of learning, you should find the following helpful in teaching your students more about them. "The basic objective of [questioning] activities is to teach students to recognize the difference between memory/ description type questions and speculation/evaluation type questions."

Closed Questions:

Closed questions are ones that have specific answers. These ask you to either remember word for word (Memory) or explain (Description) something in your own words. The answers to closed questions would be acceptable for all of us. Here are some CLOSED QUESTIONS about the American Revolution.

Memory   1. In what year was the Boston Tea Party?

Description 2. Explain why some colonists remained loyal to Britain.

Memory   3. Who was the commander-in-chief of the colonial forces?

Memory   4. What was the last battle of the Revolution?

Now write two closed questions of your own about the Revolution, remembering that:

MEMORY means to identify, define, or answer yes or no.

DESCRIPTION means to compare, contrast, or clarify something.

1. _____

   _____

2. _____

   _____

Open Questions:

Open questions are ones that have a number of possible answers.
Some of these ask you to imagine (Speculation) how something could
be different. Other open questions ask you to judge (Evaluation)
between things and decide for yourself what is better or worse or
fair or unfair. You have to make up your own mind to answer an open
question. Since everyone has a different mind, they often come up
with several different answers to the same questions. The answers
to open questions, therefore, will not be the same for everyone.
Here are some examples of OPEN QUESTIONS:

1. Why do you think the midnight ride of Paul Revere has gone into
    the history books while similar rides by others have not?

2. If you had been a British citizen, how would you have felt about
    your government's handling of the Revolutionary War?

3. How do you think a man like Thomas Paine would fit into our
    society today?

Can you see how people would have different answers to these questions?

Now write two open questions of your own concerning something that
has to do with the Revolutionary War, remembering that:

> SPECULATION means to predict, reconstruct, or conclude something.

> EVALUATION means to judge or choose something.

1. _____

   _____

2. _____

   _____

2. Mastering the Different Levels of Questions

    when: one period

    what: review survey

    how: Review students' mastery of identifying the different levels
           of questions. If students have difficulty identifying the
           four different levels of questions, review Chapters Fifth
           Grade, Sixth Grade, and Seventh Grade for purposes of clari-
           fication and practice. Follow-through activities:
           (a) Have students find questions in back of each chapter of
               their social studies text. Have them classify the
               questions they find into one of the four levels.
           (b) On the social studies topics being studied, ask students
               to write out at least one question at four different

levels: Name Columbus's three ships. Why did Columbus take three ships? Suppose you were Columbus, how many ships might you have taken? Do you think Columbus's ships were seaworthy?

Mastery Test Survey (Matching)

___m___ 1. Name one of Columbus's three ships.   m = memory question

___d___ 2. Why did Spain support Columbus?   d = description question

s = speculation question

___s___ 3. What do you suppose would have happened if all three of Columbus's ships had sunk before he could return to Spain?   e = evaluation question

___e___ 4. Is it your opinion that the world would have been better off if Columbus had not discovered America?

___d___ 5. What happened when Columbus first stepped on shore in the "New World"?

___s___ 6. Suppose you were Columbus, would you have made the same decisions about native Americans that he did?

___m___ 7. Name the country where Columbus's ship landed when first returning from the "New World."

___e___ 8. Was Columbus a "good" man?

3. Answering Open Questions

when: two periods

what: materials included

how: We need to know how to answer questions. Closed questions are easy to answer because once we have located the answer the job is finished. Open questions are more difficult to answer because they call for one to create or interpret or imagine an answer from one's own point of view. To answer an open question properly, four steps need to be taken:

CLARIFY THE QUESTION: tell what the question means to you.

PROPOSE SOLUTIONS: list several possible answers.

EXAMINE CONSEQUENCES: explain each possibility.

MAKE PERSONAL CHOICE AND JUSTIFY IT: choose the one you like best and defend it.

CLARIFY THE QUESTION

Suppose you were asked,

"What is the best way to succeed in school?"

Is that question asking you how to make good grades, or how to win friends, or how to be elected President of the eighth grade? You see, there are a lot of meanings we could each give this question and that would determine the kind of answer we would write.

This is the important part--that you and the person reading your answer both are aware of your interpretation of the question.

You might begin, therefore, by stating the question as follows:

"To succeed in school means, a student must make good grades. To make good grades you need to . . . Being successful in school means being popular . . ."

Here are a couple of other open questions for you to practice clarifying. Write a sentence after each to briefly state what you think the question is asking.

1. Imagine that you were teaching this class. What would you do differently?

   _____

   _____

   _____

2. Are you in favor of capital punishment?

   _____

   _____

   _____

PROPOSE SOLUTIONS

The second thing you must do when answering an open question is to propose solutions. Even though you don't necessarily agree, you should examine various possible answers to show that you have fully considered the question.

For instance, if you were answering the question,

"How can you make good grades in school?"

you might suggest the following possibilities:

1. Study hard.
2. Be friendly towards your teachers.
3. Cheat.

All three could be answers, but each would have different consequences.

See how many possible solutions you can propose for this question:

> "What would you do if you saw another student steal a teacher's grade book?"

1)

2)

3)

4)

5)

EXAMINE CONSEQUENCES

You can propose all kinds of solutions, but if some make no sense you really haven't accomplished much. Therefore, it is important to show that you have thought about the consequences of each possible answer.

In the example "How can you make good grades in school?" we suggested three possible ways. Now let's consider the consequences or results of each.

> "First, if we study hard we will have less time to mess around or to watch TV. There would be a lot of satisfaction from knowing that every grade has been earned. Second, to try and bribe the teacher might help, but other kids might find out, and there is no guarantee that the teacher will trade good grades for money. Finally, to cheat might work on occasion, but besides being wrong, it would be hard to do for a long period of time without getting caught!"

MAKE PERSONAL CHOICE AND JUSTIFY IT

Now you are ready for the last step which is to choose the one solution that makes the most sense and to justify it.

For instance, you might say:

"I recommend hard study because, even though it isn't fun, it will help me learn more, and that is the real reason I go to school. Good grades will often come as a result of hard study."

Read the following answer to an open question and follow the directions below it. <u>Question:</u>

"Would we be better off without television?"

<u>Answer:</u>

"I think this question is asking whether or not Americans would be happier without any television. One possibility is that we wouldn't be happier because we couldn't watch football games, or Mork and Mindy. We wouldn't know as much because we learn a lot watching TV. On the other hand, we would be happier because Dads would spend less time watching TV and more time playing with their kids. I think we would be worse off without TV because TV lets us see things that interest us."

(a) <u>Underline</u> the three possible answers offered.

(b) Underline <u>twice</u> the consequences of each possible answer.

(c) Circle the sentence that clarifies the question.

(d) What reason is given for the personal choice selected by the writer?

_____

(e) Does the personal choice fit the interpretation of the question?

(f) On a scale of 1 (poor) to 5 (excellent), how would you rate this answer?

        1   2   3   4   5

What follows is a checklist for written answers. Give the students some open questions to answer. Put some of the answers on the overhead projector or write them on the chalkboard and have students evaluate the answers according to the following checklist.

CHECKLIST FOR WRITTEN ANSWERS	Name _____ Date _____ Grade _____	
Category	Poor<——>Excellent	Comments
1. Define or clarify question	1 2 3 4 5	
2. Propose possible answers	1 2 3 4 5	
3. Examine consequences or proposed answers	1 2 3 4 5	
4. Make personal choice and support it with reasons	1 2 3 4 5	
5. Organize thoughts and write clearly	1 2 3 4 5	
6. Use correct grammar and mechanics of writing	1 2 3 4 5	

Specific Objective: Learn to identify facts and how a fact can be turned into a biased statement.

4. Recognizing Bias

    when: two periods

    what: For introductory treatment on bias, see activities and materials in Chapter Fifth Grade and Chapter Sixth Grade.

    how: (1) Hold class discussion on bias. For example:
           (a) Define bias.
           (b) Possible reasons for biased statements?
           (c) Suppose you want to get some point of view accepted, would you be apt to make a biased statement?
           (d) Do most people make biased statements at some time or another?
           (e) Do you think you can recognize a bias?
           (f) Ways to recognize bias: emotion, who says it, author with personal interest in subject
        (2) Have students bring in examples of biased writing or biased statements they have heard on TV, radio, or elsewhere.
        (3) Discuss statements brought in with entire class. Do they all agree that there is bias displayed?
        (4) As a current events activity, have students examine newspapers, popular magazines, and perhaps their own class current events magazine for examples of bias.

5. Studying Bias

    when: two periods

    what: newspapers or magazines

    how: (1) Divide students into groups and give them copies of news-
               paper articles about the same subject from two different
               sources. If different newspapers are not available,
               Time and Newsweek usually cover the same major stories
               and they can be used.
           (2) Have groups compare and contrast the stories. The fol-
               lowing form may be helpful:

Additional or inferred information from first source only	Facts stated by both sources	Additional or inferred information from second source only
1.	1.	1.
2.	2.	2.

           (3) Hold class discussion on findings.
               (a) Are groups consistent in findings?
               (b) Can a writer imply certain feelings by the way he
                   tells the facts?
               (c) How can you learn to distinguish between facts of a
                   news story and the writer's feelings?

6. Pass It On

    when: four periods

    what:

    how: (1) Divide class into groups. Each group is to write a script
               for some experience that could take place in students'
               environment.
           (2) Have group role-play experience following their script
               exactly.
           (3) Other groups must record as accurately as possible what
               they saw.
           (4) Check with script. How close were the other groups' ob-
               servations to original script?
           (5) Discuss how observations may differ, reasons for this,
               and how to be more accurate.
           Alternative suggestions: Teacher stages an impromptu event
            which the students are then asked to accurately recall.
           An old suggestion but a good one: Whisper a description of
            an event to one student who then is instructed to pass it
            on, and so on until it reaches the last student who then is
            asked to repeat the story. Comparing the final version with
            the original gives a good deal of insight into bias and
            hearsay.

7. Persuasion: The Art of Propaganda

when: two periods

what: materials included below

how: The importance of persuasion in the form of propaganda has
been emphasized starting with Chapter Fifth Grade and continuing through Chapter Eighth Grade. The media bombards society
literally day and night with a message. To be informed and
protected against the techniques of persuasion may be extremely
important to a democratic society that is obligated, if not
required, to make decisions. Below is a matching exercise
intended to test students' mastery of selected propaganda
techniques that were identified in earlier chapters. If
students have difficulty identifying the different techniques,
review Chapters Fifth, Sixth, and Seventh Grade for purposes
of clarification and practice.

___b___ 1. Everyone agrees with Joe; you get with
it and make the agreement unanimous.

___e___ 2. He's not one of us; don't listen to him.

___a___ 3. "There's a Ford in your future."

___c___ 4. Ladies and gents, you can trust me. I'm
just like you, born and raised on the
east side, worked hard with my hands like
you.

___d___ 5. I'm Reggy J. You know I can drive any car, but this is the one
I want. It's the best.

___f___ 6. The popcorn stand is open; the corn is hot and buttered. Don't
forget to stop at the popcorn stand. We made the popcorn just
for you.

___g___ 7. This great country of ours has fallen behind the other side.
It's about time we as a people take up the challenge and fight
to win.

(a) slogans

(b) bandwagon

(c) plain folks

(d) testimonial

(e) prejudice

(f) repetition

(g) arousing feelings

Follow-through activities:
(a) Ask students to identify at least three of the seven
techniques above from TV commercials, newspapers (letters
to the editor is a good place to start), radio commercials.

(b) Make up one written illustration of each of the seven
techniques above.

(c) Place students into groups, each group having their own
list of three techniques which they are to illustrate in
a role-playing. The class should try to guess the
technique.

8. Advertising

    when: two periods

    what: selected TV and radio programs

    how: This activity can be done in groups, pairs, or individually.
           Have students select popular half-hour afternoon and evening
           TV and radio shows. Include morning shows if possible. Have
           students watch and listen to the shows and time (minutes,
           seconds) the amount of the half-hour devoted to commercials
           and list what type of products were advertised. Hold a class
           discussion on the findings:

           Does the amount of time spent on advertising vary during
             different times of the day?
           Does advertising vary during the program (more advertising
             near end of program than at the beginning)?
           What age group or sex enjoys the selected show? Does the
             advertising aim at that particular group?

           If students can make the distinction, what percentage of time
           was spent on "hard sell" advertising? Do they think this
           type of advertising is effective? Are particular types of
           products advertised similarly?

9. Practice Hypothesizing

    when: two periods

    what:

    how: For an introduction to the inquiry process, see Chapter Sixth
           Grade, Activity "Inquiry: A Citizen's Obligation in a Demo-
           cratic Society."
           (1) Discuss the term hypothesis and make sure students under-
               stand it is a "rational guess."
           (2) Have each student make two personal hypotheses. See
               example below.
           (3) Have students poll rest of class to check hypothesis.
               See example.
           (4) Have students examine the current chapter they are study-
               ing in their text or supplementary materials. Have them
               practice hypothesizing by turning chapter and section
               headings into hypotheses.

Class Poll		
True	False	
✓✓✓✓✓✓✓	✓✓✓	1. Girls prefer to wear light colored clothing, boys prefer dark colored clothing.
✓✓✓✓	✓✓✓✓✓✓✓	2. Girls prefer to walk to school, boys prefer to ride bikes.

C. Purpose: Develop the skill to examine <u>values</u> and beliefs

Specific Objective: Learn to identify one's own values and beliefs and
predict whether these values will change as one
grows older.

1. <u>What Are My Values?</u>

when: one period

what: My Values form

how: (1) Have students fill out the values form below.
(2) Discuss responses with students, letting them give reasons
for their choices. Teacher must be sensitive to the
fact that some students may not want to share their
choices with the class.
(a) How did you arrive at the values you chose as most
important?
(b) Did you have a hard time deciding how to answer the
items in the future?
(c) Do some people have a hard time deciding what they
value?
(d) Are some people afraid to say what they really value
and put down what they think others value?
(e) Do you think your values are similar to your parents'
values?

MY VALUES

Check each item in the appropriate space or spaces.	Present			Future		
	Value Most	Neutral	Value Least	Value Most	Neutral	Value Least
1. Looks						
2. Good grades						
3. Money for material goods: clothes, car, stereo, etc.						
4. Independence						
5. Religion						
6. Marriage and family						
7. Popularity						
8. Athletic ability						
9. Do what parents expect						

10. Be a success in a career						
11. Have leisure time						
12. Create something (be creative)						
13. Do good for society						
14. Set a goal and work toward it						

A. Are any of your values going to be difficult to combine?

Examples: woman with family and career

leisure and successful career

B. What in the future might make it easier to reach goals?

Example: four day work week and leisure

C. Do you think your values will change when you graduate from high school or enter college? _____

If so, how? _____

_____

2. Keeping the Message Up Front

when: one period

what:

how: (1) Have students write down bumper stickers they see on cars and bring them to class.
(2) Write bumper sticker messages on board. Examples: "School's Open, Drive Carefully," "I Brake for Animals," "Hire a Vet," "America, Love It or Leave It," "Stay Off My Case," "If You Can Read This, You're Too Close."
(3) Discuss messages. Do they represent any values? What values? Can the different messages be classified into categories such as people, places, and things?
(4) If possible, get a student with a camera or provide a camera to a group who would take slide pictures of bumper stickers. The task would be to organize the slides to fit certain categories of meaning. The slide show is particularly effective in getting the point across that people are trying to deliver a message even if it is only on the back of a car.

(NOTE: Save slide show to display at Social Studies Fair; see last activity in this chapter.)

3. <u>The Message Carries the Values</u>

   when: two periods

   what: newspapers or weekly news magazines

   how: (1) Have students cut out newspaper headlines and bring them
             to class OR teacher could select headlines and run them
             off on copier.
         (2) Have students individually examine headlines and write
             down what values they feel the headlines infer and why.
             For example:

Headline	Value Inferred	Why

         (3) Hold class discussion. How do students compare on their
             inferences?

4. <u>The Immortality Game: A Question of Values</u>

   when: one period

   what: future wheel (next page)

   how: The "Immortality Game" requires the use of a future wheel.
         It calls for commitment on serious value questions. It re-
         quires a personal evaluation. It can lead to thinking
         seriously about possible consequences of alternative courses
         of action.

   <u>Information Base</u>

   Late last spring the Salk Institute developed a vaccine which,
   when injected, will stop aging for one year. It is injected
   yearly, then the animal receiving the injection will be
   frozen in time and will not age. The cost is 10 cents per
   shot. It does not need refrigeration.

   Task 1 You sit on a super-secret decision panel that will
           decide whether or not you will allow this vaccine to
           be announced and/or used. There are probabilities
           that the information is already into the underground
           but nothing has yet been substantiated.

   Task 2 If you decide to disseminate the vaccine, you must
           then suggest the method for that dissemination.
           Please be as specific as you can.

   Task 3 If you decide not to disseminate the vaccine, please
           be prepared to defend your decision.

Task 4   Using a future wheel, please place the vaccine in the center and then list the possible effects of the vaccine. List the effects of those effects and at least one more level beyond that.

Task 5   Project yourself into a time when the vaccine is available for the asking. Write a letter telling why you want to use it or why you do not.

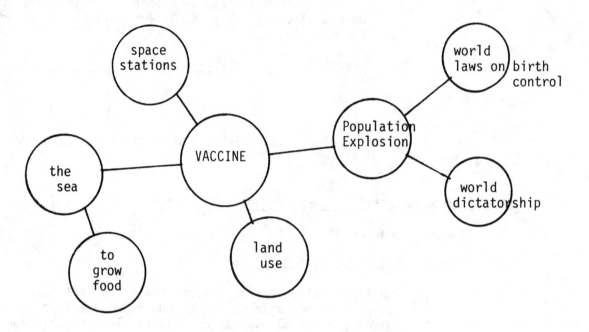

5.   Recognizing Conflicts Between Values

when: two periods

what: sets of conflicting values

how: It is quite possible, almost certain, that values will con-
       flict. Students should be aware, having participated in pre-
       vious activities in this chapter, that they may hold conflict-
       ing values. This is one reason for the emphasis on value
       clarification. Also, values may be in conflict between
       nations, organizations, and people. For example: a report-
       er's right to the privacy of his source of information
       against the government's right to keep national security
       secrets from being revealed. These conflicting values might
       be explored in the following manner.

       (a) Arrive at definition of terms such as privacy, national
           security secrets.

       (b) List possible alternatives that might be taken by re-
           porter; i.e., report because people have right to
           know, or not to report.

(c) Establish rights of government in this particular case.

(d) What might be the results of possible alternative actions?

(e) What do you think the appropriate actions would be?

Examine another set of conflicting values, perhaps one involving students:

(a) value earning money but resent having to work which takes time away from what they really want to do

(b) needing sleep, but staying up late to watch a TV program

(c) wanting a good grade but not caring to do the work

6. Does Our Country Have Values?

when: two periods

what:

how: (1) Our country's values are found in the so-called "ritualistic documents" (Declaration of Independence, Constitution including Bill of Rights, Lincoln's Gettysburg Address, etc.). In these documents such statements are found as:

We hold these truths to be self-evident: that all men are created equal, that they are endowed by their Creator with certain unalienable rights, that among these are life, liberty, and the pursuit of happiness.

. . . deriving their just powers from the consent of the governed; that whenever any form of government becomes destructive of these ends, it is the right of the people to alter or to abolish it.

Declaration of Independence

We, the people of the United States, in order to form a more perfect Union, establish justice, insure domestic tranquility, provide for the common defense, promote the general welfare, and secure the blessings of liberty to ourselves and our posterity, do ordain and establish this CONSTITUTION of the United States of America.

Preamble, Constitution

Freedom of religion, speech, press, and assembly.

Amendment 1, Bill of Rights

Four score and seven years ago our fathers brought forth on this continent a new nation, conceived in liberty, and dedicated to the proposition that all men are created equal.

. . . that these dead shall not have died in vain; that this nation, under God, shall have a new birth of freedom; and that government of the people, by the people, for the people, shall not perish from the earth.

Lincoln's Gettysburg Address

(2) Given these historic statements expressing beliefs and values of the nation, has the nation, in fact, followed these beliefs and values?

(3) Keeping the announced values of the nation in mind, examine historical events in the nineteenth and twentieth centuries, determining whether the event supported or was contrary to the announced values.

(4) Can students answer this: On balance, has the United States attempted to fulfill its announced values? What evidence is there to support students' claims?

D. Purpose: Apply knowledge through active _participation_

   Specific Objective: Identify and participate in the structure of government.

1. Student Council

    when: one week

    what: Constitution of the student council

    how: Students examine student council to see how it affects the individual.
    (1) Examine how student council is organized.

    (2) Can the student council make changes or must it do as it is told?

    (3) Is there true representation of all students on the council, i.e., special students or handicapped?

    (4) What actions does the student council consider and how does this affect each student?

    (5) What actions should the student council consider?

    (6) Attend student council meeting.

    After students have answered the above questions, they could examine what values seem to dictate actions of the student council. Are these values compatible with democracy and citizenship participation? Explain.

Specific Objective: By participating in a Social Studies Fair, students can summarize the activities by displaying materials which they created during the semester or throughout the year.

2.   Social Studies Fair

when: one week

what: materials from previous activities including jigsaw map, newspapers created by students, Bingo game, cause-and-effect railroad tracks, American symbols poster, technology mural, family geneology trees

how: The Social Studies Fair should be considered a culminating activity that comes usually at the end of the semester or school year. A fair offers the opportunity for students in a class or a number of social studies classes to display the media that they have created during the semester. Encourage students from the beginning of the year to save media that they have created. Looking back over this Chapter Eighth Grade, you will note a great many activities that call for participation through the creation of an object. Many of these activities ended with a reminder to save the media for the Social Studies Fair. They include such things as a jigsaw map, newspapers on the nineteenth century created by the students, a Bingo game, railroad tracks on cause and effect, American symbols poster, family geneology charts, slide show, etc.

Procedures:

The Fair itself should take one or two days. The planning, of course, may take several weeks. Planning should include organization and publicity committees.

Organization would be in charge of suggesting appropriate historic topics, collecting and arranging displays.

Publicity would be responsible for scheduling the visits of other classes, public announcements, posters, and information handouts.

Suggestion on organizing the display:

Each class has its own display topics OR organize in terms of time periods such as discovery, colonization, independence, westward expansion, Civil War, industrialization, technology, immigration, world power, future studies.

Suggestions for making the Fair successful:

(a) Be sure that the exhibits are supervised by students who will be there to answer questions.

(b) This is a good opportunity to use a variety of media, such as filmstrips, slides, VTR, audiotapes. The media should be organized so that at least at every other station the visitor can actively participate such as controlling the viewing of a slide show or taking part in a survey.

(c) Music and dress of a particular era would help to make display more interesting.

(d) Provide refreshments that reflect a particular era such as cornbread, sassafras tea, corn showder, maple syrup.

Notes

[1] Indiana Department of Public Instruction. 1978 Indiana textbook adoption categories for social studies. Indianapolis: Author, 1978, p. 3.

[2] Barth, J. L., & Shermis, S. S. Teaching social studies to gifted and talented students. Indianapolis: Indiana Department of Public Instruction, p. 41.

[3] Ibid., p. 42.

[4] Ibid., p. 42.

[5] Ibid., p. 43.

[6] This activity was originally developed in 1980 for "Questions Social Studies Students Ask," a Division of Innovative Education ESPA Title IV-C Research Project of the North Montgomery School Corporation, Linden, Indiana. In particular, the author wishes to recognize the contribution of James Spencer and David Horney in the development of this project. The activity has been revised for publication in this book.

INTEREST FORM

You have just completed the Chapter Eighth Grade. In an effort to have you identify activities and materials that seem most promising at this grade level to you, please fill out the following interest form.

Instructions:

Identify two activities from this chapter. Name the activities and briefly describe why these particular activities are of interest to you.

ACTIVITY 1

ACTIVITY 2

NOTES

CLARIFICATION AND SUMMARY OF SOCIAL STUDIES
CURRICULUM DEVELOPMENT
FOR FOURTH THROUGH EIGHTH GRADES

It is perfectly obvious, if you have read through each chapter, that
starting with the fourth grade the chapters become longer and more complex.
A practical explanation is that kindergarten through third grade teachers may
be required to devote no more than two and a half hours each week to social
studies, whereas in intermediate and junior high/middle school the requirements
are as much as half an hour to forty-five minutes per day. School curriculum
directors, state departments of public instruction, and state legislatures
seem more willing to prescribe both content to be taught and time to be spent
on social studies subjects above the primary grades.

The social studies curriculum for fourth grade and above hardly engenders
among teachers the feeling that someone in the field knows what should be
taught. There is substantial disagreement on the placement of social studies
content. Some states require state history in the fourth grade, others at the
seventh grade, while still others include state history in eighth grade American history. Global area studies emphasizing the non-west can be taught at
fourth, sixth, or seventh grades. American history, normally found at the
fifth and eighth grades, can also be found in the fourth and seventh grades.
Which should it be: history, government, economics, anthropology, sociology?
Of course, it is all of these depending upon the program and texts adopted.
There continues to be considerable disagreement among authorities in the field.
It is easy to be lost in the flow of arguments back and forth on what should
be taught. Social studies educators know that classroom teachers must make
decisions, that curricula be organized, books adopted, materials gathered,
even though there is no common ultimate master plan, no real sure answer to
what and how social studies must be taught. For the moment, it is important

310

to focus on those trends which may offer guidance to teachers on how to think about teaching social studies grades four through eight.

Trends: Grades Four Through Eight

1. Kindergarten through third grade foundations were to be set for the study of current events and comparative studies, with emphasis upon self, home, school, neighborhood, community (city), and regions, with the country and regions and cities in selected foreign cultures. In fourth through eighth grades these foundations were to be continued and intensified, through in-depth studies.

2. An important trend since the early 1960's was for social studies content to be organized to demonstrate specific key social science concepts, i.e., interdependence, conflict, scarcity, social control, etc. In the 1970's, in addition to the social science concepts there was pressure from special private interest groups and from federal agencies in Washington for career education, unemployment insurance education, law-related education, and courses which deal exclusively with economics education.

3. The social science concepts will be organized into a social studies program that emphasizes the integration of those concepts for the purpose of citizenship education. Clearly, the trend is toward integration of the social sciences and humanities and away from fragmentation of knowledge into discrete disciplines. Elementary textbook series are emphasizing the role of all of the social sciences and are not attempting to teach the concepts from one social science discipline.

4. A present trend is for students to be introduced to global studies at the primary and intermediate grade levels, and that introduction should be followed with an ever-increasing emphasis on comparative studies between cultures. Culture studies in the past tended to emphasize western civilization.

The obvious trend is toward a more comprehensive study which includes areas of the "non-west," the Middle East, Africa, Asia, etc.

5.   The traditional notion that the simple act of gaining information is sufficient to encourage decision-making is gradually being replaced by an alternative notion that equal emphasis should be placed on processing information, valuing, and participation. Clearly, decision-making, which some in the field define as the very heart of the social studies goal of citizenship is considered a process that requires the skills of validating and valuing. These are acquired skills, acquired over the length of a kindergarten through twelfth grade social studies citizenship education program.